New York & the Urban Dilemma

New York & the Urban Dilemma

Edited by Lester A. Sobel

Contributing editors: Mary Elizabeth Clifford,
Joseph Fickes, Chris Larson, Stephen Orlofsky
Indexer: Grace M. Ferrara

FACTS ON FILE, INC.   NEW YORK, N.Y.

New York & the Urban Dilemma

© Copyright, 1976, by Facts on File, Inc.

Published by Facts on File, Inc.,
119 West 57th Street, New York, N.Y. 10019.

Library of Congress Catalog Card No. 75-43355
ISBN 0-87196-290-X

9 8 7 6 5 4 3 2 1
PRINTED IN
THE UNITED STATES OF AMERICA

Contents

Cities in Trouble

A MERICA IS, LARGELY, A NATION of urban dwellers. With a total land area of 3,536,855 square miles, the United States has nearly three-quarters of its inhabitants crowded into 35,000 square miles or less of real estate that makes up all of the nation's metropolitan areas. The 200-year history of the nation has been marked by a tremendous long-term flow of population to America's cities. Since the 1950s, much of the migration has been from the central cities to the fringes of the cities—the suburbs. When the first U.S. census was taken, in 1790, the enumerators found 95% of Americans living in rural areas. By the time of the 1970 census, the proportion of the population in rural areas had declined to 5%, and only 27% of the nation resided outside of the 230 metropolitan areas.

There is no unanimity on the subject, but there appears to be wide agreement throughout most of the United States—in rural as well as metropolitan areas—that in a predominantly urban nation, the woes of the cities are as much national problems as they are local ones.

The troubles of the cities are numerous and chronic. They range from racial antagonisms, unemployment and inadequacy of essential services to crime, overcrowding, lack of money, excessive taxes and a collection of factors often described as "urban blight." New York' City, America's foremost municipal giant, has often served as the glaring example of what is wrong with the nation's cities. Paradoxically, as it has frequently been noted, this may be so because New York is the exemplar of what millions of people find attractive about cities. To many critics of the city as well as to its many admirers, New York is "the big apple," the natural home and inspiration of the outstanding achievements of the American civilization.

Like major cities throughout history, New York is a magnet for arts, science, culture, commerce, finance, industry and political power. It is a goal—and often a target—for the ambitious, the talented, the clever, the energetic, the industrious, the curious and the greedy.

In 1975, New York City, as before, became a focus of controversy over urban ills when its leaders appealed for state and federal rescue from financial insolvency. But while national attention was directed mainly at New York, it was generally understood that many other cities, while smaller and less conspicuous, were in equally serious trouble.

Discussing New York's plight, Sen. Abraham A. Ribicoff (D, Conn.) told the Senate Dec. 5, 1975 that "the urban centers of this nation are being crushed by the burdens of welfare, Medicaid, poor housing and many other problems. These problems are not solely of their own making. The fact is too many federal programs are designed or operated in a manner which is detrimental to the cities."

Using welfare as an example, Ribicoff pointed out that "benefits and eligibility standards vary from state to state. As a result, there is a flood of welfare recipients to high-cost urban areas like New York City where benefits are higher." He cited statistics showing that "about two-thirds of the family heads who are on relief in New York City are born outside New York State." The statistics "show a similar trend in the other states with large manufacturing and urban centers," Ribicoff declared.

According to Ribicoff: "The meaning of these figures is quite clear. New York and other urban states are assuming the welfare and Medicaid costs of other states. The problem is further complicated because while New York is paying for transient welfare cases from many parts of the nation, . . . the state is reimbursed for only 50% of the cost. Most Southern states get a much higher reimbursement, reaching up to 83%."

"New York did not invite in these outsiders now on welfare," Ribicoff continued. "On the contrary, the state of New York unsuccessfully went to court to defend its requirement that welfare recipients must live in New York City for a reasonable period of time before receiving the city's money. But this requirement was struck down by the Supreme Court. The result is New York City must pay out $1 billion yearly for welfare. This is one-fourth of the total bill, and there are few other cities in this nation who must pick up such a major portion of the welfare tab."

"There is an antiurban bias evident in many of the federal grant and assistance programs," Ribicoff charged. "Our national drug abuse program is a good example. Half of this nation's total addict population lives in New York City, but it received only 6.5% of federal government expenditures on all drug abuse programs. New York City's expenses for drug addicts last year alone were $78 million, but the federal government paid only $8 million of that $78 million.''

Ribicoff warned that the revenue-sharing system must be reformed ''if our cities are to be saved.'' ''Under the present revenue-sharing system,'' he said, ''the allocation formula used to distribute money contains built-in biases against our cities.'' He noted that New York City ''sends some $14 to $15 billion [in tax revenues] to the federal government but only gets back a little over $2 billion.''

''Even though New Yorkers now face higher taxes, they already are the highest taxed citizens in the nation,'' Ribicoff said. ''. . . These tax-burdened people paid an average of $952 per person in state and local taxes in fiscal year 1974. Massachusetts residents were second, paying $767. Hawaii's residents averaged $765; California, $739. In contrast, Alabama's citizens paid only $383 in state and local taxes. Other figures were Arkansas, $384; South Carolina, $422; Mississippi, $425; Oklahoma, $428; Kentucky, $441; Florida, $520; Tennessee, $424. If these heavy tax burdens continue, they will drive more industry and more middle-class dwellers from New York City. More and more of the 'Fortune 500' companies—those ranked annually by Fortune magazine as the nation's 500 largest industrial firms—are moving from New York City. New York City in the years from 1956 to 1968 was home base to as many as 140 of these companies and never had fewer than 130 of them. As of May [1975], the city had only 98, and more, sadly, are leaving. Employment in the city also is dropping. From a peak of 3,844,000 jobs in 1969, jobs fell by 550,000 as of September [1975].''

Sen. Hubert H. Humphrey (D, Minn.), chairman of Congress' Joint Economic Committee, had held a hearing on the financial problems of state and local governments June 20, 1975. He observed at the time that the urban ''crisis situation is not confined to New York City. Hiring freezes or layoffs, cuts in services, delays in capital expenditures and increases in taxes are the rule, not the exception. Most of our nation's largest cities have already been forced to take one or more of these actions. Cleveland has been forced to lay off 1,100 workers and cut back services to levels that previously would have been unacceptable. Detroit has had to lay off 1,500 workers and to cut back essential services. Buffalo is facing a $50 million deficit this year. But these problems are not confined to our largest cities. Wilmington, Dela. has had to reduce its fire-fighting force by 11% while other city departments have experienced personnel cuts as high as 40%. An informal telephone survey conducted by the National League of Cities of 67 small and medium sized cities indicated far more widespread problems. One-third of the cities had cut payrolls by laying off employees or through the combination of hiring freezes and attrition; over one-half had postponed essential capital expenditures; two-thirds found that their revenues had fallen short of anticipated levels; and almost half expected to enact some form of tax increase in 1975. While these budget problems that state and local governments are currently experiencing are indeed severe, they are often accompanied by difficulties in the credit markets that are just as significant. Last year, interest rates paid by state and local governments soared along with other interest rates as the Federal Reserve tightened the monetary screws. Many governments were forced to delay or cancel issues or to issue only short-term securities. However, while interest rates for most other long-term securities have declined slightly this year, yields on state and local government securities have actually continued to rise. . . ."

The problems of the cities have been the subject of increasing concern, study and action by various authorities for more than a century. A New York legislative report described the living conditions of the city's poor in 1857: "Neatness, order, cleanliness were never dreamed of in connection with the tenant house system, as it spread its localities from year to year while reckless slovenliness, discontent, privation, and ignorance were left to work out their invariable results, until the entire premises reached the level of tenant house dilapidation, containing . . . the miserable hordes that crowded beneath smouldering, water-rotted roofs of burrowed among the rats of clammy cellers."

Ten years later the legislature responded with the pioneering Tenement House Law of 1867, a health code and a demonstration rehabilitation project. Nearly a quarter of a century passed, and the crusading Jacob Riis, in 1890, expressed dismay at the lack of progress. "The 15,000 tenant houses that were the despair of the sanitarian in the past generation have swelled into 37,000, and more than twelve-hundred thousand call them home," Riis wrote. "The one way out—rapid transit to the suburbs—has brought no relief. We know now that there is no way out; that the 'system' that was the evil offspring of public neglect and private greed has come to stay, a storm center forever of our civilization. . . ."

Yet since then much has been attempted in efforts to correct the flaws of the cities. On the generally accepted theory that a basic problem in urban life was the lack of sufficient acceptable housing, Franklin D. Roosevelt's New Deal Administration pushed through the Housing Act of 1937. This law authorized American communities to establish local housing authorities and to build "low-rent" public housing units with federal subsidies. In 1970, the Housing Association of Delaware Valley summarized a widely held view of the experience of the first 30 years of public housing:

Federal money subsidized *units,* not *families.* Federal money paid for construction and capital costs of building projects—but the cost of maintaining and operating the housing was borne solely by the rent paid by tenants. People who could not afford the minimum rents to keep local housing authorities solvent did not live in public housing. In the mid-1960s, public housing began to run into sustained difficulties. While depression families of the "submerged middle class" had been able to pay minimum rents on the newly-built units . . . , the post-World War II years saw public housing acquire a whole new clientele. As young veterans and their families moved outside the cities, armed with FHA mortgages, the public housing they left behind was receiving more and more chronically poor families, many from the rural South, many black, a growing number on welfare assistance. Year after year, the cities felt the wave of in-migration of families with no place to go, nowhere to live. More and more, public housing became their home.

In the late 1940s and throughout the 1950s, local housing authorities built housing projects to house thousands of these families. Ten, 15, 20 stories and higher, these projects rose menacingly from the predominantly low-rise residential black neighborhoods in which they were placed. Horizontal problems became vertical problems. Cost limitations and Congressional scrutiny precluded any kind of amenities in these buildings. . . . Room sizes were small. Community facilities, laundry rooms, recreation space, were minimal. Many tenant families had three or more children. The resulting population densities would be unheard-of in private real estate, and were certainly higher than what the tenants had faced in their previous row-house or even tenement neighborhoods.

At the center of all these pressures—lower rental income, intense overcrowding, growing maintenance costs, lack of adequate community facilities—stood the public housing program in 1960s. It faced an ever-growing crisis. . . .

Tenant dissatisfaction with public housing was illuminated by the urban rebellions of 1964–69. In city after city, public housing projects—bleak, high-rise prisons, overcrowded, rat-infested—emerged as focal points of frustration and grievance. Central Park Village in Tampa, Florida, and Rev. Hayes Project in Newark, New Jersey, received great attention in the Report of the National Commission on Civil Disorders. So did public housing projects in Detroit, Elizabeth, Plainfield and Jersey City.

Another kind of protest—rent strikes by public housing tenants—captured public attention in 1969. By refusing to pay excessive rents for indecent, unsafe and unsanitary housing, public housing tenants dramatized the failure of the program to provide acceptable homes at rents poor people could afford to pay.

The classic rent strike in public housing was in St. Louis, Missouri. In February 1969, the St. Louis Housing Authority announced a large rent increase, necessitated by an impending financial deficit in its management operations. The increase would have raised rents an average of 40%. . . . Missouri has one of the lowest welfare allowances in the country; the increase would have forced welfare tenants in St.

Louis public housing to pay between 50% and 90% of their total welfare grant (which includes allowances for food, clothing, shelter and incidentals) for rent.

St. Louis public housing tenants, with the help of the National Tenant Organization, went on strike for eight months. When the strike was negotiated to a close in October, they had won important concessions from the Housing Authority and achieved reform of public housing in St. Louis, including tenant control of many program operations and representation on the Housing Authority Board. . . .

St. Louis was only the beginning. Public housing administrators in Washington, D.C., and other cities soon were confronted by tenant organizations who demanded that poor people no longer be penalized for the failures of Congress and the bureaucracy.

Speaking on behalf of the National Tenant Organization, Chairman Jesse Gray expressed the mood of public housing tenants when he told the Senate Subcommittee on Housing & Urban Affairs: "There is a growing consensus among tenant groups that the adequate housing of low income families cannot be achieved without government aid. . . . Until recently, the public housing program was looked upon as the best and only form of relief. But closer examination of our public housing program is bringing into serious question the adequacy of that relief. It too often duplicates the worst of the old . . . rather than striking out in bold new directions. . . . The lack of adequate shelter for all Americans in this land is a crisis of critical magnitude. The tragic relationship between landlord and tenant must be altered, be that landlord a ruthless slumlord or an efficient and impersonal government official." . . .

The Community Council of Greater New York, commenting on the explosive urban protests of the mid-1960s, had said in an Aug. 31, 1967 statement: "The deepening crisis in the ghettos is the nation's most urgent moral challenge. It also poses the greatest threat to our security as a democratic America. . . . The underlying causes of the crisis are well known. . . . Since its founding in 1925 as the Welfare Council, the Community Council has been documenting the nature and extent of the problems. The list is formidable, and despite some progress, the gap between the needs and the solutions is widening. No new studies or conferences are required . . . to identify the reasons for ghetto unrest. They include unemployment; subhuman housing; inferior education; insufficient training opportunities; meager recreation and cultural programs; racial and religious discrimination; unresponsive public services; fourth-rate health care; inequality before the law; and fragmented voluntary social assistance. Consumer exploitation, usury, traffic in vice and narcotics, and violence against persons and property abound. . . ."

Not all city leaders accepted this assessment. The NBC radio-TV program "Meet the Press" interviewed six American mayors—Peter F. Flaherty of Pittsburgh, Carl B. Stokes of Cleveland, Richard G. Lugar of Indianapolis, Sam Massell of Atlanta, Wes Uhlman of Seattle and Antonina P. Uccello of Hartford, Conn.—on a broadcast June 14, 1970. Flaherty, Stokes, Uccello and Uhlman appeared to be in total or substantial agreement that "American cities are in a crisis . . . in a fight for survival . . . on the verge of bankruptcy." Lugar, however, denied that this situation was true—for Indianapolis or for most cities. He held that "the large majority of American cities are being relatively well-managed and . . . are considerably better off than they were 10 or 20 years ago." Massell conceded that Atlanta had "critical problems, and many of them center around the need for money," but he said Atlanta seemed to get its problems later than most cities and therefore was "able to learn from the experience of others and somehow prevent the mistakes they have made." Flaherty said he thought "no large city" could survive "unless it has [financial] help from other layers of government, from state government and federal government. . . ." Lugar suggested that cities should "involve suburban [and] regional governments around them, in short, the resources that are available at fairly short range and that can make city opportunities viable." Questioned as to where he "found instances . . . [of] real progress getting suburbanites to take a voluntary interest in the city," Lugar said that "our city of Indianapolis is a prime example. . . . Our suburbanites are contributing substantially, with the same tax rates as our inner-city people, their leadership and their resources. This is true in Nashville, Tenn., in Davidson County. It is true in any number of instances where meaningful relationships are being established through the legislatures of these states and the governors, with people in the city and outside the city. . . ."

Suburban involvement in the problems of the cities is considered inescapable by many observers. Since shortly after the end of World War II there has been a "flight from the city" by middle-class and working-class whites. "Between 1950 and 1966," Paul and Linda Davidoff and Neil Newton Gold reported in the January 1970 issue of the *Journal of the American Institute of Planners*, "the population of the nation's central cities increased by 7,400,000. In the same period, the population of their suburban rings increased by 36,500,000. By 1966, more Americans lived outside of central cities in our urban configurations, than inside central cities." The central cities were left increasingly to the poor and the black—terms that frequently described the same group. At the same time, 80% of the new jobs created in the large metropolitan areas were in the suburban rings, the Davidoffs and Gold reported, whereas the central cities "not only failed to win a significant share of the new urban employment, but, in some cases, . . . have experienced a net outflow of jobs." In effect, the central cities often imported problems and, however unwillingly, exported economic resources.

During the 1950s and 1960s, more than three million black

Americans had joined the general movement of population from rural to urban areas. Most of them ended their migration in the ghettos of the central cities, where their fate often included unemployment or underemployment, substandard housing, application for welfare payments and, frequently, such city amenities as drugs, the numbers racket and victimization by criminals.

The question of money has always reared its head whenever the problems of the cities are discussed. David Rockefeller, head of the Chase Manhattan Bank of New York, had told the Subcommittee on Executive Reorganization of the Senate Government Operations Committee Nov. 29, 1966 that "city building and rebuilding will require a constantly larger share of our total national income. . . . One basic guideline seems clear: means must be found for a fairer allocation of costs among all those whom the cities serve, not only those who live within the political limits. And in the light of the increasing urbanization of the country, that is an ever-growing percentage of the population. Many of our large cities have just about reached the limits of their taxing capacity. They cannot go much further without driving away business firms, and indeed many of the present residents. Since the financial needs of the cities continue to grow, it seems to me that some means must be found to channel more federal and state funds to the cities. . . . I believe it is imperative to encourage development that will generate a source of tax revenue. . . . Deteriorating neighborhoods are a constant drain on municipal finances. While they continue to absorb a full share of services such as police and fire protection, street maintenance and sanitation, their deflated real estate values offer only diminishing assessments. Economic logic dictates that the use of real estate be in some meaningful relationship to its value. The projects we have mapped for lower Manhattan are massive and generally of a commercial, taxpaying nature. It would be inexcusably harmful to the best interests of the city as a whole, it seems to me, to take a large parcel of land in this section and devote it primarily to low-income public housing. Some critics seem to believe that each redevelopment project must be a duplicate of every other, and that each must offer the widest diversity and mixture. They would mingle high-rise apartments with single family dwellings, build a manufacturing plant above the corner grocery, and put the playground behind the foundry. Perhaps on the municipal periphery or in the suburbs we can reasonably aspire to neighborhoods of highly varied usage. But in the great downtown sections, such plans are impractical in the extreme because it is the heavy commercial concentration at the core that pays much of the bill for the pleasant communities around the edge of our cities."

Maurice H. Stans, then secretary of commerce, noted in a speech at the American University Feb. 24, 1970 that the exodus of affluent whites, industry and jobs from the central cities had caused a drastic decrease in city tax revenues. "In 1932," he said, "municipalities collected 25% of all tax revenue; today [1970], they collect 6%."

Constantinos A. Doxiadis, the Greek architect and urban planner, had testified before the Senate subcommittee Dec. 5, 1966. Doxiadis held that several elements of the urban dilemma must be treated simultaneously in attacking the cities' woes. "Mankind began the effort of solving the recent problems of cities by considering the problems of buildings only, then it moved to transportation and especially to highways; today it is considering people and social problems," Doxiadis said. "In every such attempt at placing emphasis on one element of the human settlement, mankind went astray, since all human settlements consist of five interconnected elements which cannot be separated. These are: nature, in which we live; man; society, which man forms; shells (buildings, et cetera); and networks (roads, water supply, sewers, electricity, et cetera) which he constructs. They are all equally indispensable." Doxiadis continued:

We are building multistory residences, and even though we achieve higher densities we are increasing the distance between people in what really counts, in time. People cannot come into contact easily when we pile them one on top of another. . . . The structure of our cities is such that social and racial segregation are accentuated if not directly caused; but these are only facets of the overall problem, and they cannot be dealt with separately. Man, in order to facilitate his life within his world, has created social units which provide the opportunity for closer ties which make him an integral part of the whole. Such units are the family, the neighborhood, and the small city. By our action, we have now eliminated the small city, and we are in the process of eliminating the neighborhood, and threatening even the family. Needless to say, we have no proof that what we are doing is good for man—on the conttrary we could easily prove the opposite. . . .

I think that we can say with certainty that contemporary man has failed completely in forming a proper settlement for a normal satisfactory life. Because of great new forces, people are tending to come closer together in major settlements; but in doing so they have not managed to create a better way of life, and they are doing themselves more harm than ever before. In order to enjoy the benefits of many facilities they are depriving themselves of many values. The social problems have been aggravated, new major economic problems have arisen (the city has not enough revenue and the central city has no way of financing its central role), business is declining in many downtown areas, major administrative and political problems are arising. Our cities are weaker than in the past. They are gradually becoming irrational. Is it not characteristic that the highest traffic is found in the more congested, more densely built parts with the narrowest streets? They are shapeless, and ugly; the parking lot has come to replace public gardens and squares.

In the meantime, we are destroying the values which existed in old cities, and in a very few years it will be too late. The balance is upset: Society as a whole loses (less service at higher cost); man as an individual loses (fewer facilities at higher cost); local government in most instances loses (greater responsibility at higher cost); state and federal government in most instances loses (much greater responsibility at much higher cost); many private owners lose (decay and depression in their areas). While: very few people profit (where settlements expand at no cost to them).

If we now try to understand why the situation and the problems have been aggravated, we will find that the primary cause is the dynamic change of settlements. The explosion of population, and of the economic and technological forces of which we speak, has caused problems not so much because of its size, but because it is continuous, and it causes a constant change in the whole structure of settlements and in the relationship between their elements and parts. Urban growth is not equal, as sometimes thought, to the growth of the population; it is equal to the totality of forces growing within cities, much closer to 10% than to 3%. If we look at the whole national scene we will recognize that movements of people and distribution of projects take place in a relatively reasonable way. Under the pressure of needs, people and activities are being continuously redistributed, and there are no major hindrances. If we look at the very small scale of architectural projects we find many that make sense, increasingly so with every day that passes. If, however, we look at the scale of cities and metropolitan areas we will see that the forces are in great conflict and are causing numerous problems. The reason is that the forces which are being continuously and dynamically added come up against the existing structure; the result is great conflict. As a consequence many parts and elements suffer enormously. . . .

Life in major settlements means more services for man (1) at lower cost in relation to same services provided in the countryside (and of course this is why people move to urban areas), but (2) at higher cost in relation to previous conditions without such services. . . .

Whereas problems are being continuously aggravated, we are trying to deal with them by way of insufficient means and static programs and plans. By the time these are implemented—if they are—the situation will have been aggravated even further. Obviously we are moving in a vicious circle. Only as a small example I would like to remind you of something that was mentioned by the mayor of New York: that in spite of the implementation of housing programs the number of unsound housing units increased in New York from 420,000 in 1960 to 520,000 in 1965, that is by 25 percent in 5 years. We have lately become convinced, in Detroit, that by the time the present urban renewal programs will have been implemented, much greater areas will be in need of urban renewal. . . .

. . . I have not yet seen any city in the world where the responsible officials can claim that the situation tomorrow will be better than it is today.

The [subcommittee] chairman has asked: "Why, when massive resources of our government have been poured into the cities . . . do we have an urban crisis?" . . . Perhaps the cause lies in this very fact, that we are pouring resources into the cities. The solution may lie exactly in the opposite direction, that of using resources outside the cities. . . . The solution may lie in creating new settlements to relieve those suffering from pressures, in which case we can hope to remodel the initial ones in a reasonable way. We have failed to do this, and as a result of the aggravation of the situation, we either tend to become adjusted to the existing city and gradually lose the courage to protest—we may even become adapted to it—or we try to escape. As an example of the first case I will mention the scholars who are fighting any attempt at changing the structure of the present metropolis, as if this were the correct one. As an example of the second case I will mention the escape into suburbs and new towns conceived not as parts of a whole settlement but as isolated units for a certain economic, social, or racial group. . . .

. . . Almost every measurable aspect of our life in the city proves that the situation is getting worse. The programs which we are implementing are insufficient to face our problems. Public housing, first, which is being implemented for 33 years and, after that, urban renewal for 17 years, have not saved the situation. In spite of such attempts it is getting worse. The newest program of all—the demonstration cities program—is only a small beginning in the direction of coordinated action, small in size and small as compared to the areas it must cover. If this is the situation today, it is going to be much worse in the next 5, 10, even 15 and 20 years for many cities and definitely for many aspects of our problems. Even if the best legislation is passed this year by Congress, it will be several decades before it can have direct impact on a great scale. Action taken today means results in 10, 15 years, and major changes by the end of our century. We must be prepared for an aggravation of the crisis since the real forces that shape the dynamically changing settlements are deployed years before they become physically apparent. . . .

This book is intended as a record of the urban problems of the United States during the first half of the 1970s. As most readers would probably have expected, considerably more space is devoted to New York City's problems than to those of any other city. The reasons are certainly obvious. New York is not only the nation's outstanding city. It is also the metropolis that has received most attention as the prime example of an American city in trouble. The material that follows consists largely of the record compiled by FACTS ON FILE in its weekly reports on world events. As in all FACTS ON FILE works, care was taken to keep this volume free of bias and to make it a balanced and accurate reference tool.

LESTER A. SOBEL

New York, N.Y.
May, 1976

Urban Issues as 1970s Began

Troubles Spur Flight From Cities

The mid-years of the 20th century—from the 1940s through the 1960s—were a period during which the troubles of the cities increased in intensity. The crime rate soared, racial antagonisms erupted in riot, housing continued to decay despite the erection of new public projects, unemployment was chronically high in the black ghettos, the welfare population rose and the cost of city government continued to exceed municipal revenues. These conditions continued on into the 1970s and induced many additional city-dwellers to flee to the suburbs. Those who remained in the city were, more and more, the poor and the black.

Continuing urban exodus. Statistics released by the Bureau of the Census Jan. 5, 1970 confirmed earlier reports that both white and nonwhite families were fleeing poverty areas. The figures were based on an updating of 1960 census figures by a 1968 sampling of 50,000 households in poverty areas, described as areas with the heaviest proportions of families with annual incomes below $3,000, broken homes, sub-standard housing and educational facilities and males in unskilled jobs. Most of the poverty areas were in cities with a popu-lation of 250,000 or more. The survey included 100 cities.

The bureau said whites had been fleeing poverty areas for years but the non-white migration seemed to have occurred chiefly since 1966. The bureau explained the exodus by such factors as inner-city crime and education problems, land clearance caused by urban renewal and increased availability of low-income housing outside poverty areas.

Among statistics cited by the bureau:

■The number of families living in poverty areas declined 15%—from 4.8 million to 4 million—between 1960 and March 1968.

■White families in poverty areas declined 18% and minority group families 9% during the same period. In 1968, 2.5 million whites and 1.6 million blacks lived in poverty areas.

Blacks concentrated in 15 cities. The Census Bureau reported May 18, 1971 that figures based on the 1970 census showed that half of the nation's 22.3 million Negroes now lived in 50 cities. A further breakdown of the figures revealed that one third of America's Negro population was concentrated in 15 cities.

According to the bureau, six cities had black majorities while eight others had black populations of 40% or more. The highest proportion of blacks in all cities occurred in Compton, Calif. and Washington, each with about 71%. The other cities with black populations exceeding 50% were East St. Louis, Ill., with 69.1%, Newark, N.J., with 54.2%, Gary, Ind., with 52.8% and Atlanta with 51.3%.

New York City had by far the largest black population, almost 1.7 million. The new figure represented an increase of nearly 580,000 over 1960 and raised the black proportion of New York's population to 21% from 14% in 1960. Chicago had the second largest number of blacks with slightly more than 1.1 million.

Nationwide, Negroes constituted about 11% of the total population.

The 50 cities listed by the Census Bureau:

CITY	RANK	Negro Population	Negro Percentage
New York City	1	1,666,636	21.2
Chicago	2	1,102,620	32.7
Detroit	3	660,428	43.7
Philadelphia	4	653,791	33.6
Washington	5	537,712	71.1
Los Angeles	6	503,606	17.9
Baltimore	7	420,210	46.4
Houston	8	316,551	25.7
Cleveland	9	287,841	38.3
New Orleans	10	267,308	45.0
Atlanta	11	255,051	51.3
St. Louis	12	254,191	40.9
Memphis	13	242,513	38.9
Dallas	14	210,238	24.9
Newark	15	207,458	54.2
Indianapolis	16	134,320	18.0
Birmingham	17	126,388	42.0
Cincinnati	18	125,000	27.6
Oakland	19	124,710	34.5
Jacksonville	20	118,158	22.3
Kansas City, Mo.	21	112,005	22.1
Milwaukee	22	105,088	14.7
Pittsburgh	23	104,904	20.2
Richmond	24	104,766	42.0
Boston	25	104,707	16.3
Columbus	26	99,627	18.5
San Francisco	27	96,078	13.4
Buffalo	28	94,329	20.4
Gary	29	92,695	52.8
Nashville-Davidson	30	87,851	19.6
Norfolk	31	87,261	28.3
Louisville	32	86,040	32.8
Fort Worth	33	78,324	19.9
Miami	34	76,156	22.7
Dayton	35	74,284	30.5
Charlotte	36	72,972	30.3
Mobile	37	67,356	35.4
Shreveport	38	62,162	34.1
Jackson	39	61,063	39.7
Compton Calif.	40	55,781	71.0
Tampa	41	54,720	19.7
Jersey City	42	54,595	21.0
Flint	43	54,237	28.1
Savannah	44	53,111	44.9
San Diego	45	52,961	7.6
Toledo	46	52,915	13.8
Oklahoma City	47	50,103	13.7
San Antonio	48	50,041	7.6
Rochester	49	49,647	16.8
East St. Louis	50	48,368	69.1

Integration in suburbs found slight. Preliminary studies of the 1970 U.S. census indicated very little racial integration of America's white suburbs during the 1960s, according to a Washington Post report Jan. 16, 1971.

Specialists at the Census Bureau reportedly predicted that early trends showing little suburban integration would hold true even as more detailed analyses were completed.

According to Census Bureau workers, much of the movement of blacks into the suburban areas represented simply the spillover across metropolitan lines from Negro neighborhoods. This, officials said, merely extended the size of black neighborhoods.

Meyer Zitter, assistant chief of the bureau's population division, said in a speech that "from the data now available ... for the areas already on hand, there is hardly any evidence of appreciable movement of Negroes into suburban areas, but there is much evidence of substantial increases of Negroes in central cities."

Zitter estimated that about 15% of the nation's blacks lived within metropolitan areas and outside the central cities. The figure for whites was nearly 40%. Sample surveys had indicated that about 5% of America's suburban population was black—about the same proportion as it was in 1960.

During the 1960s, there was a reported net loss of about 2½ million whites from the inner city areas and an increase of about 3 million blacks. Two-thirds of the rise in the number of black inner-city dwellers was attributable to births.

Rural population decline—The number of Americans living in rural areas (farms or towns of fewers than 2,500 people) declined during the 1960s from 30.1% to 26.5% of the population, according to Census Bureau figures reported Feb. 13. The decline, which left 53.6 million rural residents in 1970, resulted largely from an exodus of whites from rural areas of the Plains states and Appalachia regions, and of blacks from the South.

Among the causes, experts cited the increasing mechanization of agriculture and the rising level of education of the young, whose skills were more in demand in urban areas.

Final Census Bureau figures reported Aug. 24 showed the nation's farm population in 1970 at 9.7 million, a drop of nearly 6 million from 1960, and the lowest figure in at least 50 years. Farm residents constituted 4.8% of the total population, and were older than the national average.

Urban panel reports worse plight. A followup report to the 1968 Kerner Commission findings on inner-city racial problems said Sept. 23, 1971 that if present trends continued, "most cities by 1980 will be preponderantly black and brown, and totally bankrupt." The panel, headed by New York Mayor John V. Lindsay and Sen. Fred Harris (D, Okla.), was named earlier in the year by the National Urban Coalition.

In releasing the 31-page report—which was dedicated to the late Whitney M. Young Jr., a member of the 1968 National Advisory Commission on Civil Disorders headed by former Illinois Gov. Otto Kerner—Urban Coalition Chairman Sol M. Linowitz said, "We have been told by our leaders in government, and by much of the press, that the cities have 'cooled off' since the disasterous riots of 1967 and 1968." Linowitz said, "The only 'cooling off' we can detect . . . is in the commitment of the government and the American people to correct festering problems of our cities—or even to admit those problems really exist."

The panel said the "corrosive and degrading" conditions of city slums had worsened since 1968. "Housing is still the national scandal it was then," the report said. "Schools are more tedious and turbulent. The rates of crime and unemployment and disease and heroin addiction are higher. Welfare rolls are larger. And with few exceptions, the relations between minority communities and the police are just as hostile."

The commission visited Atlanta, Detroit, Los Angeles, Phoenix, Newark (N.J.) and El Paso (Tex.). The report said

the "most disturbing point" made by people they talked to was a loss of confidence in U.S. institutions. The panel said "this pervasive distrust" extended to corporations, bankers and doctors as well as government officials and institutions.

The growth of grass-roots, self-help organizations, led by "a few courageous and optimistic people working hard to recapture control of their destinies," was one hopeful trend discovered by the panel.

Agnew for aid from suburbs—Vice President Spiro T. Agnew had said March 7, 1970 that the resources of the affluent suburbs should be utilized to help solve the urban poverty problems of land, money, housing, education and jobs. Restriction of efforts to solve slum problems to the ghettoes themselves might "constitute a subtle form of racism" and encourage "segregated living and the development of racial hostility," he said.

He suggested that the suburban effort should include financial aid as well as "freer access to suburban land and suburban jobs." The suburban dweller, he said, should be aware of "the direct relationship between the economic viability of his county and city." The problems of the cities, he said, were "everybody's problems."

Agnew made the remarks in a speech before the National Alliance of Businessmen, an organization to promote hiring of the hard-core unemployed by private industry. He told the group, which had 23,520 companies participating in its program, to help "improve the linkage between the central city labor forces and areas of expanding job opportunities."

Nixon bars forced suburban integration—President Richard M. Nixon said at his press conference Jan. 4, 1971 that the government would not force the suburbs to integrate. According to Nixon:

"The law does require that there can be no federal housing funds in any community that has a policy which is discriminatory insofar as fair housing is concerned. But now, the law does not now require, or, in my opinion, allow the fed-

eral government to have forced integration of suburbs."
"We're going to carry out the law. We are going to open up opportunities for all Americans to move into housing—any housing that they're able to afford. But on the other hand, for the federal government to go further than the law, to force integration in the suburbs, I think is unrealistic. I think it would be counterproductive, and not in the interest of better race relations."

Federal, State & Local Policies

Nixon's urban policy outlined. President Nixon and members of his Administration flew to Indianapolis Feb. 5, 1970 for a meeting of the President's Urban Affairs Council attended by the mayors of 10 cities. Presidential counselor Daniel P. Moynihan presented a 10-point urban policy proposal at the meeting, the first of its kind held outside Washington. Nixon said he had brought the council to Indianapolis because he wanted his cabinet "to know what the people out in the heartland think."

Moynihan told the mayors that a basic premise of the Administration's urban policy was that "poverty and social isolation of minority groups is the single most urgent problem of American cities today," an idea reportedly put forward recently by a Presidential study panel. (The New York Times reported Feb. 1 that a task force appointed by the President Oct. 17, 1969 to study urban renewal problems had proposed as a guiding principle for federal urban policy the bringing together of various ethnic and income groups in the cities. According to the Times, the study group said in a report submitted to the President that "a major rationale for federal expenditures for urban renewal" should be to "exorcise the specter of increasing apartheid" in the cities.)

Other proposals listed by Moynihan as part of an urban plan for the 1970s included: balancing urban programs so that federal plans in one area, such as highway construction, would not contribute to problems in another area, such as housing in central cities; strengthening local governments by helping them consolidate their approach to problems as part of an overall metropolitan system; restoring fiscal vitality to local governments through programs such as the President's revenue-sharing proposals; attempting to equalize public services, such as school systems, in adjoining communities; developing programs on population growth and migration to achieve a national population balance; promoting increased state aid to cities; providing incentives to encourage cities to meet national goals; increasing information and research on urban problems; and working to protect and improve the urban environment.

The mayors who attended the council meeting were Richard Lugar of Indianapolis, Jack Maltester of San Leandro, Calif., Donald Enoch of Wichita, Kan., Lawrence Kramer of Paterson, N.J., George Seibels of Birmingham, Ala., Chris Sonnabeldt of Grand Rapids, Mich., Antonina P. Uccello of Hartford, Conn., Frank Curran of San Diego, Peter V. Demenici of Albuquerque, N.M., and Walter E. Washington of Washington, D.C.

Earlier Moynihan memo—The New York Times reported March 10 that two weeks before Nixon's inauguration as President, Moynihan had sent him a private memo saying that "the Negro lower class must be dissolved" by transforming it "into a stable working class population."

According to the Times, Moynihan acknowledged in his report to Nixon that the transformation of what he estimated at "almost half the total Negro population" would be the "work of a generation."

Moynihan said, however, that it was essential to social stability and elemental justice "that the low income, marginally employed, poorly educated, disorganized slum dwellers" should have the chance to become "truck drivers, mail carriers, assembly line workers—people with dignity, purpose, and, in the U.S., a very good standard of living indeed."

Six days after this report to Nixon,

Moynihan forwarded a second report which was actually a synopsis of a paper prepared by a Harvard University political scientist for a meeting Dec. 17, 1969 of New York City officials and administrators to discuss the state of New York City. In his memorandum to Nixon, Moynihan indicated that he agreed with the New York City report that said that the "private subsystems of authority"—the family, the community, the church and others—regulated behavior "in such a way as to make it unnecessary for the state to intervene in order to protect the public interest," and that these subsystems were breaking down in the nation's large cities.

Big-city mayors unite. The mayors of 10 big U.S. cities announced March 3, 1970 that they had joined forces to lobby for "Congressional and state action to meet city needs." Agreement on the coalition, proposed by New York City Mayor John V. Lindsay, had been reached at a Washington meeting. The mayors of New York State's six largest cities had united previously to pressure the state legislature to increase aid for cities.

In a joint announcement, the mayors said: "We believe that leaders of the major cities should speak with a common voice. . . . We share common problems and will make common cause in seeking relief." The focus of the coalition was to be five areas of pending Congressional legislation: federal revenue sharing with local government; welfare reform; federal mass transit aid; urban renewal and Model Cities; and crime control.

The group planned to develop common proposals, testify jointly before Congressional committees and make joint visits to U.S. cities. It said it planned to continue working closely with other national organizations, such as the U.S. Conference of Mayors, the National League of Cities and the National Urban Coalition.

In addition to Lindsay, the group included Mayors Joseph Alioto of San Francisco, Thomas D'Alesandro of Baltimore, Peter Flaherty of Pittsburgh, Roman Gribbs of Detroit, Harry Haskell of Wilmington, Del., Sam Massell of Atlanta, Carl Stokes of Cleveland, Wesley Uhlman of Seattle and Kevin White of Boston.

Mayors urge reordered priorities. The U.S. Conference of Mayors, meeting in Denver June 13-17, 1970, adopted a compromise resolution urging that the nation devote to urban problems money then earmarked for "programs which prudently can be deferred, such as space, military, agriculture, highway construction and research." The "priorities" resolution, with language identical to a measure adopted by the conference in 1969, was approved after a group of mayors dropped plans to push through a stronger resolution condemning expenditures for the Indochina war.

The compromise priorities resolution was sponsored by Mayor Henry W. Maier of Milwaukee. Commenting on the failure of President Nixon or Vice President Agnew to accept invitations to appear at the conference, Maier said June 16, "We're rating zero." However, he commended Housing and Urban Development (HUD) Secretary George Romney, who spoke at the conference June 15, for his efforts on behalf of the cities.

Model Cities endorsed. The administration announced Sept. 30 that it had decided to make the Model Cities program a key part of its urban aid policy. The announcement was made at a news conference by George Romney, secretary of housing and urban development, and Elliot L. Richardson, secretary of health, education and welfare.

Their plan, to utilize Model Cities funding as a means to decentralize administration of federal urban aid, was immediately endorsed by the National League of Cities and the U.S. Conference of Mayors.

An experimental project was to be instituted in 12-18 cities to test three variations of instituting more local control. One variation would be to extend aid currently limited to a Model Cities neighborhood to a citywide program with eligibility for additional federal funds. A second plan would require only an audit and review of specific grants instead of the current lengthy processing required. Under a third proposal, a mayor would have authority to review and challenge all federal programs sending funds into the city.

The Model Cities program, enacted in 1966, had been subjected to scrutiny by two Nixon Administration study groups, one appointed before the Nixon inauguration. It endorsed the program and recommended a broadening of it. But several domestic advisers to the President had serious doubts concerning the program, and a second study group was appointed.

Their report, submitted Dec. 16, 1969 but not released until Sept. 10, endorsed the program and recommended increased support for it by the President and a reduction in federal control and red tape. John R. Price, Jr., special assistant to the President, reported that Nixon "in a large measure" supported the recommendations. The program currently was being funded well below the level projected by the Johnson Administration.

Mayors planning lobbying effort. Federal revenue sharing with the states and cities was a major topic at the annual convention of the National League of Cities in Atlanta Dec. 8, 1970. Delegates (2,500 mayors, city councilmen and other representatives of cities) gave a standing ovation to New York City Mayor John V. Lindsay for his speech calling for a $10 billion revenue-sharing program in 1971.

Lindsay said: "If this country could afford to spend $17 billion on the Marshall Plan for the cities and states of Europe—if we could afford $18 billion to defend the state of South Korea—if we were willing to pour $100 billion into the villages of Vietnam for a war no general could win—then, surely, the nation can afford to share $10 billion of its revenues—now—to save our cities and suburbs and states."

Lindsay called for a coalition of governors and mayors to "lock arms" and press for the revenue-sharing program.

The delegates also heard Dec. 8 from John D. Ehrlichman, President Nixon's top domestic policy adviser, who said the Administration's proposal for a $500 million first-year allocation of federal money to the states and cities would require an "extraordinary effort" to push through Congress in 1971.

Ehrlichman also told the mayors the Administration had shifted budgetary emphasis from defense to human resources spending, but warned that the defense budget could not be cut further "without creating an impermissible deterioration of our defense capability." Lindsay had attacked the Administration for spending $80 billion on defense and for backing a supersonic transport plane while "our cities are embattled at home."

A cooperative lobbying effort by urban and state groups was announced in Atlanta Dec. 9 by John Gunther, executive director of the U.S. Conference of Mayors, following a meeting of big-city mayors.

The effort, which would be coordinated by Gunther and other conference lobbyists, was to be initiated with a drive to gain enactment of the three-year, $12 billion manpower bill that would establish a new program for jobs in public service— federal, state and local government—for those unable to find employment in private industry. The group sought the enactment of a revenue-sharing plan as a longer-range goal.

Those cooperating in the effort, in addition to the Conference of Mayors and the National League of Cities, were the National Governors Conference, the Council of State Governments, the National Association of Counties and the International Management Association.

Rockefeller urges cooperation. Nelson A. Rockefeller (R), beginning his fourth term as governor of New York, called for "effective action and coordination of all three levels of government" in his inaugural address in Albany Jan. 1, 1971. Citing a "breakdown in local government services" and "pollution of the environment," Rockefeller contended that the nation had "reached a crucial point."

Rockefeller said government's "most fundamental task" was "to make our communities places where family stability and strengthened family life and family ties can be realized in this period of social instability." He said the response to social needs had "dangerously overloaded the financial capacity of state and local governments." Stating that "we are all joined inseparably in an interdependent federal system," he said "we must all work together in common effort, to renew that system and remake our society."

During a television interview Jan. 3, Rockefeller repeated his call for federal help to meet city and state problems.

Rockefeller told the state legislature Jan. 6 that the state fiscal outlook was "bleak," that the state government, "like a family, must tighten its belt and live within its resources." Rockefeller warned that even without major new programs expenditures would rise $1.3 billion over the current budget ($7.1 billion) because of mandated increases in state aid to schools and cities and raises for state workers.

Cities cut spending. As part of a move by Cleveland Mayor Carl B. Stokes to reduce spending after voters turned down a city income tax increase, a city official said Jan. 4, 1971 that all 26 city-owned recreation halls were closed and only 77 of 500 employes of the recreation department remained on the city payroll. The department's budget was cut from $5 million to $994,000.

In Boston, Mayor Kevin H. White said Jan. 4 he would propose removing 500 employes from the city payroll and that he would ask all department heads to take a pay cut. He said he would cut spending sharply in the new city budget.

Deficit spending up. The Census Bureau reported Sept. 28, 1971 that the gap between spending and incoming revenues for municipalities in fiscal 1970 was greater than in previous years. The bureau's report on city finances for the year that ended June 30, 1970 confirmed the contention of mayors seeking more aid from state and federal governments by showing that revenues increased by 10% from the previous year and expenditures by 12%.

The study showed that municipalities, including those in the suburbs, received $32.7 billion in revenues and spent $34.2

billion for current expenses and capital outlays. In contrast to former years, the excess in expenditures over revenues was mostly due to current expenses rather than spending for buildings and equipment. Current expenses rose 14% during the year to $22.8 billion while capital outlays increased 10% to $7.1 billion.

Municipal governments collected $18.7 billion from their own sources, an increase of 11% from the former year. State and federal governments provided $7.5 billion, up 8%. The federal government spent $1.3 billion in direct aid to cities, and the amount going to each city did not always reflect population figures. Los Angeles, with a population of 2.8 million, received $5.7 million from the federal government and Nashville, with 426,029 people, received $8 million. The federal government gave $158.8 million to New York City and $90.8 million to Chicago.

Large increases in expenditures came in areas of education, police protection, health and sewage disposal services. Welfare, however, remained comparatively stable, with a spending increase of only 3%.

Mayors oppose aid cuts. Fifteen big-city mayors, members of a recently organized Legislation Action Committee of the U.S. Conference of Mayors, said Jan. 21, 1971 that they would oppose cuts in current programs for urban areas to provide money for Nixon's revenue-sharing plan. The mayors made their statement in a New York news conference in anticipation of President Nixon's presentation of revenue sharing in his State of the Union message the following day.

New York Mayor John Lindsay, head of the committee, said: "We have heard repeated reports that urban programs may be shortchanged as part of a sleight-of-hand play to finance a general revenue sharing program with a minimum of new money." He said such cuts "will add to urban tensions and urban deterioration and will, therefore, be unacceptable. The plight of the cities is too ominous to be made part of a budgetary and political shell game."

The mayors' statement said they

would seek assurances "that all monies appropriated for this fiscal year will be released for use this year and existing program levels will at the very least be maintained. We cannot tolerate the dismantling of programs built by a decade of toil in our great cities."

Revenue Sharing

Nixon proposes revenue sharing. President Nixon Jan. 22, 1971 delivered to Congress a State-of-the-Union message in which he proposed the annual sharing of $16 billion of federal revenues with state and local governments.

Major emphasis also was put on welfare reform, environmental cleanup, expansion of park lands and open spaces and a health program, including a $100 million campaign to find a cure for cancer.

In his address, broadcast by the major television networks, the President said "America has been going through a long nightmare of war and division, of crime and inflation" and was now "ready for the lift of a driving dream." He urged Congress to adopt his program and open "the way to a new American Revolution—a peaceful revolution in which power was turned back to the people—in which government at all levels was refreshed and renewed, and made truly responsive."

Nixon said his program would be presented within the context of an expansionary budget, a "full-employment" (no more than 3.8% unemployment) budget "designed to be in balance if the economy were operating at its peak potential." "By spending as if we were at full employment," he said, "we will help to bring about full employment."

He asked Congress to cooperate within this context and resist "expenditures that go beyond the limits of the full-employment budget." And he urged labor and management to make "a much greater effort" to "make their wage and price decisions in the light of the national interest and their own self-interest."

Revenue sharing—In presenting his

revenue sharing plan, which he called "historic in scope and bold in concept," Nixon said it was time "to reverse the flow of power and resources from the states and communities to Washington and start power and resources flowing back from Washington to the states and communities and, more important, to the people all across America." He viewed it as "a new partnership between the federal government and the states and localities—a partnership in which we entrust the states and localities with a larger share of the nation's responsibilities, and in which we share our federal revenues with them so that they can meet those responsibilities."

The $16 billion annual investment "in renewing state and local government" was to include $5 billion in new and unrestricted funds, "to be used as the states and localities see fit." The other $11 billion, he said, "will be provided by allocating $1 billion of new funds and converting one-third of the money going to the present narrow-purpose aid programs into federal revenue-sharing funds for six broad purposes—for urban development, rural development education, transportation, job training, and law enforcement—but with the states and localities making their own decisions on how it should be spent within each category."

For the next fiscal year, the President said, this program "would increase total federal aid to the states and localities more than 25% over the present level."

"Let us put the money where the needs are," Nixon urged. Most Americans, he said, were "simply fed up with government at all levels" and would not and should not "continue to tolerate the gap between promise and performance in government."

Chairman Wilber D. Mills (D, Ark.) of the House Ways and Means Committee which would get President Nixon's revenue sharing proposal, denounced the plan Jan. 26 as "defective" and a possible inflation risk.

In an hour-long speech on the House floor, Mills attacked unrestricted revenue sharing because he said the funds it generated might bypass the areas where it was needed most.

(Mills and Rep. John W. Byrnes [R,

Wis.], another key opponent of revenue sharing, had conferred with President Nixon at the White House Jan. 25. After the meeting, Mills said he would schedule hearings on the plan. "I am perfectly willing to have hearings," Mills said, "but not for the purpose of promoting the plan—for the purpose of killing it." Byrnes, ranking Republican member on the Ways and Means Committee, added that he and Mills had told Nixon that "we have philosophical difficulties with revenue sharing and are basically opposed to it.")

In his floor speech, Mills said revenue sharing without some government restraints would lead to unlimited spending increases by state and local governments. This increase in spending, he said, could cause inflation and lead to higher federal taxes to meet the local outlays.

While acknowledging that state and city governments had a financial problem, Mills said he did not think it was as great as some proponents of revenue sharing had said. Mills said the formula for general revenue sharing, under which money would be turned over to states mainly on the basis of population, was a "poor and wasteful" idea. Under it, Mills said, "substantial funds are given to states and localities where there is little or no need, as well as to those where there is need."

John Ehrlichman, President Nixon's chief domestic advisor, said Jan. 27 that Mills' assumptions about revenue sharing were not "well-founded." At a news briefing, Ehrlichman denied that the plan would require higher taxes or bypass areas where funds were needed most.

Among other developments:

■ In testimony before the Joint Economic Committee Jan. 27, Sol M. Linowitz, chairman of the National Urban Coalition, proposed that the $5 billion in new and unrestricted funds proposed in Nixon's plan be distributed only to states that had graduated state income taxes. Linowitz also urged that the federal government share an additional $4 billion in aid to education but that the grants be tied to changes in state and local tax practices. The coalition also proposed federal funding of a comprehensive health insurance and welfare

program and a $4 billion federal program to provide 875,000 public services jobs by 1975.

■ Vice President Spiro T. Agnew, speaking in Atlanta Jan. 27 to 250 Southern members of the National Association of Counties, criticized opponents of the revenue sharing proposal for distrusting state and local officials. Taking note of Rep. Mills' opposition, Agnew suggested that his audience's hometown residents "probably know you a lot better than Chairman Mills [of the House Ways and Means Committee], and they probably have more confidence in you than they do in him." Following the Atlanta meeting, Agnew flew to Kansas City to meet with another regional session of the association.

(Agnew had met Jan. 13 with Newark Mayor Kenneth A. Gibson, who told newsmen that Newark was "the most financially distressed city in the nation." Gibson also said Agnew had assured him that the President would not reduce existing federal aid to create funds for revenue sharing with cities and states. A spokesman for the vice president, however, said in a clarification that Agnew told Gibson the program "would contain new money, not that it would be completely new money.")

Federal budget. President Nixon Jan. 29, 1971 submitted to Congress his budget for fiscal 1972. Among items involving federal aid to urban areas:

Revenue sharing—Nixon's revenue-sharing plan was budgeted at $3.75 billion for general revenue sharing and $9.61 billion for special revenue sharing. The former program was scheduled to begin Oct. 1 and thus require only three-fourths of the planned $5 billion annual level.

Part of the $9.61 billion was to fund existing grant programs, which were to be absorbed by the special revenue sharing project Jan. 1, 1972. An additional $269 million was to be applied during the six months as a "sweetener" for the program, which had already aroused important Congressional opposition.

The block grants were to include $2.11 billion for urban community development, covering urban renewal and Model Cities programs, among others; $954 million for rural development, such as in Appalachia; $2.9 billion for education, including all elementary and secondary education funds; $1.6 billion for manpower training; $408 million for law enforcement; and $1.91 billion for transportation.

Welfare reform—Nixon urged early enactment of a welfare reform plan that would set national eligibility standards, balance training and work requirements with training and work incentives, provide financial relief to the states and set a floor under benefit payments for "all needy families with children."

Environment—Projected outlays for sewage treatment construction grants in fiscal 1972 totaled $1 billion, an increase from $422 million in fiscal 1971.

The Administration budgeted $129 million for air cleanup projects and $19 million for solid waste activity.

Housing and 'Community' agency—Fiscal 1972 outlays for the Housing and Urban Development Department were budgeted at $3.9 billion, an increase of $552 million over fiscal 1971. Construction of housing for low and moderate income families was to be subsidized at a level of 516,000 units for fiscal 1972, an increase of 50,000.

Nixon had previously proposed that HUD be reorganized, with the word "Community" replacing "Urban" and a new Community Development Special Revenue Sharing plan absorbing, after Jan. 1, 1972, Model Cities, urban renewal, rehabilitation loans and water and sewer grants. Spending for these four programs was estimated at $1.6 billion in fiscal 1971 and $2 billion for fiscal 1972 plus $150 million in revenue sharing funds.

Also under the revenue sharing project, the community action agencies of the Office of Economic Opportunity were to be within the aegis of HUD for transition to full local control by Jan. 1, 1973.

To strengthen state and local planning efforts, the budget called for a $100 million commitment in fiscal 1972, double the previous year's amount.

'General revenue sharing' plan. President Nixon Feb. 4, 1971 sent to Congress a special message and draft legislation on his "general revenue sharing" plan.

The President's "general revenue sharing" plan envisioned a $5 billion fund, automatically financed by taking 1.3% of taxable personal income each year, to be divided among the states on the basis of the state's population and its "tax effort."

As for the secondary distribution—between the states and cities—the message offered an inducement for the states and localities to work out their own "mutually acceptable formula for passing money on to the local level." The inducement was full funding of that state's share of the federal fund. States lacking their own formula would receive only 90% of their share of the federal fund, and this would be distributed under a federal formula with the states getting about half and cities and towns half.

The President presented arguments to meet criticism that taxing and spending authority should "coincide," that $5 billion was too small an amount to apply to the fiscal plight of state and local governments, that revenue sharing would necessitate new taxes, and that a better solution would be to improve the efficiency of state and local tax systems.

Nixon offered a major countering argument that accountability for tax monies depended in the end on the "accessibility" of the disbursing officials to the public and that local officials were more accessible than federal "bureaucrats." "Giving states and localities the power to spend certain federal tax monies," he said, "will increase the influence of each citizen on how those monies are used. It will make government more responsive to taxpayer pressures. It will enhance accountability."

He also contended that the revenue sharing fund would increase as the economy grew, perhaps to as much as $10 billion by 1980, that neither new taxes nor a transfer of funds from existing programs would be required, and that reform of state and local tax systems was not probable in the face of existing political pressures on state and local officials. Therefore, the best solution was to "combine the efficiencies of a centralized tax system with the efficiencies of decentralized expenditure."

The President also cited "a number of additional advantages" that would flow from revenue sharing. "The need for heavier property and sales taxes will be reduced," he said. "New job opportunities will be created at the state and local level. Competition between domestic programs and defense needs will be reduced as the state and local share of domestic spending increases. As the states and localities are renewed and revitalized, we can expect that even more energy and talent will be attracted into government at this level.

"In the final analysis, the purpose of general revenue sharing is to set our states and localities free—free to set new priorities, free to meet unmet needs, free to make their own mistakes, yes, but also free to score splendid successes which otherwise would never be realized .... Because they [state and local officials] live day in and day out with the results of their decisions, they can often measure costs and benefits with greater sensitivity and weigh them against one another with greater precision. Because they are closer to the people they serve, state and local officials will often have a fuller sense of appreciation of local perspectives and values."

Mayors attack Nixon budget. Mayors of nine major U.S. cities, in San Francisco for a meeting of the U.S. Conference of Mayors Feb. 11, attacked President Nixon's budget proposals as a "severe setback" for the cities. The mayors also assailed as "misleading" the President's special revenue sharing plan, which they feared would result in an overall reduction of federal urban aid.

New York Mayor John Lindsay, chairman of the conference's Legislation Action Committee (composed of mayors of the nation's 16 largest cities), said, "Behind the rhetoric, there is a consistent pattern of cutbacks and reductions of urban programs and a lower priority for funds for the cities." The mayors were not objecting to Nixon's general revenue sharing plan, which would supply $5 billion in new money, but to his special revenue sharing proposals not yet presented to Congress.

In a 63-page report, the mayors

charged that Nixon's budget proposals slighted the cities by funding programs at a lower level than authorized by Congress. They said the Administration was withholding $1.3 billion in urban aid already appropriated by Congress. The report said in several cases the budget would entail "reverse revenue sharing," with the federal contribution curtailed. The report cited as an example the community action program of the Office of Economic Opportunity, with federal funds reduced by $22.4 million and local governments' share in the funding increased from 20% to 25%.

(Sixteen mayors on the Legislation Action Committee appealed to Congress Feb. 8 to pass emergency legislation providing federal funds for some 150,-000 public service jobs. Lindsay, testifying before the Senate Subcommittee on Employment, Manpower and Poverty, assailed Nixon for his December 1970 veto of a manpower bill that would have funded a public-service jobs plan. The mayors said the legislation was needed to ease the cities' financial problems, reverse cutbacks in public services and reduce rising urban unemployment.)

Mayors seek help in D.C. A group of some 800 mayors assembled in Washington March 22–23, 1971 to seek additional revenue to apply to their cities' fiscal crises. The mayors met with key members of Congress, were addressed by Vice President Spiro T. Agnew, Housing and Urban Development Secretary George Romney and Sen. Edmund S. Muskie (D, Me.), and a delegation was received at the White House.

The mayors were endorsing President Nixon's proposal for general revenue sharing and were complaining about an Administration "freeze" on urban aid funds voted by Congress.

Spokesmen for the U.S. Conference of Mayors and the National League of Cities, the organizations backing the Washington effort, had told the Senate Housing & Urban Affairs Subcommittee March 3 that the funds "frozen" by the Administration totaled about $1 billion and the cities were being "shortchanged" in funds for urban renewal, Model Cities, water and sewer projects, public housing and mass transit.

The spokesmen, Mayors Lee Alexander of Syracuse and Thomas J. D'Alesandro of Baltimore, supported the general revenue sharing plan, although they felt the Administration was taking away (by impounding appropriated funds) with one hand money that it was giving to the cities (by revenue sharing) with the other hand. As for special revenue sharing, under which categorical grant programs would be consolidated into large block grant programs, they indicated that the mayors' position was tempered by the realization that "full use . . . [was not] being made of the present meager funds."

A 16-member Legislative Action Committee of the U.S. Conference of Mayors met in Washington March 10 with House Speaker Carl Albert (D, Okla.) and Majority Leader Hale Boggs (D, La.). The committee said it was "100%" for general revenue sharing but was recommending, as "the minimum amount needed to save our cities," a $10 billion funding instead of the Administration's $5 billion plan. The phrases were those of New York Mayor John V. Lindsay, who had organized the committee. Lindsay also released that day a list of 474 localities whose applications for a total of 90,289 public housing units had been approved by the federal government but not funded.

The president of the U.S. Conference of Mayors, Mayor James H. J. Tate of Philadelphia, revealed at a news conference March 10 that the committee had been trying for three months to arrange a meeting with the President. Tate attributed the Administration's resistance to the committee's efforts to Nixon's view that the requested meeting would serve as "a [political] buildup for Lindsay." (Lindsay was a potential candidate for a Presidential nomination.)

A Presidential meeting with a delegation of 16 Democratic and 12 Republican mayors attending the Washington conference was held March 23. Reportedly, consent to the meeting was given March 22 with the understanding that Lindsay, whose attendance the mayors insisted on since he was chairman of their legislative group, should not "embarrass the President" by attacking Nixon policies while at the White House. The meeting itself, according to Tate, "opened a dialogue" between the mayors and the President.

Lindsay and a group of mayors had discussed revenue sharing with Rep. Wilbur D. Mills (D, Ark.), chairman of the House Ways and Means Committee, March 22.

Conference sessions of the 800 mayors March 22 were addressed by Agnew, Muskie and Romney. Agnew attacked Congressional Democratic opponents of revenue sharing and urged the mayors not to take any "wooden alternatives."

Muskie, in a reversal of position, denounced the general revenue sharing proposal on the grounds that funds would not go to the cities needing them and that adequate safeguards against discrimination were lacking. He doubted that a "meaningful" revenue sharing would be enacted and urged, "as a viable political objective," support for a federal takeover of welfare costs.

Romney revealed details of the Administration's $2.1 billion revenue sharing plan for "community development," a consolidation of urban renewal, Model Cities, water and sewer and housing rehabilitation loans. Furthermore, he pledged that "no community will receive less annually" and "most cities will receive more" funds under the Administration plan. It called for a distribution of $1.6 billion to 247 "standard metropolitan statistical areas" on the basis of a formula incorporating the "need factors" of total population, the number of households with more than one person per room, the number of substandard housing units and the number of "poverty" families.

In addition, each city would be eligible for funds to insure that it would not lose federal aid under revenue sharing. The calculation would be based on the average federal expenditures to the city in 1965–70 for the programs to be merged under revenue sharing.

Mills criticizes revenue sharing. Rep. Wilbur D. Mills (D, Ark.), chairman of the House Ways and Means Committee, denounced President Nixon's general revenue-sharing plan May 10, 1971.

The President's plan to distribute $5

billion in federal revenues annually to the states and cities without strings, Mills said, "assumes the existence of a nonexistent surplus of revenues" and "has the dangerous potential—indeed probability . . . for destroying rather than strengthening our federal system and the independence of state and local governments."

In the long run, he said, the revenue sharing proposal would make the state governments "dependent entirely on the federal Treasury and on whatever controls Congress or the President subsequently wants to impose."

Stating his position that the legislative body that spent money should be responsible for raising it, Mills declared he was "not yet ready for a new American revolution that would remove this discipline from those who spend the revenues." The way to improve the federal-state partnership, he said, was to seek out "specific areas on a program-by-program basis and determine in a logical, rational, objective manner whether a particular program would lend itself to full federal responsibility." He said Congress intended "to provide relief to both state and local governments" and would do it "in the right way." As an example, he cited legislation pending before his committee for welfare reform by shifting more of the cost to the federal government.

Mills detailed his position on revenue sharing in an address in Nashville before a joint session of the Tennessee General Assembly. (Vice President Spiro T. Agnew had appeared before the same group May 5 to advocate support for the Administration's revenue sharing plan.)

Rep. John W. Byrnes (Wis.), the ranking Republican on Mills' committee, also attacked the Nixon general revenue sharing proposal May 10 and introduced an alternative measure. He called general revenue sharing "bad public finance and poor government" and said it was "of dubious constitutional validity" and "divorces the pleasure of providing public benefits from the odium of imposing taxes."

His "tax sharing" alternative would permit an individual to deduct 20% of his state and local income taxes from his federal income tax, and to have this amount subject to direct state taxation. He estimated that $2.5 billion could become available to the states from such a plan. In a similar procedure, he suggested that about $1 billion could be collected by the states by allowing them a larger share of the federal taxes on estates.

Mills June 9 presented another alternative at a private meeting of Democratic leaders.

According to reports, Mills' plan called for: (a) direct federal aid to cities only (not also to states, counties and other localities as in the Administration program); (b) allocation by a "need formula," taking cognizance of the incidence of welfare clients and poverty (missing from the Administration bill); (c) funding at a first-year $3.5 billion level (compared to a $5 billion level for the Administration plan) and for a limited time, perhaps three or five years (compared with a permanent program proposed by the Administration); (d) allocation by specific purpose (contrasted with the Administration's "no-strings" approach).

Proponents of the plan argued that the states would be relieved of some demand on their funds from the cities directly aided and would gain additional relief from proposed legislative changes to stabilize further increases in state costs for welfare and to hold down Medicaid costs.

The meeting, called by Democratic National Chairman Lawrence F. O'Brien, also was attended by Senate Majority Leader Mike Mansfield (Mont.) and Sen. Edmund S. Muskie (Me.), Govs. Marvin Mandel (Md.) and John J. Gilligan (Ohio) and Mayors Thomas J. D'Alesandro 3rd of Baltimore, Frank W. Burke of Louisville and Henry W. Maier of Milwaukee.

City & County Leaders Meet

International conference. Representatives of 17 nations met in Indianapolis May 25–28, 1971 for the International Conference on Cities, held under the joint auspices of the Nixon Administration and the North Atlantic Treaty Organization (NATO). Indianapolis Mayor Richard G. Lugar (R) was host to 500 delegates and 1,000 observers who discussed urban problems such as environment, housing, transportation and public health.

New York Mayor John V. Lindsay (R) declared in a speech to the meeting May 27 that the cities' problems might be dealt with more effectively if seen as the problems of "national cities." Lindsay, who was currently involved in a dispute with the governor and legislature of New York State over a budget for his city, argued that state governments usually were dominated by rural interests and discriminated against cities. He proposed a fiscal policy in which cities would deal directly with the federal government, bypassing the states.

Cleveland Mayor Carl B. Stokes suggested a similar approach to urban housing problems May 26. Stating the need for an "immense national investment," Stokes proposed that the federal government set up a program under which a family would contribute 20% of its income for housing and a national trust fund would make up the difference between the 20% and the actual cost of rent or home ownership.

Peter E. Walker, Great Britain's minister for the environment, said May 26 that his government was attacking urban problems through a centralized agency. He said transportation, housing, pollution and urban planning were all the concerns of his agency, recently established to provide a "total new approach" to urban problems.

Vice President Spiro Agnew, addressing the conferees May 28, criticized Lindsay's "national cities" proposal.

Agnew also spoke strongly in support of the Administration's decentralization and revenue sharing efforts, against yielding to the pleas of many mayors for massive and immediate federal aid.

Mayors' tour stops at Seattle. Declaring his city the "unemployment capital of the United States," Seattle Mayor Wes Uhlman welcomed members of the Legislative Action Committee of the U.S. Conference of Mayors June 1, 1971.

The touring committee of mayors, led by New York Mayor John V. Lindsay, met to mobilize support for federal legislation to provide cities with funds to hire unemployed workers.

The Seattle stop was the fourth of a national tour during which the big-city mayors hoped to dramatize urban problems. In previous months, the committee had visited Baltimore, San Francisco and New York. The group chose Seattle to discuss unemployment problems because the city had been particularly hard hit by layoffs in the aerospace industry.

At a news conference, the mayors discussed a charge that the committee had been formed to help promote Lindsay as a possible presidential candidate. San Francisco Mayor Joseph L. Alioto said the "notion that this is a political ploy just isn't so." He said the group had pressed Lindsay to serve as chairman "because we thought he was doing the most outstanding job as a mayor. As a matter of fact, I think he would do an outstanding job for the country."

Mayors urge housing pressure. The U.S. conference of mayors, meeting in Philadelphia June 12–16, 1971, unanimously urged President Nixon to deny federal funds to communities that refused to supply low- and moderate-income housing.

The housing resolution expressed "great concern" about Nixon's new housing policy, outlined by the President June 11. Nixon had said the Administration would not impose economic integration on a community.

The mayors' statement called on Nixon to "direct federal agencies administering programs such as, but not limited to, highway appropriations, public works projects and FHA mortgage loan guarantees, as well as community development projects, to advise all communities that the future availability of federal funds for these projects will depend upon the applicant community's commitment to provide low and moderate income housing and its refusal to cooperate in this regard will serve to terminate all such federal assistance."

County leaders meet. The National Association of Counties (NACO), opening its annual convention in Milwaukee July 18, 1971, drew over 2,000 representatives of counties across the nation. The distribution of federal funds, through revenue sharing or other aid programs, emerged as the conference's predominant concern.

Evidence of a shift from an emphasis on rural counties to greater concern with the problems of more densely populated counties also emerged during the convention. Pressure from representatives of the larger urban and suburban counties resulted in a change in voting within the organization from a one-county, one-vote system to a procedure based on county populations. A vocal suburban coalition took form. The NACO's incoming president was William J. Conner, executive of New Castle County, Del., which included the Wilmington suburbs.

At an opening day news conference, Clesson Y. Chikasuye, outgoing NACO president, struck the theme of the convention in urging the counties to "work out a formula together with the cities" to pressure Washington for increased federal aid.

Sen. Robert Dole of Kansas, Republican National Chairman, delivered the keynote speech July 18. Dole said he had "been asked by the White House" to make clear that "in the view of the Administration, county government is an essential part of local government and will be treated on that basis."

Nassau County (N.Y.) Executive Ralph G. Caso presented a proposal to the convention July 19 for a "suburban action team," to serve as a counterweight to the big-city mayors' Legislative Action Committee of the United States Conference of Mayors. Caso warned suburban leaders that they might be "coopted" by the mayors in cooperative lobbying in Washington.

In a 25-page document, Caso presented figures projecting a major shift of Congressional strength in 1972 from the cities to the suburbs and said, "I think it high time that the counties of this country get together on a united front to press for our own needs in Washington. . . . We just can't sit back and let the cities walk all over us."

The mayors' Legislative Action Committee was in Milwaukee July 20 as part of its national "road show" tour to publicize big-city problems. At a breakfast meeting with NACO officials, New York Mayor John Lindsay, chairman of the committee, insisted that the "cities have so much more in common in the things that unite them with the counties than divide them." However, during the group's tour of Milwaukee, Mayor Henry Maier, the host, emphasized suburban-city differences. Mayor Joseph L. Alioto of San Francisco said: "The suburbs are a kind of Robin Hood in reverse, taking from the poor and giving to the rich. Most of the federal funds are generated in the central city, yet the suburbs reap the benefits."

At an inaugural news conference July 20, NACO President Conner rejected Caso's proposal for a group to "rival" the mayors' committee. Conner said that even when the counties were allied with the cities and states, "we have barely enough muscle to get attention on Congress." Conner said that Caso's "figures prove that suburbia is an evergrowing voice in state and national affairs. . . . Once we get the clout, we don't have to get coopted. We can cooperate without surrendering our sovereignty." However, Conner also announced that the NACO had decided to establish a "council of elected county executives" that would be similar to the mayors' committee.

During speeches July 21, the closing day of the convention, Sens. Birch Bayh (D, Ind.) and Hubert H. Humphrey (D, Minn.), both considered leading contenders for the Democratic presidential nomination, drew applause when they supported federal aid to the counties as well as the cities and states. A speech by Rep. Wilbur Mills (D, Ark.), chairman of the House Ways and Means Committee, was not as well received. Mills, in a speech read by his committee counsel John M. Martin Jr., said he continued to oppose federal revenue sharing without some federal control over spending.

Welfare Burden Rises

10% on relief in big cities. A new Health, Education and Welfare Department study, reported by the Washington

Post July 16, 1971, showed more than one of 10 residents in the 26 largest U.S. cities received welfare aid. The study, based on February 1971 data, showed a 22.5% increase nationwide in the number of relief clients since the year before. The total number of persons on welfare in the U.S. was reported to be 14.2 million.

The study was the first made by HEW that focused on big-city relief rates. The closest comparable study, one based on February 1970 statistics of the 20 largest metropolitan areas, had shown 6.5% on welfare in the metropolitan areas.

The report said 10.3% of the residents of the 26 largest cities or the counties that contained them were on relief, compared with 6.9% of the entire U.S. population. Large increases in the big-city relief rolls were shown, with Washington, D.C. leading with a 58% increase over February 1970.

The report listed the following relief dependency rates for nine of the 26 largest cities:

Baltimore, 15.2%; New York, 15%; New Orleans, 14.8%; Philadelphia, 14.8%; St. Louis, 14.7%; San Francisco, 14.2%; Washington, 10.5%; Denver, 10.1%; and Jacksonville, 7.5%.

The following relief dependency rates were listed for counties containing the remaining 17 of the 26 largest cities:

Suffolk (Boston), 16.6%; Los Angeles, 12.7%; Shelby (Memphis), 9.8%; Wayne (Detroit), 9.1%; Cuyahoga (Cleveland), 8.8%; Cook and DuPage (Chicago), 8.1%; San Diego, 7.4%; Allegheny (Pittsburgh), 7%; Bexar (San Antonio), 6.7%; Franklin (Columbus, Ohio), 6.7%; Milwaukee and Washington (Milwaukee), 6.2%; Clay, Jackson and Platte (Kansas City, Mo.), 5.5%; King (Seattle), 5.2%; Dallas, 5%; Fort Bend, Harris and Montgomery (Houston), 4.2%; Maricopa (Phoenix), 4%; and Marion (Indianapolis), 3.4%.

Welfare right upheld. The Supreme Court, in a 5–3 decision March 23, 1970, ruled that welfare recipients had the constitutional right to formal hearings, complete with constitutional safe-guards, before officials can terminate their benefits. Under the court's order, procedures in use in California and New York City were declared unconstitutional.

The ruling marked the first time the Supreme Court had said that welfare officials must satisfy the Constitution's "due process of law" requirement before ending payments to welfare recipients.

The majority decision was entered by Justice William J. Brennan Jr. and joined by Justices Byron R. White, Thurgood Marshall, William O. Douglas and John M. Harlan.

Justice Hugo L. Black delivered a dissenting report and was joined by Chief Justice Warren E. Burger and Justice Potter Stewart.

Under the court order, welfare payments could not be terminated until the recipient had been given notice of the reasons he was considered to be ineligible for further benefits and an opportunity to appear with counsel at a hearing before "an impartial decision-maker" to testify and cross-examine all witnesses. The court said the welfare recipients who appeared before the hearing were entitled to counsel, but ruled that the state did not have to furnish it. After completion of the hearing, the decision-maker was required to submit a written ruling, explaining why the benefits had been terminated, if he so ruled.

The Justice Department had joined welfare officials in warning the Supreme Court that a decision in favor of the nearly nine million persons reported receiving welfare benefits could engulf welfare agencies with their demands for hearings while ineligible persons remained on relief rolls.

In his majority report, Justice Brennan said humanitarian considerations outweighed such administrative and fiscal concerns. He said welfare assistance was "not mere charity," but a means to "promote the general welfare and secure the blessings of liberty" as stated in the preamble to the Constitution. He concluded that the Constitution required that without due process of law, payments must be given without interruption to those who were eligible for them.

Justice Black, in the dissenting report, termed welfare a "gratuity" that was "nice for those who do not work but receive payments from the government—that is to say, those who do work."

Officials' visits upheld. In a 6–3 ruling Jan. 12, 1971, the Supreme Court upheld the right of state and local welfare officials to visit the homes of recipients and to cut off funds from persons who refused to let them enter their homes. The justices overturned a federal district court ruling in New York that welfare caseworkers without search warrants could not force their way into the homes of persons on public assistance. Justice Harry A. Blackmun, writing his first majority opinion since joining the Supreme Court, said the "caseworker is not a sleuth but rather, we trust, is a friend in need." He gave as a parallel one who dispenses private charity, who "naturally has an interest in and expects to know how his charitable funds are utilized and put to work."

Dissenting Justices William O. Douglas, Thurgood Marshall and William J. Brennan Jr. argued that the ruling violated the spirit of a 1967 high court decision that housing and fire inspectors did not have the right to force their way into business premises without a warrant. They said that the difference was that welfare recipients were "the lowly poor."

The case involved Mrs. Barbara James of New York City, who had refused to allow a city caseworker to enter her home in connection with welfare payments to support her young son. Welfare officials decided to cut off her payments.

Revised welfare plan offered. The Nixon Administration, under pressure from Congressional critics, revised its Family Assistance Plan (FAP) Feb. 24, 1971. The plan included an $800 million program to put 225,000 welfare recipients into city and state public jobs. The revision was presented by Health, Education and Welfare Undersecretary John G. Veneman at a closed meeting of the House Ways and Means Committee.

Rep. Wilbur D. Mills (D, Ark.), chairman of the committee, had told the Administration Feb. 10 that it must revise its FAP proposal to meet what he called the "legitimate criticism" raised during 1970 hearings by the Senate Finance Committee. Senate critics objected that the plan lacked work incentive provisions and would add too many people to relief rolls.

Under the proposal presented by Veneman, able-bodied welfare recipients would have to sign up for jobs. If private jobs were not available, they would be assigned to work in city parks, hospitals, garbage collection departments or other public service jobs that would pay at least $1.20 per hour. The federal government would pay the full cost of the program for the first year. The states would pay 25% the second year and 50% the third in an arrangement that Veneman said would encourage states to move workers to jobs in the private sector.

In other revisions, Veneman proposed that the basic allotment for a family of four be increased from $1,600 to $2,200 a year and that food stamp benefits be eliminated.

NYC suit vs. U.S. & state. New York Mayor John V. Lindsay Feb. 24, 1971 personally filed suit against federal and state government officials in an effort to have welfare costs mandated to the city declared illegal. Lindsay admitted the suit was "a long shot." Asked if he expected the action to bring political pressure for relief to the cities, he answered, "I hope it will help."

The suit argued that New York City, required to pay $549 million in welfare benefits in the current fiscal year and $600 million in the next, would be virtually bankrupted and prevented from performing local services such as police and fire protection.

The suit also contended that since New York City had the biggest annual welfare bill in the country—$1.9 billion —the city's taxpayers were unfairly deprived of "equal protection of the law."

Welfare cuts trigger New York riot. Hundreds of youths in the Brownsville section of New York City set scores of fires and fought police May 5, 1971 after day-long peaceful demonstrations by community residents against state budget cuts for welfare and related programs.

The rioting began after thousands of angry Brownsville residents closed off dozens of streets in their neighborhood with abandoned cars and trash piles to protest state budget cuts affecting welfare assistance, anti-narcotics programs, Medicaid, educational facilities and the food stamp program. Organizers of the protest later disavowed any of the actions of the rioting youths.

The residents' mid-day demonstrations were organized to protest a 10% cutback in welfare payments, made under legislation signed April 15 by Gov. Nelson A. Rockefeller.

States cut welfare funds. A Health, Education and Welfare Department (HEW) survey, reported by the Associated Press July 8, 1971, found 22 states were reducing welfare benefits or were planning to effect reductions by the end of the year. The survey, submitted to HEW Undersecretary John G. Veneman, said the findings indicated a reversal of a long trend of higher assistance for the poor.

The study of family welfare programs said cuts of up to 20% had been ordered in 10 states and reductions by the end of 1971 were possible in 12 additional states. Moves to cut benefits failed in the legislatures of four states. The study listed 1971 aid increases in four states and the District of Columbia and increases were said to be possible in three other states.

The 10 states slated for definite reductions were Alabama, Georgia, Kansas, Maine, Nebraska, New Jersey, New Mexico, New York, Rhode Island and South Dakota. The 12 states listed for possible reduction were Arizona, California, Connecticut, Delaware, Idaho, Illinois, Minnesota, New Hampshire, Oregon, Pennsylvania, Texas and Vermont.

Four states pass residency requirements—Despite a 1969 Supreme Court ruling that residency requirements for welfare benefits were unconstitutional except in cases of "compelling state interests," legislatures in four states passed one-year residency requirements in June and July. But federal courts invalidated two of the state laws by early August.

Hawaii Gov. John Burns signed legislation setting up the residency requirement June 7, to take effect June 22. The Hawaii bill was passed partly due to fear that many applicants from among an estimated total of 6,000 young people expected in the islands as part of an annual summer influx would apply.

New York Gov. Nelson Rockefeller's office announced June 23 that a welfare residency requirement bill had been signed and would take effect immediately. A three-judge federal panel in Buffalo ruled Aug. 9 that the new law was unconstitutional. A welfare residency law passed by the state had been struck down by the U.S. Supreme Court in 1969, and the new law had attempted to justify the one-year residency requirement with the "compelling governmental interest" exception suggested by the Supreme Court ruling.

The state had argued that New York was getting back only 43% from the federal government for its $8 million a year welfare program while Mississippi, with much lower benefits, was getting 78% federal reimbursement. The American Civil Liberties Union (ACLU) said relief rolls in New York increased 11% in fiscal 1971, the lowest proportionate rise in all 50 states.

One-year welfare residency requirements were approved by the Connecticut and Illinois legislatures July 1, but the Connecticut law, modeled on the New York legislation, was voided by a three-judge federal court in Hartford July 29.

California enacts welfare reform—The reform measure Aug. 11 following a compromise between Gov. Ronald Reagan and Democratic leaders of the legislature who had fought his proposals. The legislation stiffened eligibility rules, established residency requirements and tightened controls on fraud in the state's $2 billion annual welfare system.

Reagan also agreed to a provision for a cost-of-living increase mechanism for Aid to Families with Dependent Children (AFDC) recipients. AFDC clients had received no increase in California from 1957 until earlier in 1971 when courts ordered a 21% increase.

Other provisions would increase basic AFDC grants while decreasing checks for families with outside incomes. A provision made it possible to attach the wages of a father who had deserted a welfare family, and state income tax records of recipients would be open to welfare officials. Welfare rights groups planned to challenge some of the provisions in court.

Reagan signed the welfare measure

and a companion Medi-Cal reform bill Aug. 13. Savings to the state from the Medi-Cal bill were estimated at $200 million a year.

Work for those on welfare. President Nixon Aug. 20, 1971 announced a demonstration project under which welfare recipients in parts of Illinois, New York and California would be required to take public service jobs or forfeit part of their relief grants. A work requirement formed part of the President's family assistance welfare reform proposal.

Health, Education and Welfare Undersecretary John G. Veneman said Nixon had discussed the experiment with New York Gov. Nelson A. Rockefeller and Illinois Gov. Richard B. Ogilvie Aug. 18. California Gov. Ronald Reagan had met with the President Aug. 20.

New York and California had both enacted recent welfare-work legislation. The California legislation included welfare mothers and unemployed fathers.

The New York law, which took effect July 1, applied only to clients receiving general assistance, a state program not funded by the federal government. Veneman said the demonstration project would extend the New York program to include Aid to Families with Dependent Children (AFDC) clients. He said, however, that HEW foresaw no work requirements for mothers with children who needed daytime care unless daycare facilities were available.

New York City Human Resources Administrator Jules M. Sugarman said Oct. 3 that the state work-relief law had had "only a marginal effect" in reducing city welfare rolls. Sugarman said that although 20% (5,911 persons) of the city's eligible recipients had failed to comply with the work requirement according to first reports, 2,400 of these were found to have had legitimate reasons.

He said an analysis of the August relief rolls showed only a 4% drop (1,152 persons) related to noncompliance with the new law. Sugarman said 1,331 others had been taken off relief rolls for "normal" reasons.

Sugarman said he was concerned because the initial reports left a "grossly untrue" impression that 20% of the recipients were improperly on relief rolls.

Health, Education & Welfare Secretary Elliot L. Richardson Nov. 24 approved two experimental welfare plans proposed by New York state that would require some recipients to accept public service jobs, and would penalize others for failing to utilize counseling or work services. The plans were approved on condition that the state provide further financial and administration data. The plans had been developed as part of the project announced Aug. 20.

The New York plan included two parts, labeled "Public Service Work Opportunities Project" and "Incentives for Independence." In the work project, all employable members of 88,500 families, one fourth of those in the Aid to Families with Dependent Children category, would be required to work off their grants in public agencies at prevailing wage rates, accept training, or provide day care for the children of other working recipients.

The incentive plan, which was confined to three localities and was to last one year, would penalize families that refused work and counseling services, provide some full-time public sector jobs for recipients, and set up $1.50 an hour jobs for 15–18-year-old welfare schoolchildren.

HEW approved the experiment after New York state confirmed Nov. 4 that it had dropped a controversial "Brownie point" system. The system, which would have been imposed in an inner city neighborhood, a suburban and a rural county, would have sharply reduced payments to recipient families. The families could then have recouped the money by earning points for children's regular school attendance, participation in community projects or membership in Scout groups, cleaning or repairing residences or reporting the whereabouts of missing fathers.

Work rule voted for welfare aid. Congress, by voice votes of both houses, approved legislation Dec. 14, 1971 for a national work registration requirement for almost all adults receiving welfare aid, many of whom were mothers with dependent children. President Nixon signed this "workfare" bill Dec. 28.

The legislation originated in the Senate Dec. 11 as amendments introduced by Sen. Herman Talmadge (D, Ga.) to a minor Social Security bill. They were accepted by a Senate-House conference committee and adopted with little discussion by both houses Dec. 14.

The welfare work plan would require, effective July 1, 1972, all those receiving benefits under Aid to Families with Dependent Children to register for work or training unless they were children (under 16), elderly, ill, mothers with children under six years of age, or supporting someone incapacitated.

Under current law, each state determined the registrants and referred "appropriate" welfare recipients for employment.

The federal government would assume 90% of the cost of day care services for children of working mothers, and 100% of the cost of public service jobs for, the employable adults in the first year of the new program, 75% in the second year and 50% in the third year.

Although there was little debate on the bill at final passage, concern was expressed by some that enactment of the bill impaired the chances for passage of the Nixon Administration's welfare reform bill, which combined work requirements with work incentives, such as a guaranteed annual income. Rep. John W. Byrnes (Wis.), senior Republican on the House Ways and Means Committee, commented Dec. 14 that the Talmadge welfare plan "contains the stick but not the carrot."

The National Welfare Rights Organization Dec. 14 called the work requirement bill "an act of stupidity."

Poverty bill vetoed. President Nixon Dec. 9, 1971 vetoed a compromise two-year $6 billion bill extending the Office of Economic Opportunity (OEO) and setting up a $2 billion child development and day care program. The Senate failed the next day to override the veto by a 51–36 vote, seven short of the necessary two thirds.

In a strongly worded veto message, Nixon said the child care provisions would "commit the vast moral authority of the national government to the side of communal approaches to child rearing against the family-centered approach," and would create "a new army of bureaucrats." While he affirmed support for day care provisions of the House welfare reform bill and other federal child care programs, Nixon said "good public policy requires that we enhance rather than diminish both parental authority and parental involvement with children."

The bill, passed in final form by the Senate 63–17 Dec. 2 and the House 210–186 Dec. 7, would have provided free day care to all children in families with incomes up to $4,320, reduced cost day care for families earning up to $6,960, and full cost care for all other children. The programs would have been operated by local government units of at least 5,000 population, leaving the states, in Nixon's words, "relegated to an insignificant role."

Nixon had been urged to sign the bill by a wide range of legal, educational, labor, welfare, religious and women's organizations, and bipartisan groups in both Houses. Opponents claimed that costs would eventually soar, and that the day care program was unnecessary on such a scale.

Jobless aid extended. Congress gave final approval and sent to the White House Dec. 15 a bill to extend unemployment compensation an additional 13 weeks in states where the jobless rate was 6.5% or more for 13 consecutive weeks. President Nixon signed the measure Dec. 29. In a statement Dec. 30, Nixon criticized the legislation as "a sharp departure from previous practice under which employer taxes have been used to finance such aid." This program, he said, where the financing came from general tax revenues, was "another program of public welfare," he said.

Currently, the program would cost $454 million by applying to 732,000 unemployed workers in Alaska, California, Connecticut, Maine, Massachusetts, Michigan, Nevada, New Jersey, New York, Oregon, Rhode Island, Vermont, Washington and Puerto Rico.

Jobs Programs

A major effect of the long inflationary spiral and an early symptom of approaching recession was an increase in unemployment. Cities were especially hard hit, and efforts were made to provide work for the growing ranks of the unemployed.

Jobless areas rise to 65. Three more areas were added Oct. 28, 1971 to the Labor Department's list of metropolitan areas with unemployment of at least 6% of the labor force, raising the total to a 10-year high of 65.

The three additions were all in Ohio—Canton, Lorain-Elyria and Youngstown-Warren. Two cities in Indiana—South Bend and Terre Haute—were removed from the list.

At the same time, the Labor Department announced it had added eight areas to its list of smaller cities with a jobless rate of 6% or more. Three areas were dropped, leaving 785 areas on the small-city list.

The number of metropolitan areas on the 6% jobless list declined to 60 Nov. 29 with the removal of seven areas but the addition of two.

Areas put on the list earlier (Aug. 30) were Philadelphia, Boston, Fort Worth, Dayton, Ohio, Shreveport, La., Wilkes-Barre-Hazelton, Pa., Charleston, S.C., and Davenport, Iowa-Rock Island-Moline, Ill. The Labor Department added the San Francisco-Oakland and Gary-Hammond-East Chicago, Ind. areas to the list Sept. 30.

Manpower training. Nixon proposed March 4, 1971, in his second revenue-sharing message that states and cities be permitted to use federal funds to develop temporary public service jobs to train the unemployed.

In December 1970 the President had vetoed a manpower bill with a similar provision for a public service program, which, he had charged, would only create "dead-end jobs in the public sector." Nixon's new plan stipulated that a public service job could be held no longer than two years and should be regarded as

a "transitional opportunity" leading to a regular job with a public or private employer.

Under the proposal a number of existing programs would be consolidated into an annual $2 billion program of unearmarked grants to state and local governments representing 100,000 or more persons. The President stressed that his proposal was not intended to supplant or terminate any program, but to enable the "continuation, expansion or modification of each program [to] be determined . . . by the test of performance alone—and determined by the state or community which the program serves."

The President based his proposal on the idea that manpower programs were best devised and controlled at local levels free from the "bureaucratic jungle." He stressed that the plan (1) was optional, (2) allowed state and local governments to devise their own works plans, (3) freed city, county and state budgets from matching and maintenance-of-effort restrictions, and (4) dispensed with stringent accountability requirements, except for annual audits and publication of spending plans.

Of the proposed $2 billion for the program—a one-third increase over existing manpower outlays—85% would be divided among state and local governments by statutory formula according to proportionate numbers of workers, unemployed persons and low-income adults. The Labor Department would retain 15% for research, development of computerized job banks, experimental manpower programs and local staff training assistance. The proposal also contained a "trigger" feature to automatically release additional funds if the nation's unemployment level ranged 4.5% or higher for three straight months or more.

Nixon vetoes public works bill. Reaffirming an Administration policy against increasing federal spending during a time of inflation, President Nixon June 29, 1971 vetoed a bill designed to provide jobs for the unemployed through an accelerated public works program. The bill had been passed in its final form by the Senate June 8 and House June 15. Originally, the Senate had approved the bill in March primarily as an extension of the Appalachian program. The accelerated public works program had been added by the House when it adopted the bill in April. The Senate vote was 45–33 (42 D & 3 R vs. 32 R & 1 D). In the House, the vote was 275–104, with 65 Republicans joining an almost solid Democratic majority in approval.

The veto of the bill was upheld July 14 when a 57–36 Senate vote to override fell five votes short of the two-thirds necessary to cancel a veto.

The bill called for a $2 billion public works program, modeled after a Kennedy Administration program later abandoned, to provide up to 80% federal grants to areas of high unemployment to build sewers, hospitals, public buildings and other facilities.

The bill also would have provided a four-year, $1.5 billion extension of the Appalachian Regional Commission and a two-year, $2 billion extension of the Public Works and Economic Development Act financing other regional commissions.

Nixon's veto was directed at the $2 billion accelerated public works program, which he described as a "costly and time-consuming method of putting unemployed persons to work." He also said it would stimulate construction jobs, which also had little immediate effect on joblessness, instead of helping "the broad spectrum of the presently unemployed."

The President urged Congress to re-enact the other programs incorporated in the bill. He expressed support for another bill before Congress for a $2.2 billion program to provide public service jobs.

Public-service jobs approved. A $2.25 billion program to create public-service work for the unemployed was approved by 75–11 Senate vote June 29, 1971 and 343–14 House vote July 1. President Nixon, who had expressed his satisfaction with this bill when he vetoed the public-works bill, signed the measure July 12.

The bill would provide federal funds, whenever the unemployment rate reached 4.5% of the work force for three consecutive months, for 90% of the wages for emergency jobs in schools, hospitals,

parks, police and fire departments and social service agencies. A provision was included to make the funds available to local areas having a 6% jobless rate even if the national rate fell below 4.5%. Job preference would be allotted to veterans who served in Indochina or Korea within the last seven years.

A $1 billion appropriation for the program was passed by 321–76 House vote Aug. 4 and 68–10 Senate vote Aug. 6 and was signed by Nixon Aug. 9. The money was designed to provide 150,000 jobs in state, county and city governments for the unemployed.

Job accord in New Orleans. New Orleans city officials joined local representatives of the construction industry, craft unions, and a coalition of area chapters of the National Association for the Advancement of Colored People (NAACP) and the Urban League to announce July 26, 1970 their agreement on a plan to increase minority hiring and open the unions' rank-and-file membership to Negroes.

The "New Orleans Plan" was designed to place more members of minority groups, mainly blacks, in the construction industry labor pool in the New Orleans area. One official said, however, that the plan was put together to prevent the federal government from implementing more stringent racial hiring guidelines in the New Orleans area.

A similar plan had been designed for Atlanta by local groups in July but it was rejected by the NAACP and Urban League.

A spokesman for the New Orleans NAACP-Urban League coalition said the Atlanta plan had been rejected because it did not mention a minority group quota for union membership. The plan agreed to by NAACP-Urban League officials in New Orleans contained a provision calling for a 20% minority group membership in all New Orleans construction trades and crafts unions.

Housing & Urban Renewal

The problems of inadequate housing and racial segregation in housing are widely recognized as basic factors in the complex urban dilemma. Consequently, housing and urban renewal plans and efforts to eliminate discrimination usually are major elements in serious programs for dealing with the ills of the cities.

Romney assesses housing lack. Housing & Urban Development Secretary George Romney reported Jan. 8, 1970 that despite record-breaking production of federally-assisted low and middle income housing units in 1969, the nation would begin the 1970s with a housing shortage of 2,574,000 units—the greatest shortage since World War II. Romney attributed the crisis to declines in private housing starts caused by high interest rates and other factors.

Romney predicted that federally-subsidized housing starts would increase in 1970 by about 220% over the 1969 record of 165,000 units. He said the Nixon Administration was considering his proposals to ease the housing crisis by measures to attract more money to the housing market, perhaps by offering tax incentives.

Romney denied charges made by Boston Mayor Kevin H. White (D) that political considerations were involved in a HUD cutback of a grant that White had considered a commitment to Boston's urban renewal program. White, who had expected to receive about $70 million in additional funds for Boston's urban renewal projects, had been told by HUD that he would receive a maximum of $20 million. Romney said urban renewal costs had "gotten out of control" because of Johnson Administration policies that encouraged mayors to underestimate renewal costs when first applying for funds. The secretary said a study of projects in 200 cities showed that urban renewal costs had doubled over a period of years due to requests for additional funds. According to a New York Times report Jan. 9, HUD had notified 50–60 cities that funds for existing projects would be cut off after only one additional grant.

Nixon pledges housing action. President Nixon Jan. 21 pledged his Administration would "take every possible step to solve this most serious housing problem consistent with the overriding need to contain inflation." The pledge was made in a statement affirming the "top national priority" of housing.

In his statement, Nixon reaffirmed his intention to avoid unnecessary federal spending and urged "the private sector to follow this example by also postponing avoidable expenditures and increasing savings."

Paul W. McCracken, chairman of the Council of Economic Advisers, in briefing newsmen on Nixon's statement, conceded that the housing industry was "in a recession." Largely because of a severe shortage of mortgage funds, housing starts fell to an annual rate of 1.4 million in 1969—1.8 million at the start of the year and 1.2 million at the end. An "adequate" annual rate, Mc-Cracken said, would be from 1.5–1.7 million.

Mayors denounce HUD cutbacks. The executive committee of the U.S. Conference of Mayors, meeting in Washington, D.C. Jan. 28, 1970, scored Housing & Urban Development Department (HUD) cutbacks of grants for ongoing urban renewal projects. The 31 mayors on the committee issued a statement deploring what they termed HUD's departure "from the practices and moral commitments of two decades." The statement continued: "Renewal projects caught midway in the delivery of benefits for which the cities have so long pioneered their labors are now told that they are on their own" regardless of the cities' "desperate financial condition."

Budget. President Nixon Feb. 2, 1970 submitted to Congress his federal budget for fiscal 1971.

The budget for the Housing & Urban Development Department (HUD) totaled $3.3 billion. It reflected plans to increase production of housing for low and moderate income families. Outlays for all federal housing programs were scheduled to rise from $2.8 billion in 1970 to $3.6 billion, with a $615 million increase allotted for insured loans in rural areas for subsequent sale by the

Farmers Home Administration, and a $294 million rise for payments supporting low income housing.

The urban renewal and Model Cities programs were to continue at their current levels—a $1 billion authorization for urban renewal and $575 million for Model Cities. Because of the addition in both programs of carry-over funds, actual spending was projected at $1.082 billion for urban renewal ($1.049 billion in 1970) and $530 million for Model Cities ($300 million in 1970).

In other programs, outlays were to increase from $475 million to $644 million in fiscal 1971 for low rent public housing, from $272.4 million to $313 million in 1971 for metropolitan development (planning grants, technical aid, new communities, etc.), from $15 million to $25 million in 1971 for urban technology and research (including $12 million for Operation Breakthrough for utilization of new technological methods for mass production of homes).

Outlays for rent supplements were budgeted at $41.4 million ($18.7 million in 1970), for the home ownership and rental housing programs at $102 million ($19.1 million in 1970).

Outlays to enforce fair housing and employment codes in the industry were to rise to $11.3 million compared to $6.28 million in 1970.

HUD Secretary George Romney at a news conference Feb. 2 said his department's budget had been "cut to the bone" deliberately on the theory that an overall balanced budget would ease the troubled housing industry by making more capital available for private home building.

No urban funds diversion. HUD Secretary Romney, after meeting with President Nixon May 14, 1970, said the President had decided not to divert money from the Model Cities program or urban renewal to finance school desegregation and aid to racially impacted school districts. Romney said, "No city need be concerned about our following through on the projected allocations and commitments they expected."

Nixon March 24 had pledged $1.5 billion over the next two years to aid ra-

cially isolated schools, $500 million of the funds to be diverted from money budgeted for fiscal 1971 operation of other unspecified programs.

Reacting to reports that all or part of the $500 million would come from appropriations requested for Model Cities, mayors and congressmen from urban areas requested Romney to rescue the program, which had been budgeted for fiscal 1971 at only about half the level projected by the Johnson Administration.

Romney, in a May 6 letter to Rep. George H. Mahon (D, Tex.), chairman of the House Appropriations Committee, and in his May 14 meeting with the President, appeared to be responding to pleas to save Model Cities and other urban programs.

Urban renewal, housing reports. The White House released two task force reports July 22, 1970 on the urban renewal program and on low-income housing. The reports, submitted to the President Jan. 15, recommended measures to encourage building of low-income housing in the suburbs rather than concentrating it in central cities.

The report on the 21-year-old urban renewal program, prepared by a panel under the direction of Washington economist Miles L. Colean, recommended that federal aid "of all sorts" be withheld from communities that resisted housing projects for low-income families. The panel said such a measure might "break the suburban barrier around the central cities." The task force urged continuation of the urban renewal program but said that concentration of low-income housing sites in central cities tended to "perpetuate and intensify racial segregation."

The low-income housing panel also urged measures to open the suburbs to housing for the poor. The report, prepared under the direction of Barnard College professor Raymond J. Saulnier, said that some form of guaranteed income or income maintenance would do more to solve the problems of inadequate housing than "specialized categorical assistance programs." The panel also urged flexibility in interest rates on government-supported home loans, development of improved construction techniques and efforts to encourage home ownership for the poor.

(In a related development, public housing directors from 19 major U.S. cities called for increased federal aid July 22 to meet "a serious national crisis" in providing housing for the poor. Speaking at a news conference after the group met in Washington, Edward J. White Jr. of New Haven, Conn. said that, at present, 200 local housing authorities could not meet operating expenses of low-income projects "without increasing rents beyond the tenants' ability to pay.")

Nixon scored on suburban housing. In a letter to the White House, a national civil rights group Dec. 9, 1970 accused Administration officials of working against HUD Secretary George Romney's efforts to promote open housing in the nation's suburban communities. The National Committee Against Discrimination in Housing said it had asked President Nixon to "lead the nation toward development of open communities."

(President Nixon said Dec. 10 that his Administration would not use the power of the federal government "in ways not required by the law" for forced integration of suburban communities. In response to a question at his news conference, the President said he believed that "forced integration in the suburbs is not in the national interest." He said the government would act only to the extent that the law required. He said his Administration would see "as a result of acts passed by Congress, that the federal government not provide aid to housing or to urban renewal where a community has a policy of discrimination and has taken no steps to remove it.")

The co-directors of the housing group, Jack E. Wood Jr. and Edward Rutledge, said their letter expressed alarm at "apparent ambivalence" within the Nixon Administration concerning the enforcement of open housing and civil rights laws.

Romney had been instrumental in the development of plans calling for more federally subsidized housing in the sub-

urbs, but the plans had been held up after evoking considerable opposition. Attorney General John N. Mitchell had reportedly clashed with Romney over the plans. The plans were then suspended by the White House pending further discussions with the President.

The civil rights group, which had its headquarters in New York City, had played a leading role in the passage of fair housing laws and development of court rulings involving open housing.

Housing plan for Dayton suburbs. White suburbanites living on the outskirts of Dayton, Ohio were reported Dec. 16 to have accepted a voluntary plan to provide housing in their communities for the poor. Local officials reportedly approved the plan over outspoken opposition by some residents.

The arrangement, which was said to be the first of its type in the U.S., included as its keystone a plan that would dispense federally subsidized low and moderate income housing throughout the five-county area surrounding Dayton. Each community would be assigned a quota, its share of about 14,000 dwellings—most of them public housing—that were to be constructed during the next four years. If the plan were implemented, it would bring about both neighborhood and school integration in Dayton's suburbs.

Like many other cities across the U.S., Dayton had lost population while its suburbs had gained. Dayton, an industrial city of 250,000, was at the center of a metropolitan area of 842,000. While more whites quit the central-city neighborhoods, the poor became increasingly concentrated in the inner city.

The plan was unveiled in July after a long study by a commission made up of elected officials of the five counties and 29 municipalities in Southwestern Ohio. The group, known as the Miami Valley Commission, had been delegated authority to coordinate federal grants to the area.

In the plan, the commission divided the area, including Dayton, into 53 "planning units," each of them assigned a quota of subsidized dwellings under a formula that took into account the num-

ber of existing units for low income families, population and other factors.

Housing bill passed. A compromise $2.9
billion housing bill was passed by the Senate Dec. 18, 1970 and by 168–104 House
vote Dec. 19. President Nixon signed it
Jan. 1, 1971.

The final version included a new aid
program for "new communities" in
suburban-rural areas and in inner cities.
It also included authorization for an
additional $1.5 billion for urban renewal
subsidies, an additional $260 million for
Model Cities grants for fiscal 1972, federal burglary and theft insurance for
merchants and landlords in high-crime
areas where private insurance was unavailable, FHA loans of up to $15,000
(a $5,000 increase) for purchase of
mobile homes, and a rent ceiling of 25%
of income for tenants of public housing.

The "new communities" provision
called for creation of a five-member Community Development Corporation within the Housing and Urban Development
Department to administer the loan and
guarantee programs. The funds were to
go toward acquisition of land for development in new and blighted areas, loan
guarantees for long-range building plans
and grants for public services. Up to
$500 million was authorized for bonds,
debentures or other obligations incurred
nationally by private or public developers.
Additional authorizations of up to $240
million were allotted for development
loans and $5 million for planning sub-
sidies.

The House-Senate conference eliminated a Senate provision that would
have provided $750 million to pay
operating deficits of mass-transit systems.
Another Senate provision for a $10 mil-
lion annual authorization to build housing
for migrant farm workers also was
eliminated. A House-approved amendment deleted by the conferees would have
nullified the HUD requirement that
communities had to provide for low-
and moderate income housing in order
to qualify for federal subsidies for water
and sewer facilities.

Ownership program scored. The House
Banking & Currency Committee Jan. 5,

1971 released a staff report denouncing
the Federal Housing Administration
(FHA) for allowing speculation and
"sheer fraud" in a federal home ownership program. The study concerned
Section 235 of the 1968 Omnibus Housing Act, which authorized the government to insure and pay a portion of the
interest on mortgages to allow low and
moderate income familites to purchase
homes for down payments as low as
$200.

The report, which was released along
with a reply issued by HUD Secretary George Romney, charged that in
new construction of Section 235 houses,
"FHA has appraised houses for figures
that are inflated by several thousands
of dollars above the true value of the
home. The construction of these homes
is of the cheapest type of building materials, and . . . people purchasing these
houses are buying a disaster." The report
also charged that "FHA is insuring existing homes that are of such poor quality
that there is little or no possibility they
can survive the life of mortgage."

The survey, conducted in the summer
and fall of 1969, covered programs in the
following cities: Paterson, N.J.; Washington; St. Louis and Elmwood, Mo.;
Philadelphia and Pittsburgh; Seattle,
Spokane and Everett, Wash.; and Berkeley, Calif. The report said there was
"something basically wrong" in that the
"FHA views itself solely as a mortgage
insurer whose interest is in the adequacy
of the security for the loan rather than
decent, safe and sanitary housing for
people."

Romney, in his statement released with
the report, said there had been abuses in
the program due to a "dramatic work-
load increase" caused by the "massive
federal leap into the field of subsidized
home ownership." The statement had
been made to the committee Dec. 17,
1970.

The program was suspended Jan. 14,
but Romney announced Feb. 5 that he
was resuming it in selected areas.

Romney said 21 regional HUD and
Federal Housing Administration offices
would resume issuance of mortgage commitments. The suspension remained in
effect for the rest of the country. The
offices served the following states:

Maine, Rhode Island, New Mexico, Iowa, Nebraska, Montana, North and South Dakota, Utah, Wyoming and Idaho. The remaining offices covered by the order served Puerto Rico and the following cities: Albany, Hempstead and New York, N.Y.; Tampa, Fla.; Memphis; Shreveport, La.; Tulsa, Okla.; and Houston and Lubbock, Tex.

At a hearing of the House committee March 31, Romney described steps taken to end abuses in the program.

Romney said a HUD examination of the cases cited in the staff report "confirmed in major part" the findings of the committee, but he said the program had been successful in enabling an estimated 160,000 families to move into housing superior to former accommodations.

Romney also said HUD had added training programs for appraisers. He said guidelines for appraisals had been toughened and staff had been added to field offices.

HUD announced April 2 that seven additional HUD-FHA insuring offices had been reauthorized to approve mortgage commitments made in the program. The seven offices served Maryland, Delaware, Nevada, Hawaii, Sacramento and Santa Ana, Calif. and Pittsburgh.

HUD freezes aid to NY slums & Newark. Charging that New York City failed to provide "decent, safe and sanitary" housing for persons displaced by urban renewal, HUD announced Feb. 11, 1971 an immediate "embargo" of federal contributions to the city's slum clearance programs. HUD regional administrator S. William Green charged that staff audits had shown "widespread deficiencies" in city relocation efforts.

Green said he hoped the embargo would be "shortlived" but he said it would not be lifted "until the city demonstrates it has adequate relocation facilities and is complying with all federal requirements governing relocation."

Albert A. Walsh, New York housing administrator, denounced the action as "precipitous, unfounded and potentially destructive." Simeon Golar, chairman of the city Housing Authority, admitted that some families were relocated into faulty city-owned housing, but he added, "with all our problems, our [relocating] performance has been unprecedented in this city and the nation."

HUD announced April 15 that $400,-000 in aid due the Newark Housing Authority would be withheld because the agency had refused to reorganize itself as ordered in January. The authority, fourth largest in the U.S., had annual expenses of $11 million and had accumulated a $1.4 million deficit in operating its 12,721 apartments in 17 housing projects.

A team of HUD specialists had said in January the Newark agency was "top-heavy" with "many employes performing tasks of dubious value." It also charged that the director of the Newark agency was "not administrating adequately" the dual functions of public housing and urban renewal.

Answering the charges Feb. 22, the Newark authority admitted large increases in staff but said the additions had been made under HUD orders. It said other budget overruns were due to inflation.

HUD said April 15 that aid would be withheld until the agency agreed to separate the functions of administering public housing and urban renewal. The HUD regional office had said Jan. 28 that the Newark study, released that day, was one of 20 investigations of debt-ridden housing authorities in cities across the country.

U.S. halts Michigan construction. The Department of Housing and Urban Development ordered a halt Feb. 8, 1971 to further construction by private builders of federally subsidized low-income housing in the Beecher school district near Flint, Mich.

The department's action came nine months after area residents warned HUD Secretary George Romney that continued construction of the projects was having a "disastrous effect" on Beecher's schools and the community's racial balance. Beecher, with about 25,-000 residents, was 70% white and 30% black.

Officials of the Beecher district had complained to HUD that more low-income projects were being built in the five-square mile district than in any of the nearby Flint suburbs. According to HUD, 716 low-cost housing units were to be constructed in the Beecher area. At least two districts reportedly were not slated for any low-cost units.

Urban aid plan. President Nixon March 5, 1971 sent to Congress an urban assistance program that would merge major housing and urban development programs into one $2 billion plan to enable local governments to develop their own plans for urban and community redevelopment.

In an accompanying fact sheet, the President said "proliferation of separate urban development programs have brought into being independent, local bureaucracies which frequently operate outside the control of elected local officials. This has fragmented local effort and made it difficult for cities to frame a community-wide development strategy. In addition, lengthy federal reviews of applications, and the imposition of federal categorical requirements have excessively delayed renewal activities and distorted local priorities."

The President sought to reassure the cities that they would not be adversely affected by his proposal to do away with the bureaucratic structures that had governed previous programs. He said the cities could continue the old programs, such as Model Cities, by channeling funds received under the revenue sharing system to existing urban renewal agencies. He promised that no city would receive less funds than under the system of categorical grants.

Of the proposed $2 billion, $1.6 billion would be allocated to the nation's 247 urban areas with 50,000 or more persons according to a statutory formula taking into account population, degree of substandard housing and proportion of families below the poverty level. The residual $400 million would be distributed at the discretion of the Department of Housing and Urban Development, chiefly to insure that a recipient received no less under the new program than under the old. Any leftover funds would be distributed to reward communities with out-

standing programs and help those with exceptional problems.

The President said his proposal would eliminate numerous federal requirements that would free local communities to write their own rules. Matching of federal funds would also be cut out under the new plan.

Housing abandonment studied. The National Urban League and the Center for Community Change, in a survey reported April 20, 1971, said that the abandonment of housing by landlords in inner-city ghetto neighborhoods threatened to create "ghost towns." The report, titled "The National Survey of Housing Abandonment," said a massive commitment by all levels of government was needed to fight the problem.

The study said: "The central portion of our major cities cannot be allowed to continue along the road toward social and physical destruction and abandonment without endangering national, regional and metropolitan political and economic institutions." The study found that in St. Louis, with two neighborhoods where 16% of all housing was abandoned, the problem had progressed further than in the other cities surveyed. It said that "Cleveland's future is, in our opinion, very bleak."

The report found the least abandonment in Detroit and Atlanta and cited economic integration of the neighborhoods, substantial home ownership and the availability of mortgages as contributing to the better conditions in those two cities. Chicago, Hoboken, N.J. and New York were also included in the survey.

Suburban zoning laws challenged. The National Association for the Advancement of Colored People (NAACP) filed a lawsuit March 24 challenging the legality of zoning laws that prohibited construction of apartment buildings in suburban communities. It was the first time the NAACP had gone to court against suburban zoning laws.

The suit was filed in federal court in Brooklyn, N.Y. against the Town of Oyster Bay, N.Y. It charged that the town's zoning law had "foreclosed black and other nonwhite minorities from obtaining housing in the town," with results that "intensify and harden patterns of racial ghetto living in the City of New York."

Roy Wilkens, executive secretary of the NAACP, said workers employed in Oyster Bay often could not find suitable housing. He said 45 new industries had come to Oyster Bay since 1965, but that workers earning less than $17,000 a year could not afford to buy houses in the town because of the minimum lot sizes prescribed by the zoning laws.

Housing project veto upheld. The Supreme Court April 26, 1971 upheld the constitutionality of state referendum laws that allowed a majority of voters in any city, state or county to block low-rent public housing in their community.

By a 5–3 vote the court sustained California's referendum law, on the books since 1950, which required public approval of the low-rent projects before they could be built.

California voters had used the law to block construction of almost half the low-rent housing proposed for the state since its passage.

In the opinion written by Justice Hugo L. Black, the court described the law as consistent with "devotion to democracy, not to bias, discrimination or prejudice."

Chief Justice Warren E. Burger and Justices John M. Harlan, Potter Stewart and Byron White joined Black in the majority decision. Justices Harry A. Blackmun, William J. Brennan Jr. and Thurgood Marshall dissented. Justice William O. Douglas did not take part in the case.

The court had been asked in a host of friend-of-court briefs to strike down the California law on the ground that it frustrated efforts to erect low-rent public housing for the poor. Among those filing briefs were the National Urban Coalition, the National Association of Home Builders, the American Institute of Architects and the Justice Department.

The California law was challenged in a suit brought by 41 welfare families in San Jose after the city's voters reversed a decision by the city council in 1968 to build 1,000 low-rent apartments. San Jose's voters turned down the proposed construction, 68,000–58,000. A three-judge federal district court in San Francisco struck down the law as unconstitutional, saying that it violated the equal protection clause of the 14th Amendment by discriminating against the poor.

Black said for the court that the 14th Amendment's principal thrust was to outlaw legal distinctions based on race and that there was no evidence that the California referendum law was prejudicial against any racial minority. He said "this procedure for democratic decision-making" gave the voters a voice in decisions that would raise their taxes and affect the future of their community.

U.S. moves to end housing bias. The government announced federal guidelines May 21, 1971 to end the use of racial and religious designations in newspaper advertisements for housing. The Department of Housing and Urban Development (HUD), which issued the policy, said the guidelines were intended to reduce discrimination in housing.

HUD published the new guidelines in the Federal Register, a daily publication of government legal notices. Under the policy, HUD would consider the placement in advertisements of certain words, signs and symbols as clear evidence of intent to discriminate. The evidence would be used in complaints filed under the Civil Rights Act of 1968.

The guidelines would apply to designations that implied that the sale or rental of dwelling units was for the benefit of any race or religion. The restrictions would also regulate the use of human models in real estate ads.

The guidelines would ban the use of such phrases as "Jewish home, colored home" and "white private home." It would also bar the use of racial, religious and national-origin designations such as Negro, Hebrew, black, white and European. Words such as "ghetto, disadvantaged" and "restricted" would also be banned.

Panel scores housing bias. The U.S. Civil Rights Commission reported May 10, 1971 that the Nixon Administration had shown some signs of progress in enforcing civil rights laws, but said considerable strides still had to be taken.

The commission's findings came seven months after it issued a harsh report asserting that there had been a "major breakdown" in the enforcement of the rights laws. In that October 1970 report, the panel said the government had virtually abdicated its responsibility in rights enforcement.

The panel's report was summarized at a Washington news conference by the Rev. Theodore M. Hesburgh, commission chairman and president of the University of Notre Dame.

The commission used its most severe language in criticizing the Department of Housing and Urban Development (HUD) for what it said was HUD's backdown from a strong commitment of promoting racially open communities.

HUD's open community policy had so changed, the commission said, that "by April 1971" the department "now states that it is opposed to use of federal leverage to promote economic integration."

The panel said that "the harsh facts of housing economics, however, suggest that racial integration cannot be achieved unless economic integration also is achieved. Thus the change in HUD's 'open communities' policy may not only represent a narrowing of that agency's view of its fair housing responsibilities, but also may mark the beginning of the federal government's withdrawal from active participation in the effort to eliminate residential segregation."

The commission charged June 10 that the FHA's home-ownership program for low-income families had been used by the private housing and home finance industry to perpetuate segregation.

The panel, in a statement released in Washington, said the FHA "has abdicated its responsibility" in overseeing the program and "in effect, has delegated it to members of the private housing and home finance industry."

According to the commission, the private groups had misused the program by largely ignoring the intent of civil law.

The commission said that because of the FHA's ineffectiveness in running the program, housing under the plan was following the same pattern as most other housing: whites were getting new homes in the suburbs and blacks were getting homes in the central cities.

The report was based on the commission's year-long study of the home ownership program in four cities selected to provide a cross section of the nation— Denver, Little Rock, Ark., Philadelphia and St. Louis. All had operated the home ownership plan since 1968, the year it was enacted.

In all four cities, the commission reported, white and minority-group buyers were offered the housing on a segregated basis and "minority buyers received cheaper, inferior housing and smaller government subsidies than white buyers." Howard A. Glickstein, commission staff director who released the report, noted that since the document had been written, the government had issued new guidelines to curtail racially discriminatory advertising for housing. He said, however, that the new guidelines did not constitute an over all policy directive that would require enforcement of civil rights law.

HUD Secretary George Romney issued a statement contending that some of the panel's data was out of date. He also said that HUD "has in fact been engaged in a range of actions over the past several months to make all of our programs more responsive to equal opportunity objectives as well as to the consumer generally."

Nixon on housing discrimination. President Nixon, in a major position statement June 11, 1971, called racial discrimination in housing clearly unconstitutional and said it "will not be tolerated" by his Administration.

But the President repeated his earlier view that racial and economic segregation in housing were not synonymous and therefore he would not use the government's legal apparatus to force communities to accept low- and moderate-income housing against their wishes.

Nixon carefully outlined the Administration's position in his statement of more than 8,000 words. The policy was the result of nearly seven months of debate and discussion within the Administration over the limits to which federal leverage would be applied to induce local communities to integrate their housing.

Nixon pledged to enforce existing prohibitions against racial discrimination in housing, but said no federal pressure would be brought to bear against economic segregation:

"We will not seek to impose economic integration upon an existing local jurisdiction; at the same time, we will not countenance any use of economic measures as a subterfuge for racial discrimination.

"When such an action is called into question, we will study its effect. If the effect of the action is to exclude Americans from equal housing opportunity on the basis of their race, religion, or ethnic background, we will vigorously oppose it by whatever means are most appropriate—regardless of the rationale which may have cloaked the discriminatory act."

But Nixon said federal action would not include the use of U.S. sanctions to force local communities to accept housing for low- and moderate-income families. He said:

"This Administration will not attempt to impose federally assisted housing upon any community.

"We will encourage communities to discharge their responsibility for helping to provide decent housing opportunities to the Americans of low- and moderate-income who live or work within their boundaries.

"We will encourage communities to seek and accept well-conceived, well designed, well-managed housing developments—always within the community's capacity to assimilate the families who will live in them."

Elsewhere in the statement, Nixon said that based on his review of the legislative history of the 1968 Civil Rights Act, he did not believe that the act's "affirmative action" clause authorized "housing officials in federal agencies to dictate local land use policy. He said of his interpretation of the act:

"This does not mean that no federally assisted low- and moderate-income housing may be built within areas of minority concentration. It does not mean that housing officials in federal agencies should dictate local land use policies. It does mean that in choosing among the various applications for federal aid, consideration should be given to their impact on patterns of racial concentration."

In another area of his statement, Nixon said the federal government would move against zoning changes when it was determined that the rezoning had been done by a community to exclude a federally assisted housing development:

"Unlawful racial discrimination in housing extends beyond the barring of individuals from particular buildings or neighborhoods because of race. The courts have also held that, when its reasons for doing so are racial, a community may not rezone in order to exclude a federally assisted housing development. In such cases, where changes in land use regulations are made for what turns out to be a racially discriminatory purpose, the attorney general, in appropriate circumstances, will also bring legal proceedings."

The Administration's policy brought a mixed reaction. The Suburban Action Institute, which had said that only a deliberate U.S. policy of dispersing low- and moderate-income housing to the suburbs could break up the growing concentration of blacks in America's cities, said it viewed the President's statement with "keen disappointment."

The group said "racial discrimination in the suburbs is the direct and calculated result of economic discrimination." The group suggested that Nixon, by making a distinction between racial and economic discrimination, had issued an invitation for white suburbs to exclude blacks through subterfuge.

Lawyers in the Justice Department's Civil Rights Division said they were surprised and encouraged by Nixon's assertion that he would vigorously enforce the existing housing laws.

Black Jack, Mo. sued on housing—After seven months of internal debate, the Nixon Administration sued the St. Louis suburb of Black Jack, Mo. June 14, charging it with illegally rezoning land to block an integrated housing project.

Filing of the Black Jack suit in St. Louis was announced in Washington by Attorney General John N. Mitchell. The Black Jack suit, which was first recommended by the Department of Housing and Urban Development (HUD), asked the federal district court in St. Louis for an order to "permit the prompt construction" of a middle-income housing development in the suburb. The suit also asked the court to forbid racial discrimination in housing.

According to the suit, Black Jack residents incorporated their community to gain zoning power and then used that power to prohibit construction of an apartment complex. The suit charged that the rezoning violated federal civil rights laws and the Constitution.

New guidelines—HUD Secretary George Romney June 14 announced proposed new guidelines limiting federal grants for community development to communities agreeing to plan for housing for low- and moderate-income families.

Romney announced the proposed measures at the same Washington news conference at which Mitchell made known the Black Jack housing suit. Romney described the new guidelines as consistent with President Nixon's June 11 policy statement on housing. The guidelines dealt with community development and federal housing assistance, two areas of HUD responsibility. The first set of guidelines, relating to community development, would require a community that sought community development funds to provide for low- and moderate-income housing.

Romney proposed a new set of criteria for funding for federal housing assistance. He said "if a project doesn't rate at least 'adequate' on the nondiscriminatory location criterion, it will be disapproved."

HUD ruled guilty of bias. The Department of Housing and Urban Development (HUD) and HUD Secretary George W. Romney were judged guilty Sept. 10, 1971 of racial discrimination in funding construction of segregated public housing in Chicago between 1950 and 1969.

The U.S. Court of Appeals for the 7th Circuit overturned a 1970 decision by U.S. District Judge Richard B. Austin, who said that his 1969 injunction against segregated site selection and discriminatory tenant assignment by the Chicago Housing Authority had provided adequate relief.

The three-judge panel, in a unanimous opinion written by Judge F. Ryan Duffy, said HUD and Romney had violated the rights of the plaintiffs by not insisting on dispersal of public housing projects in all parts of the city, including white neighborhoods. Attorney Alexander Polikoff, who argued the case for the plaintiff, the American Civil Liberties Union, said the decision would work against President Nixon's December 1970 statement that his Administration would avoid using federal funds to force racial or economic integration in the suburbs. Noting that "HUD's authority extends beyond city limits," Polikoff said HUD had "to

come up with a new and comprehensive plan."

However, the appeals court refused to order HUD to deny financial aid to suburbs which exclude public housing, leaving the remedy to the discretion of Judge Austin.

Subsidized slum housing challenged. The Department of Housing and Urban Development (HUD) informed a U.S. court in Philadelphia Sept. 22, 1971 that a subsidized housing project approved for a predominantly Negro renewal area in North Philadelphia should have been rejected.

The decision was disclosed by the U.S. Court of Appeals for the 3rd Circuit. The court had ruled in January that HUD, in considering applications for rent supplements or mortgage insurance, had to determine whether the Philadelphia project would increase or maintain segregation. At that time, the court said HUD might not support housing projects that increased or maintained segregation unless it found that the need for renewal of a slum or additional housing in slums "clearly outweighs the disadvantage of increasing or perpetuating racial concentration."

In announcing its decision to the court, HUD said the project, Fairmount Manor, would add too much to racial concentration in the North Philadelphia area and should not have been approved. Many of those living in Fairmount Manor had been drawing federal rent subsidies. HUD's decision meant that the court would decide if the subsidies should continue.

HUD's decision came as a result of a suit filed against Fairmount Manor by the Lawyers Committee for Civil Rights Under Law on behalf of residents in the North Philadelphia neighborhood.

Housing dispersal action—HUD Sept. 29 announced guidelines to disperse subsidized housing in metropolitan areas and prevent its concentration in inner-city ghettos.

The proposed new guidelines were designed, according to HUD Secretary George Romney, "to pursue the Administration policy of not contributing to minority concentration of housing and to obey the orders of federal courts which have ruled on these questions." The guidelines would give priority to projects that avoided concentration of minorities and that provided housing for low income families in areas where services and jobs were available.

The proposal allowed exceptions if the project were to be located in an area of minority concentration but was "necessary to meet overriding housing needs which cannot otherwise feasibly be met in that housing market area." Projects could also be built in areas where the prospective residents had "strong cultural, social or economic ties."

HUD also announced guidelines on the "affirmative action" housing developers would be required to take to carry government mortgage guarantees under the 1968 fair housing act. Developers were required to advertise available housing to minority members through minority outlets.

Hamtramck renewal scored. The city of Hamtramck, Mich. and the U.S. Department of Housing and Urban Development were ordered by U.S. District Court Judge Damon J. Keith Nov. 23, 1971 to provide housing within the city to black residents forced to move by urban renewal and federal highway programs.

In a suit brought by displaced black residents of the largely Polish enclave within Detroit, Keith found that local officials had "intentionally planned and implemented urban renewal and other government projects for the purpose of removing a substantial portion of black citizens from the city." He said HUD officials had failed to act against these policies although they were aware of them since 1968.

The ruling ordered HUD and the city to devise a plan within 90 days to construct new housing or open up existing housing closed by discrimination.

The projects which prompted the suit included the conversion of largely black residential areas to industrial use in 1959, and the diversion of an interstate highway, originally intended to skirt the city, through a largely black area, isolating still another black neigh-borhood. The majority of displaced families were given no relocation assistance, and were unable to find housing in white areas, the judge found.

Nixon Administration & School Segregation

One of the persistent, troubling elements of the urban dilemma is the frequently explosive issue of racial segregation in the schools. The problem is one that involves all levels of government—federal, state and local.

Nixon outlines policy. President Nixon pledged March 24, 1970 that his Administration would not abandon or undermine the school desegregation gains made since the Supreme Court's 1954 ruling outlawing "separate but equal" educational facilities. Nixon said it was his "personal belief" that the 1954 decision "was right in both constitutional and human terms."

The President's commitment was included in an 8,000-word document on the problems of elementary and secondary school desegregation. White House officials said it was the most comprehensive statement by any president on the issue of school integration.

In his report, Nixon vowed to apply all of the government's available resources towards elimination of officially imposed, or de jure, segregation in the South's public schools. He said, however, that until the courts provided further guidance he could not require elimination of de facto segregation, in the North or South, resulting from residential housing patterns.

At the same time, President Nixon revealed that the government planned to allocate $1.5 billion over the next two years to help school districts in the North and the South alleviate the effects of racial segregation stemming from de facto segregation.

Much of the President's statement dealt with the two forms of racial segregation, de facto and de jure. Nixon said the Supreme Court had already ruled on de jure segregation when it handed down the landmark decision in Brown vs. Board of Education in 1954. The President pledged to carry out the court's mandate by relying on the "good faith" efforts of local Southern officials to comply with the court's orders.

The President said, however, that the courts had not spoken out on what, if anything, to do to overcome de facto segregation. He said that while segregation as a by-product of housing patterns was undesirable in practice, it remained fully constitutional in theory. Nixon said he was offering a set of possible remedies at an administrative level.

Nixon's suggestions encompassed two positions that he had often stated before. He repeated his opposition to student busing simply as a means of achieving racially balanced schools without improving the quality of education, and he said that he was in favor of the neighborhood-school concept.

His main proposal was to offer funds for technical assistance to public school districts in the North and South that wanted to eliminate de facto segregation on their own initiative or to mitigate the effects of segregation by providing compensatory educational guidance to minority group children in segregated schools. The President proposed $500 million for the 1971 fiscal year, beginning July 1, and an additional $1 billion in fiscal 1972.

(White House sources said later that the bulk of this money would not be used to upgrade the quality of education in slum schools, but rather, would be applied to promote forms of desegregation short of massive student busing.)

The President said it would be the purpose of his Administration "to carry out the law fully and fairly." Nixon said he had instructed Attorney General John N. Mitchell, Secretary of Health, Education and Welfare Robert H. Finch and other "appropriate officials of the government" to be guided by the basic principles and policies laid down in his statement.

The President offered these principles:

Deliberate racial segregation of pupils by official action is unlawful, wherever it exists. In the words of the Supreme Court, it must be eliminated "root and branch"—and it must be eliminated at once.

Segregation of teachers must be eliminated. To this end, each school system in this nation, North and South, East and West, must move immediately, as the Supreme Court has ruled, toward a goal under which "in each school the ratio of white to Negro faculty members is substantially the same as it is throughout the system."

With respect to school facilities, school administrators throughout the nation, North and South, East and West, must move immediately, in conformance with the Court's ruling, to assure that schools within individual school districts do not discriminate with respect to the quality of facilities or the quality of education delivered to the children within the district.

In devising local compliance plans primary weight should be given to the considered judgment of local school boards—provided they act in good faith and within constitutional limits.

The neighborhood school will be deemed the most appropriate base for such a system.

Transportation of pupils beyond normal geographic school zones for the purpose of achieving racial balance will not be required.

Federal advice and assistance will be made available on request, but Federal officials should not go beyond the requirements of law in attempting to impose their own judgment on the local school district.

School boards will be encouraged to be flexible and creative in formulating plans that are educationally sound and that result in effective desegregation.

Racial imbalance in a school system may be partly de jure in origin, and partly de facto. In such a case, it is appropriate to insist on remedy for the de jure portion, which is unlawful, without insisting on a remedy for the lawful de facto portion.

De facto racial separation, resulting genuinely from housing patterns, exists in the South as well as the North; in neither area should this condition by itself be cause for Federal enforcement actions. De jure segregation brought about by deliberate school-board gerrymandering exists in the North, as the South; in both areas this must be remedied. In all respects, the law should be applied equally, North and South, East and West.

The President also outlined what he called his "policies for progress:"

In those communities facing desegregation orders, the leaders of the communities will be encouraged to lead—not in defiance, but in smoothing the way of compliance. One clear lesson of experience is that local leadership is a fundamental factor in determining success or failure. Where leadership has been present, where it has been mobilized, where it has been effective, many districts have found that they could, after all, desegregate their schools successfully. Where local leadership has failed, the community has failed—and the schools and the children have borne the brunt of that failure.

We shall launch a concerted, sustained and honest effort to assemble and evaluate the lessons of experience: To determine what methods of school desegregation have worked, in what situations, and why—and also what has not worked. The Cabinet-level working group I recently appointed will have as one of its principal functions amassing just this sort of information and helping make it available to the communities in need of assistance.

We shall attempt to develop a far greater body of reliable data than now exists on the effects of various integration patterns on the learning process. Our effort must always be to preserve the educational benefit for the children.

We shall explore ways of sharing more broadly the burdens of social transition that have been laid disproportionately on the schools—ways, that is, of shifting to other public institutions a greater share of the task of undoing the effects of racial isolation.

The President said the federal government was limited in its enforcement of school desegregation orders. "If we are to be realists," Nixon said, "we must recognize that in a free society there are limits to the amount of government coercion that can reasonably be used; that in achieving desegregation we must proceed with the least possible disruption of the education of the nation's children. . . ."

Little change seen—HEW Secretary Robert H. Finch indicated April 7 that Nixon's statement would cause little or no change in his department's enforcement of school desegregation rules.

Finch told newsmen that he and his HEW aides foresaw no change in the department's practice of busing as one means of enforcing either court-ordered or HEW-ordered school desegregation in the South.

Finch said that since nearly 90% of the South's public schools used student busing "it's not as though we're calling for a whole new lot of buses."

One of Finch's key aides, Jerry H. Rader, HEW's equal educational opportunity director, said that where busing already was used to maintain segregation, there would be little problem in rearranging it to accommodate school desegregation.

Finch said the task of determining whether discrimination was de jure or de facto would be "very, very difficult" and that it would have to be done on a school-by-school basis.

J. Stanley Pottinger, the new director of HEW's Office of Civil Rights, acknowledged that HEW policy on school segregation would apply, apparently, only to de jure segregation.

But James E. Allen Jr., U.S. commissioner of education, said in a statement that was made public April 27 that "in the position of national leadership which I occupy I shall continue to emphasize the educational value of integration and the educational deprivation of segregation regardless of cause." He called on educators to intensify their efforts to achieve school desegregation and to take the lead by educating others about "the harmful educational effects of segregation on all our people."

Allen's office distributed the commissioner's statement after it was inserted into the record of a Senate subcommittee hearing the week of April 20.

'Unreasonable' busing scored. Attorney General John N. Mitchell said April 16 that every citizen had "the right to reject unreasonable requirements of busing and to send their children to neighborhood schools." Mitchell said this right was "just as important as the right of all of our citizens to be assigned [to the schools] without regard to their race." Mitchell's antibusing remarks drew cheers and applause from many of the 1,200 Republicans who were attending the party's 1970 leadership conference in Washington, D.C.

The attorney general told the GOP leaders that despite the balancing of constitutional rights and antibusing rights, the Nixon Administration "has brought about more school desegregation than any previous administration."

Nixon seeks school funds. President Nixon asked Congress May 21, 1970 to appropriate $1.5 billion over the next two years to be used primarily to help finance desegregation of Southern schools and to spur Northern school districts to integrate voluntarily.

In his message, Nixon asserted that racial isolation was injurious to children of both races and that "desegregation is vital to quality education." He said the school aid act would establish three categories of aid:

■Aid to districts that were under federal court orders or under pressure from HEW to eliminate de jure segregation, caused by official local or state policy. Most of these districts were in the South.

■Aid to districts that sought to voluntarily reduce, eliminate or prevent de facto segregation, caused by residential patterns. These districts were for the most part in the North.

■Aid to districts in which de facto segregation persisted, for the purpose of helping establish special interracial or intercultural educational programs. Where such programs were impracticable, programs would be designed to overcome the educational disadvantages that stemmed from racial isolation.

Two-thirds of the funds would be dispensed among the states "according to the proportion of the nation's minority students in each state." The other third was to be allocated by HEW.

A White House official denied that the bill leaned heavily in favor of the Southern states. According to the language of the bill, those school districts that were required by law to desegregate, largely in the South, would receive extra incentive to obey the desegregation arrangements. Asked why no such similar incentives were being made to Northern school districts, the official said the Administration's first priority was to end Southern school segregation.

The official also said that the bill had been drawn flexibly to permit local school districts to use the money to finance busing of students to achieve desegregation as long as the district could show that the busing was not aimed "solely to achieve racial balance," which was prohibited by law.

According to White House sources, the President's message asked Congress for $150 million immediately on an "emergency basis," $350 million more in fiscal 1971 and $1 billion in fiscal 1972. The emergency $150 million was earmarked for use by the time schools reopened for the fall term in September. It would be allocated by the secretary of health, education and welfare.

U.S. pledges integration drive. Three of the Nixon Administration's chief civil rights officers pledged in separate statements June 25–29, 1970 that the government would force recalcitrant Southern school districts to comply with school desegregation orders when their schools reopened for the fall term.

One of the officials, Jerris Leonard, chief of the Justice Department's Civil

Rights Division, warned that unless state and local officials worked out acceptable desegregation arrangements for their districts, the government would begin filing desegregation suits against their districts.

The first disclosure that a concerted effort was under way to force compliance was made June 25 by Elliot L. Richardson, the new secretary of health, education and welfare. He said the government was prepared to halt federal funds to school districts that continued to ignore desegregation orders.

Richardson also said the government would prosecute any discrimination against black students or faculty members in otherwise desegregated schools. He said that the "ending of officially sanctioned racial discrimination should and must go beyond the assignment of students by race. This means desegregation not only at the point of entry but integrating education within the building as well."

Leonard's statement warning Southern school administrators that they faced possible court action was made June 26 during a week of meetings with Southern public school officials in Augusta, Ga. Leonard told the officials that no further delay would be tolerated in about 50 school districts that had avoided court scrutiny while maintaining token integration arrangements under freedom-of-choice school plans. Most of the 50 districts under government observation were reported to be in the South. Leonard said that a single suit would be filed against the State of Mississippi if the 27 districts in the state that had refused to comply with desegregation laws failed to act by July 1. (The government announced June 29 that it had filed a desegregation suit in federal district court in Jackson, Miss., charging the Brookhaven Municipal Separate School District of Lincoln with maintaining a dual educational system based on race.)

School suits start—The Justice Department July 9 filed suits against 46 Deep South school districts as it began its threatened action against districts without acceptable desegregation plans.

Attorney General John N. Mitchell

announced that the department had sued the state of Mississippi and a number of individual school systems in South Carolina, Arkansas and Florida.

The government, filing the suits simultaneously in seven federal courts, asked for immediate orders to bring the districts into compliance with the law before the start of the 1970–71 school year.

Focus shifts North. The Nixon Administration promised Jan. 14, 1971 to start efforts to increase the rate of school integration in the North. The Administration held that the South already had more integrated school systems than did the North.

Announcement of the government's intended drive was made by Elliot L. Richardson, secretary of health, education and welfare (HEW). Richardson said HEW's Office of Civil Rights had found after a survey that only a slight change had occurred in the rate of school integration in the North and West since 1968.

According to the survey, the percentage of blacks attending integrated schools in the North and West rose from 27.6% to 27.7%.

This compared with a two-year rise of 19.7% in the percentage of Negro schoolchildren attending integrated schools in the South. According to HEW data, the rate increased from 18.4% to 38.1%.

HEW's figures marked a change in Administration procedure. Earlier data had used figures relating to school districts rather than pupils. In the earlier reports, the Administration had asserted that 97% of all school districts in the South were desegregated. However, civil rights groups challenged the statistics, claiming that students, rather than districts, should be counted.

Richardson said the new figures "show clearly and dramatically that unprecedented progress has been made in school desegregation since 1968."

"The pupil desegregation battle in the South has been brought to the point where the only remaining steps are to follow up the job," Richardson said. "But the back of [segregation] has been broken."

Integration failure in North—A House

subcommittee was told in New York City May 21 that voluntary school integration in the North was failing.

New York state officials and educators told members of the General Education Subcommittee of the House Education and Labor Committee that neighborhood housing patterns stood in the way of increased school integration.

Dr. Harvey B. Scribner, chancellor of New York City's schools, said that "because this nation is composed of black housing areas and white housing areas, and because this pattern is not likely to change overnight, school integration plans will frequently have to transcend school district bondaries."

School integration in South cited. The federal government released the results of a nationwide survey June 17 showing that public school integration in the South had increased dramatically in the last two years.

Other figures, contained in the survey made public by the Department of Health, Education and Welfare (HEW), indicated that school integration in many of the North's large cities had shown a significant decline over the same two-year period.

According to HEW: of the total Negro students in the U.S., the percentage attending majority white schools increased from 23% in the fall of 1968 to 33% in the fall of 1970. The increase was attributed by HEW almost wholly to the increase in integration in the South.

In the 11 Southern states, HEW's data showed, the percentage of Negroes in schools with a white majority rose from 18% in 1968 to 39% in 1970. In the North and West, integration remained steady at 27%. Increased integration in some areas of the North and West was offset by declines in big cities.

New York, Detroit, Philadelphia, St. Louis, Boston, San Francisco and Minneapolis all showed a drop in the percentage of Negro students in schools with a white majority.

Los Angeles, Newark, N.J., San Diego and Denver were among the large cities in the North and West showing an increase in school integration.

Following is the table compiled by the

Department of Health, Education and Welfare on the rate of integration in the nation's 100 largest school districts:

	Total Negroes (In Percentages)		Negroes in White Schools	
District	1968	1970	1968	1970
New York	31.5	34.5	19.7	16.3
Los Angeles	22.6	24.1	4.7	5.9
Chicago	52.9	54.8	3.2	3.0
Detroit	59.2	63.8	9.0	5.8
Philadelphia...........	58.8	60.5	9.6	7.4
Houston...............	33.3	35.6	5.3	8.4
Dade Co. (Miami).......	24.3	25.4	12.4	21.7
Baltimore City.........	65.1	67.1	7.7	9.4
Dallas.................	30.8	33.8	2.1	2.7
Cleveland..............	55.9	57.6	4.8	4.2
Memphis	53.6	51.5	2.6	6.5
Washington	93.5	94.6	0.9	1.2
Milwaukee.............	23.9	26.0	12.4	12.2
San Diego.............	11.6	12.4	25.1	32.1
Duval Co., Fla. (Jacksonville)..........	28.2	29.4	12.6	25.6
St. Louis, Mo.	63.5	65.6	7.1	2.5
Orleans Parish, La. (New Orleans).........	67.1	69.5	8.8	7.8
Indianapolis...........	33.7	35.8	22.4	20.5
Atlanta................	61.7	68.7	5.4	6.6
Denver	14.1	14.7	20.0	44.6
Boston	27.1	29.8	23.3	18.0
Nashville-Davidson Co., Tenn.	24.1	24.6	16.8	25.0
San Francisco	27.5	28.5	15.5	14.2
Cincinnati	42.9	45.0	21.9	16.9
Seattle	11.0	12.8	44.8	40.6
Charlotte-Mecklenburg Co.	29.2	30.8	27.7	90.7
Newark	72.5	72.2	2.1	2.9
Tulsa.................	12.2	13.7	15.6	27.5
San Antonio...........	14.7	15.3	10.6	9.3
Portland, Ore.	8.1	9.2	57.4	62.1
Pittsburgh	39.2	40.3	21.3	23.3
Kansas City, Mo.	46.8	50.2	14.0	9.3
Buffalo	36.6	38.5	27.0	26.8
Mobile Co., Ala.	41.7	44.5	10.9	18.2
Oakland, Calif.	55.2	56.9	5.5	6.5
Minneapolis...........	7.5	8.9	70.8	57.6
Birmingham, Ala........	51.4	54.6	7.2	15.8
Toledo, Ohio	26.7	26.6	22.6	24.1
Dayton, Ohio..........	38.3	40.7	10.9	13.0
Akron, Ohio	25.8	27.3	37.7	36.5
Norfolk, Va.	41.9	44.9	11.5	32.9
Louisville.............	46.1	48.3	13.5	11.7
St. Paul..............	5.8	6.4	87.6	64.6
Richmond	68.3	64.2	6.4	11.7
Gary, Ind.	61.6	64.7	3.1	3.5
Rochester, N.Y.........	28.9	33.1	45.6	40.9

Suburban school plan rejected. After a day and a half of acrimonious debate between two of its leading civil rights advocates, the Senate April 24, 1971 voted down, 51-35, a proposal to force suburban communities to integrate their schools with neighboring inner-city public schools within 12 years.

Discussion on the proposal was marked by exchanges between Sen. Abraham A. Ribicoff (D, Conn.), the proposal's sponsor, and Sen. Jacob K. Javits (R, N.Y.), who spoke against it.

At one point, Ribicoff charged Javits with "hypocrisy" for being "unwilling to accept desegregation for his state, though he is willing to shove it down the throats of the senators from Mississippi." Looking directly at Javits, Ribicoff said: "I don't think you have the guts to face your liberal constituents who have moved to the suburbs to avoid sending their children to school with blacks."

Ribicoff had introduced his proposal March 16 as an amendment to a $1.4 billion bill designed to assist school districts in desegregating.

Javits said the "essential basis" for his opposition to the amendment was that if it was accepted it might jeopardize the bill which he was instrumental in drawing up. Javits said April 20 that the plan to integrate suburban schools "is Senator Ribicoff's idea. It may be a good one, and it may be a bad one, but I think it will sink this bill, and my people sent me here to achieve results."

Ribicoff's amendment would have required all schools within a metropolitan area to have a percentage of minority students at least equal to half the percentage of minority students in the entire metropolitan area.

Desegregation Developments

N.Y. antibusing law invalid. A New York State antibusing law was ruled unconstitutional Oct. 1, 1970 by a three-judge federal court in Buffalo. The law had barred appointed school boards from shuffling pupil assignment plans to achieve racial balance without the consent of their parents.

The law had been copied by school administrators in the Deep South seeking to forestall desegregation in their district's classrooms.

The judges held in their 24-page decision that the law violated the U.S. Constitution because it "constitutes an explicit and invidious racial classification and denies equal protection of the law." They granted a permanent injunction against all future enforcement of the law.

The law, which was enacted in May 1969, applied to appointed school boards, but not to elected school boards. The litigation challenging the law was brought by a group of black and white Buffalo parents.

The judges said that an examination of the objectives and effect of the law "supports the proposition that the statute serves to continue segregation in the school and thus significantly encourages and involves the state in racial discrimination."

N.C. busing held valid. North Carolina's Supreme Court Jan. 20, 1971 sustained the state's policy of providing school buses for city-dwelling children involved in desegregation programs as long as the state used funds to transport children from rural areas to their schools.

The decision struck down a lower court injunction that would have prohibited the state from using funds for busing. The injunction was not in effect pending the decision of the state Supreme Court.

In effect, the court's action gave the state legislature the choice of continuing busing for all children who needed it, or dropping it altogether. In either case the state would have to apply its decision uniformly to rural and city children.

Supreme Court upholds busing. The Supreme Court, in a series of unanimous decisions, told the Charlotte-Mecklenburg County, N.C. joint school system and all the other school districts of the South April 20, 1971 that busing as a means of dismantling dual school systems was constitutional.

The rulings brought to a close final legal efforts by Southern school boards to stave off busing students to achieve racially-balanced schools.

Chief Justice Warren E. Burger wrote the opinions for the entire court in the four cases on which it ruled.

In addition to upholding a far-reaching school desegregation plan for the Charlotte-Mecklenburg district, the court struck down as unconstitutional an anti-busing statute enacted by the North Carolina legislature, ordered Mobile, Ala. school officials to use "all available techniques" to correct segregation in their schools and overturned a Georgia Supreme Court ruling that had said certain desegregation efforts in Athens were unconstitutional.

"Desegregation plans cannot be limited to the walk-in school," Burger wrote for the court. The justices held that busing schoolchildren was proper unless "the time or distance is so great as to risk either the health of the children or significantly impinge on the educational process." The court added that at times busing was an indispensible method of eliminating "the last vestiges" of racial segregation.

The court made it clear, however, that the rulings in the Charlotte and its companion cases did not apply to de facto segregation, caused by neighborhood housing patterns and found most often in the North.

In upholding the constitutionality of busing, the court brushed aside the arguments of the Nixon Administration and the Justice Department, which had backed Southern school officials. Justice Department lawyers had urged the court to let Southern school districts assign students to schools in their own neighborhoods even if it slowed down the pace of desegregation.

Lawyers for the Southern districts argued that in the North, communities were allowed to have neighborhood schools and that it would be discriminatory if the South were not allowed the same "privilege."

The court imposed some limits on its decisions. It stopped short of ordering the elimination of all-black schools or of requiring racial balance in the schools. In addition, the court said that young children may be improper subjects for busing if it was over long distances.

The major portion of what Burger described as "guidelines" for the "assistance of school authorities and courts" came in a 28-page decision involving the Charlotte school district. The court upheld the action of U.S. Judge James B. McMillan who approved a school desegregation plan that required massive crosstown busing of schoolchildren to increase the incidence of integration. His ruling was overturned by a U.S. appeals court on the grounds that it was unreasonable and burdensome. In upholding McMillan's decision, the court said the Charlotte school board had failed to propose an acceptable alternative plan and that McMillan was forced to draw up his own.

In the other North Carolina case, the justices ruled that the legislature violated the Constitution when it enacted an anti-busing law and that the statute, "apparently neutral" and "color-blind" in form, "would render illusionary" the concept of a unitary school system. Burger wrote that bus transportation had been an "integral part of all public educational systems" and that it was unlikely that an effective remedy could be devised "without continued reliance upon.it."

In the Mobile case, the justices overturned a desegregation plan that city officials had devised and ordered further desegregation.

The court held in the Athens, Ga. action that, contrary to the ruling of the Georgia Supreme Court, Athens and its surrounding county (Clarke) were within the law to take race into account in devising their own voluntary desegregation plans. White parents had challenged the efforts on the grounds that they violated the 14th Amendment.

Nixon disavows Austin busing. President Nixon Aug. 3, 1971 dissociated himself from his Administration's proposal for a school desegregation plan for Austin, Tex. that would require extensive crosstown busing.

In disavowing the plan drawn up by the Department of Health, Education and Welfare (HEW), Nixon reasserted his strong opposition to busing as a means of racial balance:

"I am against busing as that term is commonly used in school desegregation cases. I have consistently opposed the busing of our nation's schoolchildren to achieve a racial balance, and I am opposed to the busing of children simply for the sake of busing."

Nixon also directed HEW Secretary Elliot L. Richardson and Attorney General John N. Mitchell to "work with

individual school districts to hold busing to the minimum required by law" as Southern school districts altered desegregation plans to comply with the Supreme Court's April 20 ruling upholding busing.

The President left no doubt, however, that his Administration would continue to enforce the order of the court, including court-ordered busing.

Nixon said the Justice Department would appeal on "limited constitutional grounds" the ruling by a federal district court judge in Austin that the Austin school board bus elementary students as part of a desegregation plan.

(The judge, Jack Roberts, July 19 had accepted the board's plan for the creation of centers for fine arts, social sciences, avocations and science and to bus elementary schoolchildren to the centers for periodic "cultural" experiences.)

The President said Mitchell had advised him that he "must appeal" the board's plan for periodic interracial sessions "because that decision is inconsistent" with the Supreme Court's ruling.

Nixon also instructed Richardson to submit to Congress an amendment to the proposed Emergency School Assistance Act that would "expressly prohibit" using any of the act's $1.5 billion for busing.

New Jersey school lines to stand. A three-judge federal court in Newark, N.J. May 18, 1971 let stand New Jersey's public school district lines despite its finding that the boundaries had led to "extreme racial imbalance in some districts."

The court said that the segregation in some New Jersey districts was directly traceable to local housing patterns that discriminated against Negroes. The panel then said that the issue of school segregation caused by neighborhood patterns had been left unresolved when the U.S. Supreme Court failed to rule on it in its latest series of school desegregation cases.

The suit asking for new boundaries was filed in the name of two black Jersey City schoolchildren as a class action on behalf of all black New Jersey students.

An attorney for the plaintiffs said that the case eventually could test the constitutionality of de facto school segregation in the North if the Supreme Court agreed to hear an appeal.

Pennsylvania school balance ordered. Pennsylvania's Human Relations Commission ordered the Philadelphia and Pittsburgh school districts June 18, 1971 to "eliminate" racial imbalance by speeding integration in their schools.

Philadelphia was directed to integrate 20% of its schools which had failed to meet integration standards by September and all such recalcitrant schools by 1974. The Pittsburgh district was handed a similar order.

The Pennsylvania Human Relations Commission was a 16-year-old state agency empowered by state law to act to end discrimination in education, employment, housing and public accommodations.

Nearly 60% of the students in Philadelphia were black, while 40% of Pittsburgh's student population was black. According to commission figures, about 25% of Pittsburgh's black students were in schools with a white majority. In Philadelphia, 7.4% of the black pupils were attending majority white schools.

The order required that by September 1974 no school have an enrollment with more than 79% of the students members of one race. That order was to be carried out even if widespread busing was necessary to achieve the integration.

Busing resistance in North, West. For the first time since the Supreme Court ordered an end to racial segregation in public education in 1954, resistance to court-ordered integration centered in the North and West as schools reopened for the fall Aug. 30–Sept. 8, 1971.

In the South, which for years had been the citadel of resistance to integrated schooling, newly desegregated schools reopened quietly and without major incident, even those with new busing plans.

Some federal and state officials had voiced fears over the possibility that there would be widespread and turbulent protests over the flood of new busing plans ordered for school districts across the nation. Except in a few communities, there were no extensive protests.

Southern school officials expressed satisfaction with the way in which the latest round of school integration was achieved with a minimum of friction and tension. Unofficial statistics indicated that about 500,000 of the South's school children would be involved in new integration during the 1971–72 academic year.

The stiffest resistance to busing and newly implemented integration plans was focused in the North and West.

In Pontiac, Mich., eight white students and one black youth were injured Sept. 8 in fights during protests against a busing plan. Earlier, arsonists set firebombs that gutted 10 school buses that were to have been used to carry out the integration plan.

The protests in Pontiac over busing were among the most violent in the U.S. Protesters carrying American flags marched in front of the school bus depot Sept. 8 daring bus drivers to run them down. Police arrested nine persons at the depot, but busing opponents vowed to continue their protests. One group, the National Action Group, the center of white opposition to busing in Pontiac, demanded that the schools be closed but the Pontiac school board refused.

Pontiac School Superintendent Dana Whitmer said Sept. 8 that attendance on the second day of classes was about the same as opening day, with 60% of the children attending classes. But the figures showed that a high percentage of white parents were heeding a boycott. More than 75% of Pontiac's 8,000 black students were in classes. Total student enrollment was 24,000.

Parents of about 300 children assigned to a new racially-balanced elementary school in Boston refused Sept. 8 to enroll their children in the new school and instead took them to the neighborhood schools they attended the previous term. There was no violence.

Minimum of disruption in South— Throughout the Southern and Border states most school districts reopened newly desegregated schools with a minimum of disruption.

Even in most of the districts where children were riding buses out of their neighborhoods to distant integrated public schools, there was little protest activity.

There were scattered protests in Chattanooga, Tenn., Columbus, Ga., Kannapolis, N.C. and Pembroke, N. C. And in Norfolk, Va., controversy over a court-ordered plan increasing the number of pupils bused to achieve racial integration led the school board to delay for at least a week the reopening of Norfolk's schools.

In Chattanooga, public protests over new integration plans resulted in the absence of more than 3,000 students when the city's schools opened. A bomb damaged a high school Sept. 6, but city and police officials insisted that they had found no relationship between the explosion and the opening of the city's schools.

A dynamite bomb damaged two classrooms in a vacant school Sept. 1 in Columbus. Schools in Columbus were set to reopen despite a jurisdictional dispute between a state judge and the federal courts over a desegregation plan.

In Kannapolis, an elementary school was damaged by eight firebombs. Schools remained open Sept. 4.

Indian parents armed with hatchets and machetes staged a demonstration Sept. 2 in Pembroke to protest the busing of their children.

In Little Rock, Ark., schools reopened Aug. 30 with new busing and pairing plans which produced a consistent 2-1 white-black ratio throughout Little Rock's 24,000-pupil system. There was no public opposition in the city where federal troops once protected black schoolchildren from angry whites.

More than 110,000 children returned to integrated classrooms in Birmingham, Ala., and in adjacent Jefferson County Aug. 30 without incident.

Downstate in Mobile, more than 6,000 schoolchildren were bused out of their neighborhoods. Despite a suggestion by Gov. George C. Wallace

that the city defy the court-ordered busing plan, the new busing arrangement worked smoothly and did not evoke appreciable opposition.

In Nashville, Tenn., elementary school children registered without incident Sept. 8. There was some opposition, however, to a federal court-ordered busing plan

A final effort to block implementation of the busing plan had failed Sept. 2 when Supreme Court Justice Potter Stewart refused to stay its implementation. Under the plan, about 47,000 of the city's 96,000 pupils were to be bused.

Boston school integration ordered. The Massachusetts Commission Against Discrimination directed the Boston school system June 23, 1971 to complete the integration in the city's public schools by the opening of the 1972 school year.

In ordering the integration, the commission said it had found that Boston's open enrollment arrangement was discriminatory against nonwhites and failed to eliminate racial imbalance caused by housing patterns. The commission, a state agency, directed the city's School Committee to establish a central administration to eliminate the alleged discrimination.

In its 21-page report, the commission said Boston's system, which was drawn up to achieve school balance by the voluntary transfer of students, was not achieving the desired effect. According to the commission, statistics compiled by the school department showed that "only a small percentage of black students actually achieve admission to schools having a high white enrollment."

The School Committee Sept. 22 discontinued its efforts to integrate a new multimillion dollar school in a black neighborhood in the face of organized protests by parents.

Efforts at integrating the school had begun Sept. 8, but withered when black and white parents refused to send their children to the school.

As a result of the committee's decision, the new school opened classes Sept. 22 with a ratio of four black students to each white student enrolled. The Lee School, an $8 million complex, had 1,200 students. The committee's action also meant that two other nearby schools would remain predominantly white and would be able to enroll children who up until the committee's decision had been attending without credit in defiance of the law.

Because of the failure to integrate the school, the state withheld $14 million in operating funds from the Boston school system.

The Department of Health, Education & Welfare (HEW) formally notified Boston school officials Dec. 1 that they were violating the 1964 Civil Rights Act by following policies that tended to create segregated school attendance patterns. Boston was the largest Northern school system to be so charged.

HEW noted that the Boston School Committee had maintained two types of intermediate school grade structures since 1965, when it had announced a plan to convert all junior high schools (grades 7-9) to middle schools (grades 6-8). The committee only implemented the plan in four schools, which had since become predominantly nonwhite, as had the elementary and high schools with meshing grade structures. While the resulting segregation may not have been deliberate, according to J. Stanley Pottinger, director of HEW's Office for Civil Rights, school officials "knew, or should have known, racial isolation was occurring. The burden is on them to do something about it."

Other examples of discriminatory policies in Boston which had been uncovered by earlier investigations by the Massachusetts Department of Education included cases of busing nonwhites past predominantly white schools with empty seats, nearly adjacent elementary schools totally segregated by race, and an all-white high school in a district that included large numbers of nonwhites.

Chicago to get new faculty plan. Chicago School Superintendent James F. Redmond in early June 1971 unveiled a new plan designed to broaden the integration of the city's public school teachers.

The new plan would recast the city's public school faculties so that no Chicago school would have a staff more than 75% white or 75% black.

The plan was drawn up to meet a federal demand for greater integration of the city's public school teachers. The Department of Health, Education and Welfare (HEW) had recommended a 65-35 ratio of white to black teachers in predominantly white schools and the reverse in schools with a black majority.

Redmond said the new balance would be achieved by assigning all newly appointed teachers or teachers with temporary assignments to black or white schools in a manner that would achieve the integration intended by the plan.

Columbia (S.C.) plan approved. The Nixon Administration June 6, 1970 approved a school desegregation plan for Columbia, S.C. that left four all-black elementary schools unchanged and eight others nearly 95% black. The plan, drawn up by Columbia school administrators after two of the President's chief civil rights officers told them that delay was no longer possible, was accepted by J. Stanley Pottinger, director of the Department of Health, Education and Welfare's (HEW) Office of Civil Rights.

The plan followed closely the outline of President Nixon's March 24 school desegregation policy statement.

Under the provisions of the plan, the faculty ratio in all of Columbia's schools would be approximately 65% white and 35% black, and 750 of the district's 1,900 teachers would be assigned across racial lines.

Fifteen of the 19 junior and senior high schools in the district would be reshuffled to have an enrollment that would be 35% to 40% black, including a formerly all-black high school. The other four would have an enrollment that would be more than 70% black. Fifteen of the city's 43 elementary schools would remain more than 80% black and 11 would remain more than 80% white.

There would be no busing of students except in cases where it was needed to relieve overcrowding.

Denver school integration ordered. A U.S. District Court judge May 23, 1970 ordered the Denver public school system to desegregate 15 of its minority-group schools by 1972 and enact sweeping changes at two others. Judge William E. Doyle, ruling in a segregation suit filed against the Denver Board of Education by eight Denver families, said desegregation was essential to improving the quality of education at the 17 schools.

Each of the schools had an enrollment of at least 70% black or Spanish-American, with the exception of one, which was 60% black. The drawing up of desegregation plans was left to the school district and the plaintiff's lawyers, but Doyle set down several guidelines. He ordered the 14 elementary schools covered by his ruling to be desegregated by the fall of 1972. At least seven of them had to be desegregated by the fall of 1971. When integrated, each school had to have a white, non-Spanish enrollment of more than 50%. Doyle also ordered one predominantly Spanish-American junior high school fully desegregated by the fall of 1972.

Doyle also touched on the sensitive issue of student busing. (In February nearly one-third of Denver's school buses were dynamited in a parking lot.)

Doyle said mandatory busing should be avoided "to the extent possible" but that it "may well be necessary to effectuate much of the court's plan."

Michigan district held segregated. A federal hearing examiner for the Department of Health, Education and Welfare ruled Sept. 28, 1970, for the first time, that a Northern school district had violated the nation's civil rights laws by illegally segregating its elementary school pupils.

The examiner recommended that $275,000 in federal aid be withheld from the Ferndale, Mich. school district.

Horace H. Robbins, the hearing examiner, said he found that local and state zoning laws contributed to school segregation in the district. He supported the government contention that Ferndale officials in 1926 opened the U.S. Grant school to segregate black students after racial disorders in Ferndale in 1925. Robbins said that "the school board's course of conduct for 44 years has been

consistently one of segregating the Negro children residing in the Grant area and the township from the Ferndale city elementary schools."

HEW, which had initiated the action against the district in April 1969, contended that Ferndale intentionally segregated its elementary schools by assigning all but 31 of its 396 black school children to the Grant school.

Court voids Houston school plan. A freedom-of-choice school plan that had been in effect for two years in Houston, Tex., the nation's sixth largest school district, was voided June 1, 1970 by a federal court judge. Judge Ben C. Connally said the plan "has been administered fairly and without discrimination," but did not achieve a sufficiently high degree of integration.

The Houston school board had been moving voluntarily to discard the plan in favor of a new one. An equidistant zoning plan, which was one of seven plans proposed by the Houston Board of Education and submitted to the court, was approved by Connally to be implemented as the replacement for the vacated freedom-of-choice arrangement.

The equidistant zoning plan called for the drawing of lines an equal distance from the adjoining schools of the same grade level. Students within one zone would not be permitted to attend a school in another zone even if the student's family changed residences during the school year.

Connally called the plan another "chapter in the effort to disestablish the dual school system and create a unitary system." He said he was unalterably opposed to busing students to achieve racial balance in the schools.

The judge also ordered the faculties of Houston's schools reassigned to bring about a racial balance of 68% white and 32% black in each school.

Jackson, Miss. ruling. U.S. District Court Judge Dan Russell issued a permanent order Oct. 20, 1971 enjoining the State of Mississippi from interfering with a desegregation plan for public schools in Jackson or withholding funds from the

Jackson district because of busing.

Russell ordered the state tax commission, state auditor and attorney general not to interfere with implementation of a court-approved desegregation plan.

Jackson officials had sought relief from the federal court after Gov. John Bell Williams directed state agencies Sept. 11 to withhold education funds until the system showed that it was not using the money for busing purposes.

Minneapolis pairs schools. The Minneapolis board of education Sept. 18, 1971 began to offset school segregation fostered by neighborhood housing patterns by pairing two of its elementary schools as part of an integration plan.

Under the pairing program, all the children in the upper three grades of a virtually all-white school were bused to a school nearby that was 56% black. All children from kindergarten through the third grade were bused from the predominantly black school to the formerly white school. The pairing gave each school an enrollment that was about 25% black or Indian.

Nashville busing ordered. A federal district judge in Nashville, Tenn. June 28, 1971 approved a crosstown busing plan submitted by the Nixon Administration to desegregate the Nashville-Davidson County public school system.

Judge L. Clure Morton adopted the integration plan drawn up by the Department of Health, Education and Welfare (HEW) with some modifications.

The plan as approved required the daily busing of about 47,000 students, an increase of some 13,500 over the number bused during the 1970–71 school year. The Nashville-Davidson school system, the second largest in Tennessee, had an enrollment of about 95,000 students. Under the plan, the system's all-black schools would be completely eliminated, although 36 of the system's 141 schools would remain mostly white.

Pasadena plan approved. A federal district court judge in Los Angeles March 4, 1970 approved a plan submitted by school administrators in Pasadena, Calif. to integrate the city's elementary and secondary public schools. Judge Manuel L. Real had ordered the district to formulate a plan Jan. 20.

Real rejected a petition by the attorneys general of three Southern states —Alabama, Mississippi and Louisiana— to enter the case as a "friend of the court."

The Southern officials had sought to enter the Pasadena case because in their view the time allowed Pasadena educators to design a desegregation arrangement was excessive. The Southerners contended that the California district should be ordered to "integrate now," which, according to the attorneys general, was the order handed down to their states.

The Pasadena case was the first of the government's suits against Northern school districts to be acted upon. The ruling ordered that the plan submitted by the Pasadena district must produce no school with a majority of nonwhite students.

(The suit was filed in August 1968 by the parents of three schoolgirls. The Justice Department joined the suit in November 1968.)

The plan approved by Judge Real called for busing students up to 10 miles within zones set up inside the Pasadena district.

The plan was implemented when the Pasadena schools reopened for the fall term. Under its terms, 30,000 students were to be bused at a cost of $1 million to Pasadena and three neighboring communities which were involved in the busing arrangement.

Pasadena residents Oct. 14 narrowly defeated three referenda to recall three members of the school board who had supported the integration plan.

Pontiac busing review refused. The Supreme Court Oct. 26, 1971 refused to hear an appeal by the Pontiac, Mich. school board of a court-ordered busing plan that had evoked widespread community opposition and violence by the Michigan Ku Klux Klan.

By refusing to hear the case, the court

avoided ruling on the controversial issue of busing in the North to achieve racially-balanced schools.

For the most part, school segregation in the North was fostered by neighborhood housing patterns, or de facto segregation. In the South, school segregation was generally the result of officially constituted acts or de jure segregation. The court had yet to rule on de facto segregation.

The court's action in the Pontiac case meant that lower court judges would remain free to order school busing plans in other Northern school cases.

The court did not give reasons for refusing to hear the appeal by the Pontiac school board, which maintained that school segregation in Pontiac was a result of neighborhood patterns and not of discriminatory actions by either school or public officials.

FBI agents Sept. 9 had arrested six Ku Klux Klan members in connection with the bombing of 10 Pontiac school buses.

The vehicles, which were bombed Aug. 30, were part of Pontiac's fleet of 90 school buses being used to carry out the court-ordered integration plan involving the busing of 8,700 schoolchildren.

Richmond school plan ordered. A federal judge in Richmond, Va., who for two years had heard arguments over various desegregation plans for the city's public schools, ordered officials April 5, 1971 to go ahead with a plan that would increase busing of schoolchildren by about 50%.

The plan approved by U.S. District Court Judge Robert R. Merhige affected all the city's 50 public schools. Of about 50,000 pupils, 20,000 would be bused to increase the incidence of desegregation.

Earlier plans submitted to Merhige by the Department of Health, Education and Welfare (HEW) and backed by the Richmond School Board had no provisions for busing students for desegregation purposes.

Under the plan ordered by Merhige, the city was required to buy 56 more school buses at a cost estimated at $500,000 for the first year. Each high school and elementary school would have a student population of at least 17% white or 33% black under the new plan.

San Francisco order. Federal District Judge Stanley A. Weigel said in San Francisco April 28, 1971 that the city's Board of Education was responsible for widespread school segregation. On Weigel's orders, the board June 4 adopted a busing plan designed to fully integrate the city's elementary schools in September.

Weigel said he found that only 29% of the 48,000 pupils in the city's 102 elementary schools were black, but that 80% of the blacks were concentrated in 27 schools.

Weigel said the district had advanced segregation by zoning new schools and attendance boundaries in a manner that perpetuated the racial imbalance.

Busing sparks Trenton violence. Trenton, N.J., public schools were shut down Oct. 29–30, 1970 because of racial disorders stemming from the city school board's decision to implement a student busing plan. The board voted Nov. 1 to reopen the schools, and a dusk-to-dawn curfew that had been imposed on Trenton Oct. 29 was ordered relaxed by Mayor Arthur J. Holland.

The violence erupted Oct. 29 when fighting broke out between 100 black and white youths at a school in the city's predominantly Italian section. The fighting spread into the downtown district when bands of black youths surged into the area, hurling bottles at policemen and breaking store windows. State troopers joined local police and county detectives in bringing the disorders to an end.

The fighting was apparently triggered by the board's decision to implement a busing plan to achieve racial balance in the schools.

The state commissioner of education Nov. 14 annulled Trenton's controversial school busing plan in the wake of a boycott by white parents who had kept their children at home rather than have them bused to schools outside their neighborhoods.

In a 26-page decision canceling the plan, Commissioner Carl Marburger said that "meaningful school integration cannot be achieved by the involuntary busing of children in urban areas where the majority of the public school youngsters consist of children of the nation's minority groups."

D.C. busing to suburb ended. The Washington, D.C. Board of Education Sept. 25, 1971 ended a three-year program of busing black schoolchildren from the District of Columbia to a predominantly all-white school in a Maryland suburb.

The board canceled the experimental busing by vote. Reasons ranged from budget limitations to black pride.

The cancellation meant that 31 black pupils from inner-city schools would be required to return to an elementary school in their neighborhood, one of the city's poorest. The 31 children had been attending a virtually all-white school in Montgomery County. It would have cost the D.C. district almost $58,000 to have the children attend the suburban school in 1971-72.

Other School Problems

Urban school disruptions studied. A study commissioned by the U.S. Office of Education, in a report Oct. 3, 1970, said that 85% of 683 urban high schools surveyed had experienced some type of disruption over the last three years. According to the survey, the high schools reported racial factors involved in a majority of the disruptions characterized as student walkouts, riots or "abnormal unruliness among students."

Other types of disruptions reported were teachers' strikes, arson or other property damage, student-teacher physical confrontations, picketing and presence of unruly non-school persons. For the purpose of the survey, prepared at the request of former Education Commissioner James E. Allen Jr., a disruption was defined as "any event which significantly interrupts the education of students."

Dr. Stephen K. Bailey, who directed

the Syracuse University Research Corp. unit that conducted the study, said the report was an "unsettling story of an unsettling reality" and that the number and seriousness of incidents would "continue to increase unless met head-on with some imaginative program." He said a "widespread and volatile situation" existed in urban high schools.

The study found that racially integrated high schools were more likely to experience disruption than predominantly white or black schools. However, the report said that without even considering moral objections, the solution of segregated schools to cut down on disruptions was unacceptable. The study said: "A segregated educational system would hardly train the young for an integrated future when they become adults."

In integrated schools where the percentage of black students exceeded the percentage of black staff members, the survey found that disruptions were more numerous and more likely to have a racial basis. Field researchers sent to high schools in 19 cities found some evidence of what the report called "black revenge" as a factor in disruptions. The report said: "We note that most urban black young people are fully aware of the long and ugly centuries of disgrace in which they and their kind were oppressed purely on the basis of color."

As contributing causes of disruption, the report cited the success of civil rights protests and "the ripple effect on high schools of repeated college and university disruption." The study also noted the impact of minority group pressures on traditionally middle-class oriented public schools and the stresses of slum life.

In dealing with disruptions, the study group concluded that traditional methods—such as suspension, expulsion, in-school detention, referral to parental discipline or police arrest—often produced "perverse and counter-productive results." The study cited examples of experimental programs that had reported some success in limiting disruptions: Berkeley (Calif.) High School, which employed young adult security personnel recruited from the same neighborhoods as the students; Kettering High School in Detroit, which used young, specially trained and well educated policemen; a New York City program of special schools to help disruptive students; and experiments to de-emphasize school "bigness" and "academic rigidities" such as the new John Adams High School in Portland, Ore., organized into "houses" with 300 students each.

Federal share in school aid drops. The National Education Association (NEA), in its annual report of "estimates of school statistics," said the nation's public schools would cost a record $42.4 billion in 1970–71. However, the federal government's share of funding the schools would drop for the third straight year. NEA said federal contributions, which reached 8% of the school dollar in 1967–68, would drop to 6.9% of the total in the current school year. The report was issued Jan. 11, 1971.

The actual amount of federal funding for 1970–71 was estimated at $2.9 billion, up $126 million over the previous year. State contributions were placed at $17.2 billion and local governments at $21.8 billion.

Tax revolt threatens Missouri schools. School systems in suburban St. Louis suffered tax revolts in 1970 as voters repeatedly failed to approve tax levies. Schools serving 80,000 students were faced with financial crisis. The situation in the Missouri schools paralleled a similar crisis that caused Youngstown, Ohio schools to close for five weeks in the winter of 1968–69.

One Missouri district, Riverview, closed its schools to 9,000 students for two weeks before voters finally approved a school levy Dec. 9 in the seventh vote of the year. Officials in the Hazelwood district, serving 24,000 students, also threatened to close the schools after voters repeatedly turned down levies.

Schools in two districts, St. Charles with 9,000 students and Wentzville with 7,000 students, were kept closed until voters approved tax levies. The St. Charles levy won in a Sept. 26 vote and the schools opened one month late Sept. 29. Wentzville schools opened Oct. 2 after the district's levy was approved Sept. 30.

In the Fergusson-Florissant district with 20,000 pupils, a levy was approved Sept. 29. School closings were averted for 10,000 students in the Ritenour district after a levy was approved Sept. 30 after being rejected in four previous votes.

Financing by property tax invalid. The California Supreme Court Aug. 30, 1971 ruled, 6–1, that the school financing system based on property taxes favored affluent districts and discriminated against children in poorer neighborhoods. The ruling, written by Justice Ralph L. Sullivan, examined a series of U.S. Supreme Court decisions and held that the property-tax system "must fall before the equal protection clause" of the 14th Amendment, which guaranteed every citizen "the equal protection of the laws."

The ruling sent the case back to lower courts where it had been previously dismissed due to a finding that the plaintiffs had no standing to bring suit. The lower courts were instructed to hold hearings to discover a more equitable school financing system.

The California system, followed in virtually every state, raised 56% of the school revenues from local property taxes, 35% from the state and about 9% from federal grants. The California court held that affluent districts could spend more per pupil and, at the same time, have lower property taxes. The ruling objected that the system "makes the quality of a child's education a function of the wealth of his parents and neighborhoods."

Similar suits had been filed in Illinois, Michigan, Texas and Virginia but had met with little success.

Nationalization of big-city schools asked—Dr. Mark R. Shedd, superintendent of the Philadelphia school system, told the Senate Select Committee on Equal Educational Opportunity Sept. 21

that the "urban schools of this country are dying . . . from financial strangulation." Shedd proposed that the government nationalize the funding and operation of the 25 largest urban public school systems.

Shedd said the "job of rescuing the nation's urban schools from disaster simply has become too big for the limited resources of state and local governments to accomplish." He said property taxes were an insufficient basis to finance urban schools and that most of the revenues of big cities went to fund other services whereas the major share of suburban tax money could go to education.

'Open admissions' begins in NYC. The City University of New York began its fall term Sept. 14, 1970, its first term under an open admissions policy designed to increase college opportunity for poor and minority group students. Under the new policy, every city high school graduate who applied was assured a place in one of the system's 16 senior and community colleges regardless of grades. Tuition remained free.

Commenting on insufficient funds, lack of space and students poorly prepared for college level work, Dr. Albert H. Bowker, university chancellor, said Sept. 13 that open admission was "a critical test" for public higher education and that "with all our planning and effort, failure is possible."

Municipal Labor Problems

Cities across the country were beset by strikes or threatened strikes of municipal workers, often in disregard of laws that forbade strikes by government employes. Raises in pay and improvements in fringe benefits resulting from some of the confrontations added to the financial woes troubling the cities.

N.Y. transit pact, fare rise. A New York City transit strike was averted by an agreement Jan. 1, 1970, three hours past a strike deadline, providing for

an 18% wage increase over two years. The settlement was followed by an increase from 20¢ to 30¢ in the transit fare—effective Jan. 4.

The agreement was announced by Mayor John V. Lindsay. Applying to about 35,000 bus and subway workers represented by the Transport Workers Union and the Amalgamated Transit Union, the pact called for an immediate 8% wage hike and a 10% additional hike July 1, 1971 (pre-pact average wage: $4.02 an hour).

The settlement was expected to cost $120 million over the two-year life of the new contracts.

The fare hike, approved Jan. 2 by the Metropolitan Transportation Authority (MTA), a state agency controlling city transit operations, was to help offset an estimated transit deficit of $120 million for the fiscal year ending June 30, a deficit not taking into account the cost of the new contract.

Cincinnati city workers strike. A 31-day strike in Cincinnati by 2,400 city employes ended Feb. 5, 1970 on the basis of a 13-month contract calling for pay raises of from 22¢ to 54¢ an hour. About 1,400 workers received a 30¢ hourly wage boost.

The workers were members of the State, County & Municipal Employes (SCME) union. The work stoppage resulted in a massive garbage pileup and a lack of street maintenance and waterworks service. Police and firemen were not involved.

During the strike, a sewage treatment plant had to be closed for repairs and 260 million gallons of raw sewage poured into the Ohio River in violation of an interstate agreement. Three strike leaders were jailed for nine days for violating a picketing ban. Two had been sentenced to 20 days each, the third for 10 days, plus fines, but the union refused to negotiate until a court-ordered release was obtained.

The pact also provided for reinstatement of striking employes, who had been informed by the city midway in the strike that they faced dismissal if absent after three days.

San Francisco employes strike. A strike by San Francisco municipal workers closed down the city's schools and transit system and curtailed health services March 13-16, 1970. About 14,000 of the 22,000 city employes were involved. The strike was called by four unions in a dispute with the Board of Supervisors over the size of a proposed wage increase package. The strike ended with agreement on a $6 million package, a $1,250,000 increase over the board's pre-strike offer.

The schools and transit system were shut down when drivers and teachers, who were not members of the striking unions, refused to cross picket lines. The agreement was reached shortly after strike leaders announced their intention to extend picket lines to the city's piers and airport.

37-day Atlanta civic strike. In 1970, Atlanta city employes went on strike for 37 days in a wage dispute with the city administration. The strike, which began March 17, ended April 22 with agreement on a one-step 4.3% pay increase for most of the 2,314 employes involved. The workers, whose pre-pact wages were $355 a month to start and $438 after five years, had sought a 4.5% raise. They were members of the AFL-CIO American Federation of State, County and Municipal Employes union.

Mayor Sam Massell announced March 20 that 1,400 of the absent employes were discharged, and the city tried to hire replacements March 21, but only a few persons applied. City prisoners were then employed in garbage pickups. After the settlement, Massell said those discharged would be rehired without prejudice.

City strikes in Washington State. In Seattle, garbage workers, members of the International Brotherhood of Teamsters, ended a six-day walkout April 8, 1970 with agreement on a three-year pact with a total pay raise of $1.22 more an

hour; Tacoma city workers (transit and garbage service) ended a two-day work stoppage April 25 when an arbitration board was set up to hear Teamsters' demands for higher wages.

Teachers' strikes. Communities in New Jersey were hit by a series of teachers' strikes from January through March 1970. Although many teachers' contracts involved were not due to expire until summer, a state law required communities to submit school budgets in February; this apparently accounted for the strikes and wage disputes. Teachers in the state's two largest school systems, Newark and Jersey City, violated court injunctions to strike for higher wages.

In Newark, N.J. the city's Teachers Union, a local of the AFL-CIO American Federation of Teachers (AFT), voted Feb. 25 to end a 23-day strike against the city's 84 elementary and high schools, serving more than 78,000 students. The strike settlement gave the teachers an average annual salary increase of $2,200 with wages to range from $8,000-$13,-100 a year beginning in September.

In Jersey City, a strike by the Jersey City Education Association, an affiliate of the National Education Association (NEA), closed all of the city's 34 elementary and high schools Feb. 9. They ended the strike after agreeing March 4 on a two-year contract with raises providing for a basic annual salary scale ranging from $8,700 to $14,100 in the second year of the contract. The maximum salary for teachers with doctoral degrees would rise to $15,600. The increases ranged up to about $3,350.

The United Teachers of Los Angeles (UTLA) voted May 13 to end a month-long strike and to forego a 5% raise offer so that the funds could go for educational improvements. Although wages were at issue during the strike, which began April 13, the teachers consistently had maintained that the main problem was a cutback in funds that would cause a $42 million deficit in the city's school budget for the coming year.

Schools had remained open during the strike, but about half of the city's

25,000 teachers remained off the job. UTLA represented about 22,000 teachers. Student absenteeism was estimated at 30–40%. Non-teaching school employes, represented by AFL-CIO Service Employes Local 99, had joined the strike April 24.

A Toledo, Ohio strike ended Oct. 2 when teachers ratified a new pay schedule providing from $100 to $1,000 in pay increases. Most of the city's 2,-500 striking teachers had already returned to work following a court injunction Sept. 18. The strike had begun Sept. 2.

The 11,500-member Philadelphia Federation of Teachers struck Oct. 16 after a 30-day truce, negotiated after a two-day delay in opening the term in September, expired without a contract settlement. The city's 275 schools, serving 295,000 students, resumed full operations Oct. 21 after preliminary agreement on a two-year contract package valued at $57.3 million.

Full agreement on the contract was reached Nov. 6 and ratified by the teachers Nov. 11. The contract provided an average annual pay increase of $1,050. An agreement on hour increases required by state laws governing the length of the school day gave teachers working overtime payment at extra-curricular rates.

A teachers' strike ended Nov. 23 in East St. Louis, Ill. after an American Federation of Teachers local and the school board agreed to a settlement to end a walkout that had been in progress since the beginning of the term. The 44 schools in the district, serving 23,000 students, had opened under a court order Oct. 5 and were operating at one-third capacity, staffed by 240 non-union and newly hired teachers.

Under the settlement, 600 striking teachers returned to their jobs but lost seniority and tenure. They had asked no pay increases during the strike, and it was estimated that the teachers lost more than $1 million in wages and benefits during the walkout. The strikers lost seniority and tenure because they resigned during the strike to avoid a court order that they return to work.

The Pittsburgh Federation of Teach-ers voted Jan. 10, 1971 to accept a $900 annual pay increase in a pact ending a walkout that began Jan. 4. It was the first settlement in the city's week-long labor crisis, which affected garbage collection and the two largest daily newspapers as well as the city's 110 public schools serving 73,000 students.

The agreement, which raised starting salaries for teachers with bachelor's degrees to $8,500 a year and with master's degrees to $8,900 a year, also provided for negotiations to improve discipline and a pledge by the school board to hire 86 new teachers. Smaller classes had been one of the union demands.

The Newark (N.J.) Teachers Union and the city's board of education agreed April 18 to a contract settlement proposed by Mayor Kenneth A. Gibson, ending an 11-week teachers' strike. The strike, which began Feb. 1, was the second in less than a year in Newark and was the longest in the history of any major American city.

The strike raised racial tensions in the city, although both black and white teachers were among the 50% of the Newark teachers who remained out of class. The board kept the city's 84 schools open to almost 80,000 students in the system, but attendance was reduced by 50% throughout the strike.

NTU President Mrs. Carole Graves, herself a black, charged that the racial issue was being exploited by Jesse Jacob, president of the board of education, and Imamu Amiri Baraka (LeRoi Jones), a leading black playwright who headed the Committee for a Unified NewArk. Mrs. Graves, who had been accused of being a tool of the white teachers, said Feb. 13, "this is just a labor-management fight. Jesse Jacob and LeRoi Jones interject this racial business because it's a good way to break the union and get control of the schools."

The five-man black and Puerto Rican majority on the board of education opposed the union demands for binding arbitration and release from certain non-classroom duties such as supervising children in the halls and lunchroom. They charged that the teachers, many of whom lived outside Newark in the suburbs, were unsympathetic to the needs of black children. About 55% of Newark's residents were black and another 10% were Puerto Rican.

White enrollment in the schools was about 15%, but about 60% of the teachers were white.

From the beginning of the strike, acts of violence exacerbated the tensions. Mrs. Graves charged Feb. 1 that her car had been firebombed and windows in her home broken. About 15 men and women strikers, both black and white, were beaten with clubs and fists Feb. 2 by about 25 black youths.

Mrs. Graves and two other union officials were jailed March 4 for violating a court injunction against the strike. The three were released April 14. Some picketing teachers were arrested during the course of the strike, and the board suspended 347 of the strikers March 30.

Mayor Gibson's contract proposal came after two tumultuous public meetings April 6 and 7 when the board rejected a settlement which had been informally agreed to earlier. Gibson's plan, presented April 16 and approved by both sides April 18, was a compromise proposal.

Under Gibson's proposal, a "special task force of concerned citizens" was to be appointed to review the city's education problems, which included a 30% dropout rate in the high schools. The two-year contract also gave the teachers $500 raises in the second year. The union, an affiliate of the AFL-CIO American Federation of Teachers, had first demanded a $2,000 raise in the $8,-000 annual starting salary, but wages were never a primary issue in the strike.

N.Y. police strike. About 85% of New York City's 27,400 patrolmen engaged in a wildcat strike Jan. 14–19, 1971 but did not win a resolution of the pay dispute involved.

Essential service was maintained during the strike, and there was no evidence of a crime upsurge.

The pay dispute involved the salary ratio between sergeants, who had received a wage increase, and patrolmen, who demanded retroactive $100-a-month raises to maintain the 3.5–3 ratio they con-

tended was written into the contract which expired Dec. 31, 1970.

The patrolmen's raises could cost $2,700 in back pay to each patrolman, or a total of $60 million–$70 million. They could also trigger other similar demands, since contracts with firemen and sanitationmen also expired Dec. 31, 1970.

The strike action was opposed by the Patrolmen's Benevolent Association, the policemen's union, but spread to 85% of the force and drew sympathy walkouts by security officers in transit, housing and social service work. It ended Jan. 19 when PBA delegates voted resumption of customary duties.

Milwaukee police strike—About 95% of Milwaukee's 2,000-man police force stayed off the job Jan. 23–26 in a contract dispute that also remained unresolved. The massive sick-call observance, or "blue flu," ended Jan. 27 under a court order interpreting the action as a strike and setting a deadline for return to work.

Crime rate up 11% in 1970. The Federal Bureau of Investigation reported March 28, 1971 that in 1970 the nationwide crime rate was 11% above the 1961 level.

Despite the nationwide rise, 10 of the most populous cities reported a decline in the number of offenses known to the police. They were Chicago, Cleveland, Kansas City, Mo., Louisville, Oakland, Calif., Pittsburgh, St. Louis, St. Paul, Minn., Seattle and Washington.

The FBI indicated that the incidence of crime was increasing in the suburbs. According to the statistics, there was a 6% rise in the number of reported crimes in cities with populations of a quarter of a million or more. Police in suburban communities reported a 15% increase in the number of crimes reported.

The FBI cautioned the public "against drawing conclusions by making direct comparisons between cities due to the existence of numerous factors which affect the amount and type of crime from place to place."

In a statement accompanying an Aug. 31 report, Attorney General John N. Mitchell noted that crime in large cities had risen only 6% in 1970 after rising 9% in 1969 and 18% in 1968.

According to the figures, Miami had the highest major crime rate of any U.S. city, with 5,342.8 crimes per 100,000 population. The San Francisco-Oakland area was second, with 5,329.3. New York City had the third highest, with 5,220.

New York's chief medical examiner released statistics July 8 showing that the city's murder rate in the first six months of 1971 had risen 30% over the same period of 1970.

The figures showed that from January through June there were 714 homicide victims. Over the same period in 1970, there were 548 homicides.

Gains in war vs. crime. Attorney General Mitchell said Jan. 19, 1971 that the Nixon Administration was making headway in curbing crime.

Despite the nationwide crime figures, Mitchell said crime had actually been reduced in the District of Columbia and in 23 cities with populations exceeding 100,000. He added that more accurate FBI data and better crime reporting, however, had created a "paper crime wave" that made it appear as if crime was still on the rise.

Mitchell's assertion was made during a news conference review of his two years as attorney general.

In addition to holding down crime, the achievements listed in Mitchell's report included enactment of three major crime bills, an increase in the convictions of "high echelon organized crime leaders" and reduction of street crime in Baltimore, Kansas City, Pittsburgh, St. Louis and Seattle and an increase in the number of discrimination suits involving Mexican-Americans, Negroes, women and Puerto Ricans.

Grants for war on crime. Attorney General Mitchell Jan. 18, 1970 announced grants of $236 million in federal funds in fiscal 1970 to help cities and states fight crime and improve their criminal justice systems. Mitchell said the grants, for programs under the Justice Department's Law Enforcement Assistance Administration (LEAA), were a "promising

beginning for the federal-state partnership to defeat crime in the streets."

The allocations included $215 million to states and cities for action programs. The grants were to be matched in part by funds provided by the recipients. Mitchell said the action grants were awarded on the basis of population. California received $17.3 million and New York $16.4 million.

States were to receive $21 million in fiscal '70 grants for planning purposes. In fiscal 1969, LEAA's first year of operation, most of the $63 million budget was spent for planning projects and for setting up anticrime machinery in each state.

Crime control act signed. The Omnibus Crime Control Act of 1970, cleared by both houses of Congress Dec. 17, 1970, was signed by the President Jan. 2, 1971. It authorized $3.55 billion for federal law enforcement aid to state and communities in fiscal 1971–73.

Designed to help local police forces increase their effectiveness, the act refocused the aid to concentrate more on urban high-crime areas.

Nixon's anticrime plan. President Nixon asked Congress March 2, 1971 to approve a $500 million outlay in "special" revenue sharing funds to help states and cities in their fight against crime.

The $500 million in special crime-fighting funds would be distributed to the states on the basis of population. California was to receive the single largest grant—$41.1 million—and Alaska was to receive the least—$623,000. The District of Columbia would receive $1,565,000.

Nixon's proposal called for a total federal expenditure of $711 million. Of that total, $211 million was earmarked for programs administered by the Justice Department's Law Enforcement Assistance Administration. The remaining $500 million was to be allocated to the states by the Justice Department. The states would be able to use the funds as they saw fit.

The President said his plan provided

"the benefits of federal assistance without the burdens of assistance built into the present grant programs."

Under the Nixon plan, the states would not be required to "match" special revenue payments with their own funds. The states would not be required to maintain their present expenditures on law enforcement to qualify for federal funds.

(The Justice Department's fiscal 1972 appropriation, cleared by Congress Aug. 3 and signed by Nixon Aug. 10, provided $698,919,000 for the Law Enforcement Assistance Administration.)

1972 : Urban Problems in an Election Year

City Issues Debated

The problems of the cities were among major issues debated during 1972 in the nation's 46th Presidential election. President Richard M. Nixon and Vice President Spiro T. Agnew, the Republican candidates, were reelected in a landslide victory Nov. 7 over Democratic Presidential nominee George S. McGovern and Vice Presidential candidate R. Sargent Shriver Jr.

Political positions. The official programs of the two parties on urban affairs were detailed in their 1972 platforms.

Democratic platform—The Democratic Party platform, adopted July 11–21, included the following statements on urban issues:

Always the vital center of our civilization, the American city since World War II has been suffering growing pains, caused partly by the change of the core city into a metropolitan city and partly by the movement of people from towns and rural areas into the cities.

The burgeoning of the suburbs—thrust outward with too little concern for social, economic and environmental consequences—has both broadened the city's limits and deepened human and neighborhood needs.

The Nixon Administration has failed to meet most of these needs. It has met the problem of urban decay with tired, decaying "solutions" that are unworthy of the name. It could act to revitalize our urban areas; instead, we see only rising crime, fear and flight, ra-

cial and economic polarization, loss of confidence and depletion of community resources.

This Administration has ignored the cities and suburbs, permitting taxes to rise and services to decline; housing to deteriorate faster than it can be replaced, and morale to suffer. It actually has impounded funds appropriated by a Democratic Congress to help cities in crisis.

The Administration has ignored the needs of city and suburban residents for public services, for property tax relief and for the planning and coordination that alone can assure that housing, jobs, schools and transportation are built and maintained in suitable locations and in needed numbers and quality.

Meanwhile, the Nixon Administration has forgotten small-town America, too, refusing to provide facilities that would make it an attractive alternative to city living.

This has become the American crisis of the 1970's. Today, our highest national priority is clear and precise: To deal effectively—and now—with the massive, complex and urgent needs of our cities, suburbs and towns.

The federal government cannot solve all the problems of these communities. Too often, federal bureaucracy has failed to deliver the services and keep the promises that are made. But only the federal government can be the catalyst to focus attention and resources on the needs of every neighborhood in America.

Under the Nixon Administration, piecemeal measures, poorly funded and haphazardly applied, have proved almost totally inadequate. Words have not halted the decline of neighborhoods. Words have not relieved the plight of tenants in poorly managed, shoddy housing. Our scarce urban dollars have been wasted, and even the Republican Secretary of Housing and Urban Development has admitted it.

The Democratic Party pledges to stop the rot in our cities, suburbs and towns, and stop it now. We pledge commitment, coordination, planning and funds:

Commitment to make our communities places where we are proud to raise our children;

67

Coordination and planning to help all levels of government achieve the same goals to ensure that physical facilities meet human needs and to ensure that land—a scarce resource—is used in ways that meet the needs of the entire nation; and

Funds to reduce the burden of the inequitable property tax and to help local government meet legitimate and growing demands for public . . . services.

The nation's urban areas must and can be habitable. They are not only centers of commerce and trade, but also repositories of history and culture, expressing the richness and variety of their region and of the larger society. They are worthy of the best America can offer. They are America.

Partnership Among Governments

The federal government must assist local communities to plan for their orderly growth and development, to improve conditions and opportunities for all their citizens and to build the public facilities they need.

Effective planning must be done on a regional basis. New means of planning are needed that are practical and realistic, but that go beyond the limits of jurisdictional lines. If local government is to be responsive to citizen needs, public services and programs must efficiently be coordinated and evolved through comprehensive regional planning and decision-making. Government activities should take account of the future as well as the present.

In aiding the reform of state and local government, federal authority must insist that local decisions take into account the views and needs of all citizens, white and black, haves and have-nots, young and old, Spanish and other non-English-speaking, urban, suburban and rural.

Americans ask more and more of their local governments, but the regressive property tax structure makes it impossible for cities and counties to deliver. The Democratic Party is committed to ensure that state and local governments have the funds and the capacity to achieve community service and development goals—goals that are nationally recognized. To this end:

■ We fully support general revenue sharing and the principle that the federal income tax should be used to raise more revenues for local use;

■ We pledge adequate federal funds to halt property tax increases and to begin to roll them back. Turning over federal funds to local governments will permit salaries of underpaid state and local government employees to climb to acceptable levels; and it will reduce tax pressures on the aged, the poor, Spanish and other non-English-speaking Americans and young couples starting out in life;

■ We further commit ourselves to reorganize categorical grant programs. They should be consolidated, expanded and simplified. Funding should be adequate, dependable, sustained, long-term and related to state and local fiscal timetables and priorities. There should be full funding of all programs, without the impounding of funds by the Executive Branch to thwart the will of Congress. And there should be performance standards governing the distribution of all federal funds to state and local governments; and

■ We support efforts to eliminate gaps and costly overlaps in services delivered by different levels of government.

Urban Growth Policy

The Nixon Administration has neither developed an effective urban growth policy designed to meet

critical problems, nor concerned itself with the needed re-creation of the quality of life in our cities, large and small. Instead, it has severely over-administered and underfunded existing federal aid programs. Through word and deed, the Administration has widened the gulf between city and suburb, between core and fringe, between haves and have-nots.

The nation's urban growth policies are seen most clearly in the legitimate complaints of suburban householders over rising taxes and of center-city families over houses that are falling apart and services that are often non-existent. And it is here, in center city, that the failure of Nixon Administration policies is most clear to all who live there.

The Democratic Party pledges:

■ A national urban growth policy to promote a balance of population among cities, suburbs, small towns and rural areas, while providing social and economic opportunities for everyone. America needs a logical urban growth policy, instead of today's inadvertent, chaotic and haphazard one that doesn't work. An urban growth policy that truly deals with our tax and mortgage insurance and highway policies will require the use of federal policies as leverage on private investment;

■ A policy on housing—including low- and middle-income housing—that will concentrate effort in areas where there are jobs, transportation, schools, health care and commercial facilities. Problems of overgrowth are not caused so much by land scarcity, as by the wrong distribution of people and the inadequate servicing of their needs; and

■ A policy to experiment with alternative strategies to reserve land for future development—land banks—and a policy to recoup publicly created land values for public benefit.

The Cities

Many of the worst problems in America are centered in our cities. Countless problems contribute to their plight: decay in housing, the drain of welfare, crime and violence, racism, failing schools, joblessness and poor mass transit, lack of planning for land use and services.

The Democratic Party pledges itself to change the disastrous policies of the Nixon Administration toward the cities and to reverse the steady process of decay and dissolution. We will renew the battle begun under the Kennedy and Johnson Administrations to improve the quality of life in our cities. In addition to pledging the resources critically needed, we commit ourselves to these actions:

■ Help localities to develop their own solutions to their most pressing problems—the federal government should not stifle or usurp local initiative;

■ Carry out programs developed elsewhere in this Platform to assure every American decent shelter, freedom from hunger, good health care, the opportunity to work, adequate income and a decent education;

■ Provide sufficient management and planning funds for cities, to let them increase staff capacity and improve means of allocating resources;

■ Distribute funds according to standards that will provide center cities with enough resources to revitalize old neighborhoods and build new ones, to expand and improve community services and to help local governments better to plan and deliver these services; and

■ Create and fund a housing strategy that will recognize that housing is neighborhood and community as well as shelter—a strategy that will serve all the nation's urban areas and all the American people.

Housing and Community Development

The 1949 Housing Act pledged "a decent home and suitable living environment for every American family." Twenty-three years later, this goal is still far away. Under this Administration, there simply has been no progress in meeting our housing needs, despite the Democratic Housing Act of 1968. We must build 2.6 million homes a year, including two-thirds of a million units of federally-subsidized low- and middle-income housing. These targets are not being met. And the lack of housing is particularly critical for people with low and middle incomes.

■ In the cities, widespread deterioration and abandonment are destroying once sound homes and apartments, and often entire neighborhoods, faster than new homes are built.

■ Federal housing policy creates walled compounds of poor, elderly and ethnic minorities, isolating them in the center city. These harmful policies include the Administration's approach to urban renewal, discrimination against the center city by the Federal Housing Administration, highway policies that destroy neighborhoods and create ghettos . . .

■ Millions of lower- and middle-class Americans —each year the income level is higher—are priced out of housing because of sharply rising costs.

Under Republican leadership, the Federal Housing Administration (FHA) has become the biggest slumlord in the country. Some unsophisticated home buyers have purchased homes with FHA mortgage insurance or subsidies. These consumers, relying on FHA appraisals to protect them, often have been exploited by real estate speculators and dishonest builders. Unable to repair or maintain these houses, the buyers often have no choice but to abandon them. As a result, the FHA will acquire a quarter million of these abandoned houses at a cost to the taxpayers of billions of dollars.

Under the Republican Administration, the emphasis has been on housing subsidies for the people who build and sell houses rather than for those people who need and live in them. In many cases, the only decent shelter provided is a tax shelter.

To correct this inequity the Democratic Party pledges:

■ To overhaul completely the FHA to make it a consumer-oriented agency;

■ To use the full faith and credit of the Treasury to provide direct, low-interest loans to finance the construction and purchase of decent housing for the American people; and

■ To insist on building practices, inspection standards and management that will assure quality housing.

The next Administration must build and conserve housing that not only meets the basic need for shelter, but also provides a wider choice of quality housing and living environments. To meet this challenge, the Democratic Party commits itself to a housing approach that:

■ Prevents the decay and abandonment of homes and neighborhoods. Major rehabilitation programs to conserve and rehabilitate housing are needed. Consumers should be aided in purchasing homes, and low-income housing foreclosed by the FHA should be provided to poor families at minimal cost

as an urban land grant. These houses should be rehabilitated and lived in, not left to rot;

■ Provides federal funds for preservation of existing neighborhoods. Local communities should decide whether they want renewal or preservation. Choosing preservation should not mean steady deterioration and inadequate facilities;

■ Provides for improved housing quality for all families through strict enforcement of housing quality standards and full compliance with state and local health and safety laws;

■ Provides effective incentives to reduce housing costs—to the benefit of poor and middle-income families alike—through effective use of unused, undeveloped land, reform of building practices and the use of new building techniques, including factory-made and modular construction;

■ Assures that residents have a strong voice in determining the destiny of their own neighborhoods;

■ Promotes free choice in housing—the right of all families, regardless of race, color, religion or income, to choose among a wide range of homes and neighborhoods in urban, suburban and rural areas— through the greater use of grants to individuals for housing, the development of new communities offering diversified housing and neighborhood options and the enforcement of fair housing laws; and

■ Assures fair and equitable relationships between landlords and tenants.

New Towns

New towns meet the direct housing and community needs of only a small part of our population. To do more, new towns must be developed in concert with massive efforts to revitalize central cities and enhance the quality of life in still growing suburban areas.

The Democratic Party pledges:

■ To strengthen the administration of the New Towns program; to reduce onerous review requirements that delay the start of New Towns and thus thwart Congressional mandates; to release already appropriated monies and provide new planning and development funds needed to assure the quality of life in New Towns; and

■ To assure coordination between development of New Towns and renewed efforts to improve the quality of life in established urban and suburban areas. We also promise to use effectively the development of New Towns to increase housing choices for people now living in central and suburban areas.

Transportation

Urban problems cannot be separated from transportation problems. Whether tying communities together, connecting one community to another or linking our cities and towns to rural areas, good transportation is essential to the social and economic life of any community. . . .

Today, however, the automobile is the principal form of transportation in urban areas. The private automobile has made a major contribution to economic growth and prosperity in this century. But now we must have better balanced transportation—more of it public. Today, 15 times as much federal aid goes to highways as to mass transit; tomorrow this must change. At the same time, it is important to preserve and improve transportation in America's rural areas, to end the crisis in rural mobility.

The Democratic Party pledges:

■ To create a single Transportation Trust Fund, to replace the Highway Trust Fund, with such additional funds as necessary to meet our transportation crisis substantially from federal resources. This fund will allocate monies for capital projects on a regional basis, permitting each region to determine its own needs under guidelines that will ensure a balanced transportation system and adequate funding of mass transit facilities.

Moreover, we will:

■ Assist local transit systems to meet their capital and operating needs;

■ End the deterioration of rail and rural transportation and promote a flexible rural transportation system based on local, state and regional needs;

■ Take steps to meet the particular transportation problems of the elderly, the handicapped and others with special needs; and

■ Assist development of airport terminals, facilities and access to them, with due regard to impact on environment and community. . . .

School Finance

Achieving educational excellence requires adequate financial support. But today local property taxes—which do not keep pace with inflation—can no longer support educational needs. Continued reliance on this revenue source imposes needless hardship on the American family without supplying the means for good schools. At the same time, the Nixon recession has sapped the resources of state government, and the Administration's insensitivity to school children has meant inadequate federal expenditures in education.

The next Democratic Administration should:

■ Support equalization in spending among school districts. We support Court decisions holding unconstitutional the disparities in school expenditures produced by dependence on local property taxes. We pledge equality of spending as a way to improve schools and to assure equality of access to good education for all children;

■ Increase federal financial aid for elementary and secondary education to enhance achievement of quality education anywhere, by fully funding the programs passed by the Congress and by fully funding ESEA Title I;

■ Step up efforts to meet the special needs and costs of educationally disadvantaged children handicapped by poverty, disability or non-English-speaking family background;

■ Channel financial aid by a Constitutional formula to children in non-public schools;

■ Support suburban-urban cooperation in education to share resources and expenses;

■ Develop and implement the retraining of displaced black and other minority teachers affected by desegregation; and

■ Continue with full federal funding the breakfast and lunch programs for all children and the development of other programs to combat hunger. . . .

Equal Access to Quality Education

The Supreme Court of the United States in Brown v Board of Education established the Constitutional principle that states may not discriminate between school children on the basis of their race and that separate but equal has no place in our public educa-

tion system. Eighteen years later the provision of integration is not a reality.

We support the goal of desegregation as a means to achieve equal access to quality education for all our children. There are many ways to desegregate schools: School attendance lines may be redrawn; schools may be paired; larger physical facilities may be built to serve larger, more diverse enrollments; magnet schools or educational parks may be used. Transportation of students is another tool to accomplish desegregation. It must continue to be available according to Supreme Court decisions to eliminate legally imposed segregation and improve the quality of education for all children.

Bilingual Education

Ten per cent of school children in the United States speak a language other than English in their homes and communities. The largest of the linguistic and cultural groups—Spanish-speaking and American Indians—are also among the poorest people in the United States. Increasing evidence indicates an almost total failure of public education to educate these children.

The drop-out rates of Spanish-speaking and Indian children are the worst of any children in the country. The injury is compounded when such children are placed in special "compensatory" programs or programs for the "dumb" or the "retarded" on the basis of tests and evaluations conducted in English.

The passage of the Bilingual Education Act of 1967 began a commitment by the nation to do something about the injustices committed against the bilingual child. But for 1972-73, Congress appropriated $35 million—enough to serve only two percent of the children who need help.

The next Democratic Administration should:

■ Increase federal support for bilingual, bicultural educational programs, pre-school through secondary school, including funding of bilingual Adult Basic Education:

■ Ensure sufficient teacher training and curriculum development for such schools;

■ Implement an affirmative action program to train and to hire bilingual-bicultural Spanish-speaking persons at all levels in the educational system;

■ Provide inventories for state and local districts to initiate bilingual-bicultural education programs;

■ Require testing of bilingual-bicultural children in their own languages; and

■ Prohibit discrimination against bilingual-bicultural children in school. . . .

Crime, Law & Justice

We advocate and seek a society and a government in which there is an attitude of respect for the law and for those who seek its enforcement and an insistence on the part of our citizens that the judiciary be ever mindful of their primary duty and function of punishing the guilty and protecting the innocent. We will insist on prompt, fair and equal treatment for all persons before the bar of justice.

The problem of crime in America is real, immediate and fundamental; its costs to the nation are staggering; nearly three-quarters of a million victims of violent crime in one year alone; more than 15,000 murders, billions of dollars of property loss.

The indirect, intangible costs are even more

ominous. A frightened nation is not a free nation. Its citizens are prisoners, suspicious of the people they meet, restricted in when they go out and when they return, threatened even in their own homes. Unless goverment at all levels can restore a sense of confidence and security to its people, there is the ever-present danger that alarm will turn to panic, triggering short-cut remedies that jeopardize hard-won liberties.

When law enforcement breaks down, not only the victims of street violence suffer; the worker's health and safety is imperiled by unsafe, illegal conditions on the job; the society is defenseless against fraud and pollution; most tragically of all, parents and communities are ravaged by traffic in dangerous drugs.

The Nixon Administration campaigned on a pledge to reduce crime—to strengthen the "peace forces" against the "criminal forces." Despite claims to the contrary, that pledge has been broken:

Violent crime has increased by one-third, to the highest levels in our history;

Fueled by the immense profits of narcotics traffic, organized crime has thrust its corruption farther and farther, into law enforcement agencies and the halls of Justice;

The Department of Justice has become the hand-maiden of the White House political apparatus, offering favors to those special interests which buy their "law" in Washington;

The Justice Department has failed to enforce laws protecting key legal rights, such as the Voting Rights Act of 1965;

Nixon and Mitchell use federal crime control funds for political purposes, squandering $1.5 billion;

To reverse this course, through equal enforcement of the law, and to rebuild justice the Democratic Party believes:

The impact of crime in America cuts across racial, geographic and economic lines;

Hard-line rhetoric, pandering to emotion, is both futile and destructive;

We can protect all people without undermining fundamental liberties by ceasing to use "law and order" as justification for repression and political persecution, and by ceasing to use stop-gap measures as preventive detention, "no-knock" entry, surveillance, promiscuous and unauthorized use of wire taps, harrassment, and secret dossiers; and

The problems of crime and drug abuse cannot be isolated from the social and economic conditions that give rise to them.

Preventing Crime

Effective law enforcement requires tough planning and action. This Administration has given us nothing but tough words. Together with unequal law enforcement by police, prosecutors and judges, the result is a "turnstile" system of injustice, where most of those who commit crime are not arrested, most of those arrested are not prosecuted, and many of those prosecuted are not convicted. Under this Administration, the conviction rate for federal prosecutions has declined to one-half its former level. Tens of thousands of offenders simply never appear in court and are heard from again only when they commit another crime. This system does not deter crime. It invites it. It will be changed only when all levels of government act to return firmness and fairness to every part of the criminal justice system.

Fear of crime, and firm action against it, is not racism. Indeed the greatest victims of crime today—whether of business fraud or of the narcotics plague—are the people of the ghetto, black and brown. Fear

now stalks their streets far more than it does the suburbs.

So that Americans can again live without fear of each other the Democratic Party believes:

There must be equally stringent law enforcement for rich and poor, corporate and individual offenders;

Citizens must be actively involved with the police in a joint effort;

Police forces must be upgraded, and recruiting of highly qualified and motivated policemen must be made easier through federally-assisted pay commensurate with the difficulty and importance of their job, and improved training with comprehensive scholarship and financial support for anyone who is serving or will contract to serve for an appropriate period of police service;

The complex job of policing requires a sensitivity to the changing social demands of the communities in which police operate;

We must provide the police with increased technological facilities and support more efficient use of police resources, both human and material;

When a person is arrested, both justice and effective deterrence of crime require that he be speedily tried, convicted or acquitted, and if convicted, promptly sentenced. To this end we support financial assistance to local courts, prosecutors, and independent defense counsel for expansion, streamlining, and upgrading, with trial in 60 days as the goal;

To train local and state police officers, a Police Academy on a par with the other service academies should be established as well as an Academy of Judicial Administration;

We will provide every assistance to our law enforcement agencies at federal and local levels in the training of personnel and the improvement of techniques and will encourage mutual cooperation between each in its own sphere of responsibility;

We will support needed legislation and action to seek out and bring to justice the criminal organizations of national scope operating in our country;

We will provide leadership and action in a national effort against the usage of drugs and drug addiction, attacking this problem at every level and every source in a full scale campaign to drive this evil from our society. We recognize drug addiction as a health problem and pledge that emphasis will be put on rehabilitation of addicts;

We will provide increased emphasis in the area of juvenile delinquency and juvenile offenses in order to deter and rehabilitate young offenders;

There must be laws to control the improper use of hand guns.

A comprehensive fully-funded program is needed to improve juvenile justice, to ensure minimum standards, to expand research into rehabilitation techniques, including alternatives to reform schools and coordinate existing programs for treating juvenile delinquency; and

The block-grant system of the Law Enforcement Assistance Administration which has produced ineffectiveness, waste and corruption should be eliminated. Funds should go directly to operating agencies that are committed to change and improvement in local law enforcement, including agencies concerned with research, rehabilitation, training and treatment.

Narcotic Drugs

Drug addiction and alcoholism are health problems. Drugs prey on children, destroy lives and communities, force crimes to satisfy addicts, corrupt police and government and finance the expansion of organized crime. A massive national effort, equal to the scale and complexity of the problem, is essential. The next Democratic Administration should support:

A massive law enforcement effort, supported by increased funds and personnel, against the suppliers and distributors of heroin and other dangerous drugs, with increased penalties for major narcotics traffickers;

Full use of all existing resources to halt the illegal entry of narcotics into the United States, including suspension of economic and military assistance to any country that fails to take appropriate steps to prevent narcotic drugs produced or processed in that country from entering the United States illegally, and increases in customs personnel fighting smuggling of hard drugs;

An all-out investigative and prosecutory effort against corruption in government and law enforcement. Where corruption exists it is a major factor in permitting criminal activity, especially large-scale narcotic distribution, to flourish. It also destroys respect for the law in all who are conscious of its operation. We are determined that our children—whether in the ghetto or in a suburban high school—shall no longer be able to see a pusher protected from prosecution, openly plying his trade;

Strict regulation and vigorous enforcement of existing quotas regulating production and distribution of dangerous drugs, including amphetamines and barbiturates, to prevent diversion into illegal markets, with legislation for strong *criminal* penalties against drug manufacturers engaging in illegal overproduction, distribution and importation;

Expanded research into dangerous drugs and their abuse, focusing especially on heroin addiction among the young and development of effective, non-addictive heroin treatment methods;

Concentration of law enforcement efforts on major suppliers and distributors, with most individual users diverted into treatment before prosecution;

Immediate placement in medical or psychiatric treatment, available to any individual drug abuser without fear of disclosure or harrassment. Work opportunities should be provided for addicts in treatment by supported work and other programs; and

Drug education in schools based on fact, not scare tactics to teach young people the dangers of different drugs, and full treatment opportunities for youthful drug abusers. Hard drug trafficking in schools must be met with the strongest possible law enforcement.

Organized and Professional Crime

We are determined to exert the maximum power and authority of the federal government to protect the many victims who cannot help themselves against great criminal combinations.

Against the organized criminal syndicates, we pledge an expanded federal enforcement effort; one not restricted to criminals of any particular ethnic group, but which recognizes that organized crime in the United States cuts across all boundaries of race, national origin and class.

Against white-collar crime, we pledge to enforce the maximum penalties provided by law. Justice cannot survive when, as too often is the case, a boy who steals a television set is sentenced to a long jail term, while a stock manipulator who steals millions is only commanded to sin no more.

At least where life or personal injury are at stake, we pledge to seek expanded criminal penalties for the violation of federal laws. Employers who violate the worker safety and health laws, or manufacturers who knowingly sell unsafe products or drugs profit

from death and injury as knowingly as the common mugger. They deserve equally severe punishment. ...

Republican platform—The 1972 Republican platform, adopted Aug. 22, included these statements on urban issues:

Education

We take pride in our leadership these last four years in lifting both quality and equality in American education—from pre-school to graduate school —working toward higher standards than ever before.

Our two most pressing needs in the 1970's are the provision of quality education for all children, and equitable financing of steadily rising costs. We pledge our best efforts to deal effectively with both.

Months ago President Nixon sent Congress a two-part comprehensive proposal on school busing. The first is the Student Transportation Moratorium Act of 1972—legislation to halt immediately all further court-ordered busing and give Congress time to devise permanent new arrangements for assuring desegregated, quality education.

The details of such arrangements are spelled out in a companion bill, the Equal Educational Opportunities Act. This measure would:

■ Provide $2.5 billion in Federal aid funds to help promote quality education while preserving neighborhood schools.

■ Accord equal educational opportunities to all children.

■ Include an educational bill of rights for Spanish-speaking people, Americans Indians, and others who face special language problems in schools.

■ Offer, for the first time, a real chance for good schooling for the hundreds of thousands of children who live in urban centers.

■ Assure that the people's elected representatives in Congress play their proper role in developing specific methods for protecting the rights guaranteed by the 14th Amendment, rather than leaving this task to judges appointed for life.

We are committed to guaranteeing equality of educational opportunity and to completing the process of ending *de jure* school segregation.

At the same time, we are irrevocably opposed to busing for racial balance. Such busing fails its stated objective—improved learning opportunities—while it achieves results no one wants—division within communities and hostility between classes and races. We regard it as unnecessary, counter-productive and wrong.

We favor better education for all children, and more transportation for some children. We favor the neighborhood school concept. We favor the decisive actions the President has proposed to support these ends. If it is necessary to accomplish these purposes, we would favor consideration of an appropriate amendment to the Constitution.

In the field of school finance, we favor a coordinated effort among all levels of government to break the pattern of excessive reliance on local property taxes to pay educational costs.

By every measure, our record in the field of education is exceptionally strong. The United States Office of Education is operating this year under its highest budget ever some $5.1 billion. Federal aid to elementary and secondary education has increased

60% over the past four years. Federal aid for college students has more than tripled.

We are proud of these accomplishments. We pledge to carry them forward in a manner consistent with our conviction that the Federal government should assist but never control the educational process. But we also believe that the output of results, not the input of dollars, is the best yardstick of effectiveness in education. When this Administration took office in 1969, it found American schools deficient at many points. Our reform initiatives have included:

■ An Office of Child Development to coordinate all Federal programs targeted on the first five years of life and to make the Head Start program work better;

■ A Right to Read Program, aimed at massive gains in reading ability among Americans of all ages;

■ A Career Education curriculum which will help to prepare students for the world of work;

■ A National Institute of Education to be a center for research on the learning process; and

■ A proposed National Foundation for Higher Education.

We have also proposed grant and loan programs to support a national commitment that no qualified student should be barred from college by lack of money. The Education Amendment of 1972 embodied substantial portions of that proposal and marked the nation's most far-reaching commitment to make higher education available to all.

Our non-public schools, both church-oriented and non-sectarian, have been our special concern. The President has emphasized the indispensable role these schools play in our educational system—from the standpoint of the large numbers of pupils they serve, the competition and diversity they help to maintain in American education, and the values they help to teach—and he has stated his determination to help halt the accelerating trend of non-public school closures.

We believe that means which are consistent with the Constitution can be devised for channeling public financial aid to support the education of all children in schools of their parents' choice, non-public as well as public. One way to provide such aid appears to be through the granting of income tax credits.

For the future, we also pledge Special Revenue Sharing for Education, continued work to develop and implement the Career Education concept, and continued efforts to establish a student financial aid system to bring higher education within the reach of any qualified person.

Welfare Reform

The nation's welfare system is a mess. It simply must be reformed.

The system, essentially unchanged since the 1930's, has turned into a human and fiscal nightmare. It penalizes the poor. It provides discriminatory benefits. It kills any incentives its victims might have to work their way out of the morass.

Among its victims are the taxpayers. Since 1961 the Federal cost of welfare has skyrocketed over 10 times from slightly over $1 billion then to more than $11 billion now. State and local costs add to this gigantic expenditure. And here are things we are paying for:

■ The present system drains work incentive from the employed poor, as they see welfare families making as much or more on the dole.

■ Its discriminatory benefits continue to ensnare the needy, aged, blind and disabled in a web of inefficient rules and economic contradictions.

■ It continues to break up poor families, since a father's presence makes his family ineligible for benefits in many states. Its dehumanizing life-style thus threatens to envelop yet another "welfare generation."

■ Its injustices and costs threaten to alienate taxpayer support for welfare programs of any kind.

Perhaps nowhere else is there a greater contrast in policy and philosophy than between the Administration's remedy for the welfare ills and the financial orgy proposed by our political opposition.

President Nixon proposed to change our welfare system "to provide each person with a means of escape from welfare into dignity." His goals were these:

■ A decent level of payment to genuinely needy welfare recipients regardless of where they live.

■ Incentives not to loaf, but to work.

■ Requiring all adults who apply for welfare to register for work and job training and to accept work or training. The only exceptions would be the aged, blind and disabled and mothers of preschool children.

■ Expanding job training and child care facilities so that recipients can accept employment.

■ Temporary supplements to the incomes of the working poor to enable them to support their families while continuing to work.

■ Uniform Federal payment standards for all welfare recipients.

In companion actions, our efforts to improve the nutrition of poor people resulted in basic reforms in the food stamp program. The number of recipients increased from some three million to 13 million, and now 8.4 million needy children participate in the school lunch program, almost three times the number that participated in 1968.

Now, nearly 10,000 nutrition aides work in low-income communities. In 1968 there were none.

We all feel compassion for those who through no fault of their own cannot adequately care for themselves. We all want to help these men, women and children achieve a decent standard of living and become self-supporting.

We continue to insist, however, that there are too many people on this country's welfare rolls who should not be there. With effective cooperation from the Congress, we pledge to stop these abuses.

We flatly oppose programs or policies which embrace the principle of a government-guaranteed income. We reject as unconstitutional the idea that all citizens have the right to be supported by the government, regardless of their ability or desire to support themselves and their families.

We pledge to continue to push strongly for sound welfare reform until meaningful and helpful change is enacted into law by the Congress.

Law Enforcement

We have solid evidence that our unrelenting war on crime is being won. The American people know that once again the thrust of justice in our society will be to protect the law-abiding citizenry against the criminal, rather than absolving the criminal of the consequences of his own desperate acts.

Serious crimes rose only 1% during the first quarter of this year—down from 6% last year and

13% the year before. From 1960 to 1968 major crime went up 122%.

The fact is, in the first quarter of 1972, 80 of our 155 largest cities had an actual decline in reported crime.

In our nation's capital, our anti-crime programs have been fully implemented. Through such measures as increased police, street lighting, a Narcotics Treatment Administration, court reform and special prosecuting units for major offenders we have steadily dropped the crime rate since November 1969. By the first quarter of this year, the serious crime rate was down to half its all-time high.

When our Administration took office, a mood of lawlessness was spreading rapidly, undermining the legal and moral foundations of our society. We moved at once to stop violence in America. We have:

■ Greatly increased Federal aid to state and local law enforcement agencies across the country, with more than $1.5 billion spent on 50,000 crime-fighting projects.

■ Augmented Justice Department funding four-fold and provided more marshals, more judges, more narcotics agents, more Assistant United States attorneys in the field.

■ Raised the Law Enforcement Assistance Administration budget ten-fold, earmarking $575 million of the $850 million for 1973 to upgrade state and local police and courts through revenue sharing.

■ Added 600 new special agents to the FBI.

■ Raised Federal spending on juvenile delinquency from $15 million to more than $180 million and proposed legislation to launch a series of model youth services.

■ Appointed attorneys general with a keen sense of the rights of both defendants and victims, and determination to enforce the laws.

■ Appointed judges whose respect for the rights of the accused is balanced by an appreciation of the legitimate needs of law enforcement.

■ Added to the Supreme Court distinguished lawyers of firm judicial temperament and fidelity to the Constitution.

Even more fundamentally, we have established a renewed climate of respect for law and law enforcement. Now those responsible for enforcing the law know they have the full backing of their government.

We recognize that programs involving work release, study release and half-way houses have contributed substantially to the rehabilitation of offenders and we support these programs. We further support training programs for the staffs in our correctional institutions and will continue to see that minority group staff members are recruited to work in these institutions.

The Fight Against Organized Crime. To most of us, organized criminal activity seems remote and unreal —yet syndicates supply the narcotics pushed on our youth, corrupt local officials, terrify legitimate businesses and fence goods stolen from our homes. This Administration strongly supported the Organized Crime Control Act of 1970, and under our Strike Force concept we have combined Federal enforcement agencies to wage a concerted assault on organized crime. We have expanded the number of these strike forces and set a high priority for a new campaign against the syndicates.

Last year we obtained indictments against more than 2,600 members or associates of organized

crime syndicates—more than triple the number indicted in 1968.

At last we have the lawless elements in our society on the run.

Drug Abuse. The permissiveness of the 1960's left no legacy more insidious than drug abuse. In that decade narcotics became widely available, most tragically among our young people. The use of drugs became endowed with a sheen of false glamour identified with social protest.

By the time our Nation awakened to this cancerous social ill, it found no major combat weapons available.

Soon after we took office, our research disclosed there were perhaps hundreds of thousands of heroin users in the United States. Their cravings multiplied violence and crime. We found many more were abusing other drugs, such as amphetamines and barbiturates. Marijuana had become commonplace. All this was spurred by criminals using modern methods of mass distribution against outnumbered authorities lacking adequate countermeasures.

We quickly launched a massive assault against drug abuse.

We intercepted the supply of dangerous drugs at points of entry and impeded their internal distribution. The budget for international narcotics control was raised from $5 million to over $50 million. Narcotics control coordinators were appointed in 59 United States embassies overseas to work directly with foreign governments in stopping drug traffic. We have narcotics action agreements with over 20 countries. Turkey has announced a total ban on opium production and, with our cooperation, France has seized major heroin laboratories and drugs.

To inhibit the distribution of heroin in our own country, we increased the law enforcement budget for drug control more than 10 times—from $20 million to $244 million.

We are disrupting major narcotics distribution in wholesale networks through the combined efforts of the Bureau of Narcotics and Dangerous Drugs, Customs operations at our borders, and a specially created unit of over 400 Internal Revenue agents who conduct systematic tax investigations of targeted middle and upper echelon traffickers, smugglers, and financiers. Last January we established the Office of Drug Abuse Law Enforcement to disrupt street and mid-level heroin traffickers.

We established the "Heroin Hot Line"—a nationwide toll free phone number (800/368-5363)—to give the public a single number for reporting information on heroin pushers.

Last year we added 2,000 more Federal narcotics agents, and the Bureau of Narcotics and Dangerous Drugs has trained over 170,000 state and local personnel.

And we are getting results. This past year four times as much heroin was seized as in the year this Administration took office. Since 1969, the number of drug-related arrests has nearly doubled.

For drug abuse prevention and treatment we increased the budget from $46 million to over $485 million.

The demand for illicit drugs is being reduced through a massive effort directed by a newly created office in the White House. Federally funded drug treatment and rehabilitation programs were more than doubled last fiscal year, and Federal programs now have the capacity to treat more than 60,000 drug abusers a year.

To alert the public, particularly the youth, to the

dangers of drugs, we established a National Clearinghouse for Drug Abuse Information in 1970 as well as a $3.5 million Drug Education and Training Program.

We realize that the problem of drug abuse cannot be quickly solved, but we have launched a massive effort where practically none existed before. Nor will we relax this campaign:

■ We pledge to seek further international agreements to restrict the production and movement of dangerous drugs.

■ We pledge to expand our programs of education, rehabilitation, training, and treatment. We will do more than ever before to conduct research into the complex psychological regions of disappointment and alienation which have led many young people to turn desperately toward drugs.

■ We firmly oppose efforts to make drugs easily available. We equally oppose the legalization of marijuana. We intend to solve problems, not create bigger ones by legalizing drugs of unknown physical impact.

■ We pledge the most intensive law enforcement war ever waged. We are determined to drive the pushers of dangerous drugs from the streets, schools, and neighborhoods of America.

Community Development

For more than a quarter century the Federal Government has sought to assist in the conservation and rebuilding of our urban centers. Yet, after the spending of billions of dollars and the commitment of billions more to future years, we now know that many existing programs are unsuited to the complex problems of the 1970's. Programs cast in the mold of the "big government" philosophy of the 1930's are simply incapable of meeting the challenges of today.

Our Party stands, therefore, for major reform of Federal community development programs and the development of a new philosophy to cope with urban ills.

Republican urban strategy rejects throwing good money after bad money. Instead, through fundamental fiscal, management and program reforms, we have created a new Federal partnership through which state, county and municipal governments can best cope with specific problems such as education, crime, drug abuse, transportation, pollution and housing.

We believe the urban problems of today fall into these categories:

■ The fiscal crises of state, county, and municipal governments.

■ The need for a better quality and greater availability of urban services.

■ The continual requirement of physical development.

■ The need for better locally designed, locally implemented, locally controlled solutions to the problems of individual urban areas.

In the last category—the importance of grass roots planning and participation—our Republican Party has made its most important contribution to solving urban problems.

We hold that government planners should be guided by the people through their locally elected representatives. We believe that real solutions require the full participation of the private sector.

To help ease the fiscal crises of state, county and municipal governments, we pledge increased Federal assistance—assistance we have more than doubled in the past four years. And, as stressed elsewhere in this platform, we remain committed to General Revenue Sharing, which could reduce the oppressive property tax.

Our proposals for Special Revenue Sharing for Urban Development, transportation, manpower and law enforcement—all still bottled up by the opposition Congress—are designed to make our towns and cities places where Americans can once again live and work without physical or environmental hazard. Urban areas are already benefiting from major funding increases which we fought for in the Law Enforcement Assistance Administration programs and in our $10 billion mass transit program.

Urban areas are also benefiting from our New Legacy of Parks program, which is bringing recreational opportunities closer to where people live.

We are committed also to the physical development of urban areas. We have quadrupled subsidized housing starts for low and moderate income families since 1969, and effected substantial increases for construction of municipal waste treatment facilities.

We strongly oppose the use of housing or community development programs to impose arbitrary housing patterns on unwilling communities. Neither do we favor dispersing large numbers of people away from their homes and neighborhoods against their will. We do believe in providing communties, with their full consent, guidance and cooperation, with the means and incentives to increase the quantity and quality of housing in conjunction with providing increased access to jobs for their low income citizens.

We also pledge to carry forward our policy of encouraging the development of new towns in order to afford all Americans a wider range of residential choices. Additionally, our Special Revenue Sharing for Urban and Rural Community Development, together with General Revenue Sharing and nationwide welfare reform, are basic building blocks for a balanced policy of national growth, leading to better lives for all Americans, whether they dwell in cities, suburbs or rural areas.

Our party recognizes counties as viable units of regional government with a major role in modernizing and restructuring local services, eliminating duplication and increasing local cooperation. We urge Federal and State governments, in implementing national goals and programs, to utilize the valuable resources of counties as area-wide, general-purpose governments.

Housing

Our Republican Administration has made more and better housing available to more of our citizens than ever before.

We are building two-and-a-third million new homes a year—65% more than the average in the eight years of the two previous Administrations. Progress has not been in numbers alone; housing quality has also risen to an all-time high—far above that of any other country.

We will maintain and increase this pattern of growth. We are determined to attain the goal of a decent home for every American.

Significant numbers of Americans still lack the means for decent housing, and in such cases—where special need exists—we will continue to apply public resources to help people acquire better apartments and homes.

We further pledge:

■ Continued housing production for low and moderate income families, which has sharply increased since President Nixon took office.

■ Improvement of housing subsidy programs and expansion of mortgage credit activities of Federal housing agencies as necessary to keep Americans the best-housed people in the world.

■ Continued development of technological and management innovations to lower housing costs—a program begun by Operation Breakthrough, which is assisting in the development of new methods for more economical production of low-cost, high-quality homes.

We urge prompt action by state, county and municipal governments to seek solutions to the serious problems caused by abandoned buildings in urban areas.

Transportation

When President Nixon took office a crisis in transportation was imminent, as indicated by declining mass transportation service, mounting highway deaths, congested urban streets, long delays at airports and airport terminals, deterioration of passenger train service, and a dwindling Merchant Marine. Within two years the President had proposed and signed into law:

■ A $10 billion, 12-year program—the Urban Mass Transportation Act of 1970—to infuse new life into mass transportation systems and help relieve urban congestion. . . .

■ The Rail Passenger Service Act of 1970 to streamline and improve the nation's passenger train service.

■ New research and development projects, including automatic people movers, improved Metroliner and Turbo-trains, quieter aircraft jet engines, air pollution reduction for mass transportation vehicles, and experimental safety automobiles. We strongly support these research and development initiatives of the Department of Transportation. . . .

To reduce traffic and highway deaths, the National Highway Traffic Safety Administration has been reorganized and expanded, with dramatic results. In 1971, the number of traffic deaths per hundred million miles driven was the lowest in history.

To help restore decision-making to the people, we have proposed a new Single Urban Fund providing almost $2 billion a year by 1975 to state and metropolitan areas to assist local authorities in solving their own transportation problems in their own way.

Our proposal for Special Revenue Sharing for Transportation would also help governments close to the people meet local needs and provide greater freedom to achieve a proper balance among the nation's major transportation modes.

Campaign Statements

McGovern's plans. Among McGovern's campaign statements on urban issues:

Increased urban aid pledged—McGovern stressed the need to increase urban

aid at a press conference in Washington Sept. 28 with 10 Democratic mayors. "The major enemy of this country is not in Hanoi," he said. "It's the collapse of our cities due to inadequate resources."

McGovern said "the sharpest differences" between himself and Nixon were ones directly affecting the cities. "The things he vetoes," he said, "like education, day care centers, job training, public service employment—are bills I would not veto. I would be urging the Congress to expand."

McGovern proposed to put some $26 billion in federal funds—recuperable from the war effort, the military budget and tax loopholes—in an effort to help the cities create jobs, strengthen law enforcement, provide property tax relief and improve housing, schools and transit systems.

A "Mayors for McGovern-Shriver" was launched at the news conference, headed by Mayors John Lindsay of New York, Joseph Alioto of San Francisco and Roman Gribbs of Detroit.

A McGovern urban affairs policy panel, headed by Newark Mayor Kenneth Gibson, also was announced.

Proposals to curb street crime—A program to curb crime in the streets was outlined by McGovern before a group of civil and political leaders in New York City Oct. 3. He said the issue had "number one" domestic priority for him.

McGovern accused the Nixon Administration of masking "a record of astounding failure in the field of crime behind a veil of 'law and order' rhetoric which grows more strident as the muggings and murders and rapes in our cities continue to rise." He said those really "permissive" toward crime were those "who thwarted gun control" and who had not stopped the flow of drugs from southeast Asia.

McGovern proposed an aid cutoff to such nations permitting heroin traffic to the U.S., special federal aid to high crime areas, a ban on small handguns, increased educational aid for policemen, and accelerated court procedure.

Urban aid advisers' program—McGovern's urban affairs policy panel presented proposals Oct. 21 for a $6 billion public service jobs program to help reduce urban jobless rates, a $1.5 billion program to combat crime and drug abuse and a $2 billion program, from additional revenue-sharing funds, to improve local police and fire protection, child-care centers and recreation facilities.

The panel recommended a shift from public housing projects to housing allowances to families, a warranty program to protect homeowners against builder inadequacies comparable to car-warranty protection, local zoning reform and new financing techniques for public service facilities.

The panel, headed by Newark Mayor Kenneth A. Gibson, also proposed allocating $15 billion a year to state and local governments to help relieve educational costs covered by property taxes and to equalize local tax structures.

Nixon says crime rise halted. President Nixon said Oct. 15 his administration had "fought the frightening trend of crime and anarchy to a standstill." He made the claim in a paid political radio broadcast.

He said his court appointments had made the Constitution "more secure," his Justice Department personnel had brought "backbone" to national law enforcement and "the raging heroin epidemic" of the last decade had been stemmed.

He pledged to continue to battle "the criminal forces in America" by appointing more "strict constructionists" to the courts, revising the federal criminal code and providing more funds to local law enforcement agencies.

The President also denounced "permissiveness" and promised action to protect the "moral and legal values" of the nation in a second term. "I will work unceasingly to halt the erosion of moral fiber in American life," he asserted, "and the denial of individual accountability for individual action."

Nixon cited statistics that critics claimed were misleading. He said serious crime in the eight years before he took office had risen by 122% but only 1% in the first half of 1972, and that in Washington, which had been the "crime capital of the world" in 1968, his Administration had cut the crime rate in half.

Serious crimes in the country increased by 30% in the first three years of the Nixon Administration, according to FBI statistics, and in Washington a change in the recording of serious crimes contributed to the previously reported decline.

Democratic presidential nominee George McGovern protested later Oct. 15 that the President was making fraudulent claims and that "the falsification of D.C. crime statistics has been extensively documented."

Nixon on urban affairs. Citing his commitment to America's cities, President Nixon said in a radio speech Oct. 31 that while his predecessors had fruitlessly spent billions of dollars on urban problems, he had spent more while putting it to better use.

Nixon emphasized his belief that the money spent on urban problems in his Administration had been well spent because he had cut red tape, decentralized decision-making, and restored to the local authorities the power to spend money as they saw fit.

Nixon described his urban strategy as one that not only gives the cities the money it needs, but also gives them "the freedom they need to use those dollars effectively."

Jobs & Welfare

Job training program resubmitted. President Nixon renewed a request to Congress Feb. 7 for a $2 billion manpower program. In a special message stressing a shift of control in manpower programs from federal to local government, the President called for enactment of an Administration program proposed in 1971 for distributing $1.7 billion in unearmarked grants to states, cities and counties for training the unemployed and underemployed. Under Nixon's proposals:

Current manpower training programs would be consolidated under the revenue sharing plan and some programs commanding powerful support in Congress, such as Neighborhood Youth Corps,

JOBS and Operation Mainstream, would be replaced.

Another $300 million would be administered by the Labor Department for national job training programs.

House kills works bill. In its first major action after the recess for the Democratic National Convention, the House defeated July 19, by a largely partisan 206–189 vote, a Democratic-sponsored bill for an 18-month, $5 billion program of grants for local water and sewer projects, designed to provide at least 500,000 new jobs.

The vote came after an amendment was passed by a 205–192 vote to suspend any grants in years in which the federal budget deficit was $20 billion or more. The fiscal 1973 budget deficit was currently estimated as at least $27 billion.

5% said ineligible. Health, Education and Welfare (HEW) Deputy Undersecretary Richard P. Nathan reported Jan. 3 that 4.9% of all welfare recipients nationally were ineligible, according to an April 1971 survey, resulting in annual government losses of about $500 million.

Nathan, at a news conference at which Administration officials pressed for Congressional action on President Nixon's welfare reform program, said "most of the errors were honest," and "more than half were agency errors," which could be eliminated by "transfering responsibility and making payments to a new, uniform and automated national system."

Suspected cases of fraud remained at less than .4% of recipients, Nathan said.

State work plans OKd. The Department of Health, Education and Welfare (HEW) announced June 6 it had reapproved experimental welfare reform programs proposed by New York and California.

The New York plan included an Incentives for Independence program in sections of three counties that would penalize welfare families that refused work and counseling services, and provide part-time jobs at $1.50 an hour for welfare schoolchildren 15–18; and a

Public Service Work Opportunities Project to require employable individuals in about one-fourth of the state's caseload of families with dependent children to accept training or community service jobs.

The California plan would place 30,000 welfare recipients in jobs and training. The first group of recipients was summoned to discuss employment alternatives June 15. An earlier California proposal that would reportedly have covered all the state's welfare recipients had been dropped due to HEW opposition.

'Workfare' in effect. The "workfare" program enacted by Congress in 1971 to require about 1.5 million welfare recipients to register for work or training went into effect July 1, 1972.

Assistant Secretary of Labor Malcolm R. Lovell Jr. said the first year's goal would be to provide jobs or training for 200,000 men and women in the aid to families with dependent children category.

Welfare roll growth slowed. HEW reported Oct. 17 that the rate of growth in welfare rolls and in total welfare-Medicaid payments had slowed in fiscal 1972 to the lowest levels since 1966.

In the year ending June 30, slightly more than 15 million persons were on public assistance rolls, a 5% increase over the previous year. Federal-state-local costs reached $18.2 billion, a 17.4% increase in the year. The corresponding fiscal 1971 figures had been 17.2% and 28.3%. HEW attributed the slowdown to rising employment, and to stricter state eligibility and cost controls.

The rolls rose a further 16,000 to 15,071,000 in July, but costs fell $13 million to $1.6 billion, HEW reported Nov. 24.

U.S. threatens welfare cuts. The Department of Health, Education and Welfare (HEW) said Dec. 4 it would withhold up to $689 million in welfare payments in 1973 to states that had failed to institute adequate procedures to eliminate ineligible recipients and overpayments.

HEW said it had moved in order to "restore public confidence" in the welfare program. John D. Twiname, administrator of the Social and Rehabilitation Service of HEW, cited a March survey which estimated that 6.8% of families in the Aid to Families with Dependent Children (AFDC) program were ineligible, as were 4.9% of adult blind, disabled and aged beneficiaries. Some 13.8% of AFDC families were found to be receiving overpayments, as were 9.7% in the other programs. Underpayments were found in the cases of 7.6% and 5.6% of recipients respectively.

In the 21 states that had not investigated the required percentage of cases to determine ineligibility rates, funds would be reduced according to the national average. HEW said it expected that as many as 700,000 persons in the AFDC program and 147,000 in the other programs would be cut from the rolls, if the new policy were fully effective.

Twiname said "we can't continue in a business as usual way," since "during the campaign, people of all political spectra were getting large amounts of heat about welfare spending." He said Caspar W. Weinberger, HEW secretary-designate, fully supported the new policy.

But HEW Undersecretary John G. Veneman said Dec. 13 that HEW had agreed to delay the cuts from Jan. 1, 1973 to April 1 to give state officials adequate notice. (Weinberger then announced April 4, 1973 that HEW had decided not to make the cuts but to give the states two years to reduce improper payments.)

Housing & Urban Development

Budget. President Nixon submitted his fiscal 1973 budget to Congress Jan. 24, 1972. A $2.3 billion revenue-sharing program designed for community development was provided to replace programs for urban renewal, model cities, open space, neighborhood facilities and rehabilitation loans. The budget total for fiscal 1973 was only $1.8 billion, but President Nixon promised to request

another $490 million if Congress enacted the plan.

Total fiscal 1973 outlays for the Department of Housing and Urban Development would increase $805 million to $4.8 billion.

The department estimated that 566,-000 subsidized housing units would be started in fiscal 1973.

Commitments to subsidized apartments would be reduced in fiscal 1973 to a $150 million level from the $200 million level in fiscal 1972.

The program was plagued with problems, and the Administration planned to focus on quality rather than quantity. Funds were budgeted to develop a way to counter the growing problem of abandonment of the inner-city housing that was under federal subsidy.

Housing dispersal set. The Department of Housing and Urban Development (HUD) published final regulations effective Feb. 7 on site selection for subsidized housing, that were expected to curtail most construction in urban renewal and model cities areas, in order to promote housing opportunities for moderate income families outside the often segregated central cities.

The new regulations, reported Jan. 16, would disallow a "superior" priority rating for projects in the areas. Although "adequate" ratings could be assigned, the location would have to be in a housing market area with few minority residents, or in an integrated area in which the new project would not alter the population balance, or in a minority area whose minority residents had access to adequate housing outside the area.

"Overriding housing needs" in a minority area would merit an exception, provided the "overriding need" were not caused by discrimination. A former provision was eliminated that had allowed minority area projects "if prospective residents of the project or residents of the project area express a desire for it," since HUD feared the provision was "unworkable and would have been abused."

A HUD spokesman denied Jan. 15 the department would "turn our backs

on the problem of the inner city."
HUD rules limited subsidies in inner
cities, in suburbs in which projects had
already been built, and in outlying areas
far from jobs or transportation.

D.C. metro housing plan. The Metropolitan Washington Council of Government, an advisory group composed of
elected officials from 14 suburban cities
and counties in Virginia and Maryland
and representatives of the Presidentially
appointed government of the District of
Columbia, unanimously approved a
formula to allocate all future federal
housing subsidies among their constit-
uencies, it was reported Jan. 15.
Slightly over half the units provided
for the D.C. area would go to Montgomery County, Md. and Fairfax County,
Va., which together accounted for only
13.5% of all government owned or aided
units completed or being built in the
area as of October 1971. The District
itself, which had 58.7% of the area's
units, would receive only 20.3% under
the new plan. Arlington, Va., which had
no units despite massive federal facilities
within its borders, would be allocated
9% in the future.
Enforcement of the plan, which had
been urged on the council in October
1971 by HUD Secretary George Romney, would be voluntary. Under federal
programs, public housing required local
government cooperation, and subsidized
housing usually required local private
sponsors.

D.C. message. In a special message
to Congress on the District of Columbia
Feb. 4, President Nixon supported more
Congressional representation for the
district (a voting representative) and a
five-year-old plan to establish a 4,000-
unit "new town" in the northeastern
section of the district.

GSA housing role enforced. U.S. District Court Judge Orrin G. Judd ruled in
New York April 19 that the General
Services Administration must determine that an adequate supply of low-
income integrated housing existed be-

fore building a federal facility in any
area.
Judge Judd refused, however, to bar
operation of a $25 million Internal
Revenue Service center in Brookhaven,
L.I. because it was largely completed. He
agreed to a demand by the plaintiffs,
the National Committee Against Discrimination in Housing and a community
fair housing group, that 220 units of surplus housing at the Suffolk County Air
Force Base be opened to low-income
residents.
The ruling was based on a 1970 Presidential Executive Order, requiring a
housing survey before the siting of major facilities.

New Jersey housing plan asked. New
Jersey Gov. William T. Cahill proposed
March 27 a statewide housing planning
program that would encourage localities to abandon zoning practices that
excluded poor and moderate income
families.
Under the plan, the state government
would determine statewide housing needs
every two years, and allocate the needs
among the 21 counties on the basis of
size, need and capacity. Six months later
the county planning boards would allocate their quotas among municipalities,
none of whom, however, would be forced
to accept. The plan aimed at voluntary
local action to end "systematic exclusion" of the poor from the affluent suburbs.
Cahill warned that if localities failed
to abandon restrictive zoning practices
intended to prohibit all but private dwellings on large plots or luxury apartment
houses, the courts would intervene and
might cause "the ultimate destruction of
local control." The state had estimated
that only half of New Jersey's needed
100,000 new units were being built annually.

HUD concedes subsidy abuses. An audit
by the Department of Housing and Urban Development (HUD) of federal
mortgage subsidy programs, released
by HUD Secretary George Romney,
confirmed earlier reports of widespread
financial and construction abuses. Romney told the House Banking and Cur-

rency Committee that his agency had implemented administrative reforms in reponse to the findings, it was reported Feb. 27.

According to the audit, cost per unit in the "section 236" program of the 1968 Housing Act had run substantially higher than in privately financed housing because of excessive fees and land markups and other fraudulent practices inadequately policed by the Federal Housing Administration (FHA). Rents under the program, which subsidized apartment house mortgages, were consequently higher then for comparable apartments on the private market.

High vacancy rates, resulting partly from locations near junkyards, factories, power lines and former lake beds, were high enough to cause or threaten frequent defaulting of section 236 mortgages. HUD had fired seven employes for "wrongdoing" under the program, Romney reported, and referred 27 alleged violations to the Justice Department. Grand jury probes with HUD cooperation were investigating projects in Philadelphia, New York, Newark, N.J., and Detroit.

In the "section 235" program, which subsidized new and used private home mortgages for moderate income families, some 26% of a sample of 700 new houses and 43% of a sample of used homes contained serious property, safety, health or "livability" deficiencies. HUD referred 362 alleged section 235 violations for Justice Department investigation, including false applications and fraudulent repair certificates.

Romney had told the National Association of Home Builders convention in Houston Jan. 25 that a new emphasis on quality might disqualify as many as 200,000 of a possible 550,000 subsidized units to be built in 1972. In 1971, about 25% of a record 2.1 million new housing units in the U.S. were built with some form of federal subsidy.

House committee scores HUD. In a unanimous report disclosed June 22, the House Government Operations Committee charged that "incompetent administration" by the Department of Housing and Urban Development (HUD) of inner city private home loan guarantees

threatened to cost the government up to $200 million in Detroit alone. According to the committee:

"Unscrupulous speculators" had bought dilapidated houses, made "cosmetic repairs," and sold them at greatly inflated prices. Purchasers soon abandoned the mortgages in droves, and by April, HUD had bought 8,000 homes guaranteed by the Federal Housing Administration (FHA). Another 18,000–20,000 homes were in default and likely to be purchased by HUD, which was losing as much as $10,000 each on houses it attempted to resell.

The committee said HUD had allowed FHA appraisers to overvalue "structurally unsound houses," had not sufficiently advised poor home buyers and had not turned over enough cases for prosecution. The committee urged HUD to purge its staff of lax appraisers, and to cease dealing with "undesirable brokers and mortgagees." Twenty-one Detroit mortgage lenders had default records of at least 10%, with the rate in some cases reaching 40% for welfare recipients, the report noted.

HUD Secretary George Romney said the department was in the midst of "sweeping reforms." In any case, he said, the Detroit situation was not indicative of its housing programs nationally.

Another appraisal of the Detroit affair, issued by the Mortgage Bankers Association of Michigan, was reported July 6. According to an association report, speculators raised the price on each house so that the federally guaranteed long term low interest rate would yield the same monthly payments as conventional mortgages. The sellers "realized excessive profits and fled from the city," leaving buyers with overpriced, inadequate homes.

The report called for more government construction of subsidized housing in inner cities, and asked the government to subsidize home sales by poor people to prevent wholesale abandonment.

Housing bill dies. The House Rules Committee refused by a 9–5 vote Sept. 27 to approve a $10.6 billion omnibus housing and mass transit aid bill. The following day the Banking and Currency Committee, which had reported the bill Sept. 19, voted to extend current housing programs through the end of the fiscal year, killing all chances for the new bill, which had been approved in different form by the Senate in March. Banking Committee Chairman Wright Patman (D, Tex.), while asking for consideration by the full House, had criticized the bill in the committee report for ignoring the massive scandals and failures that had plagued the section 235 and 236 housing subsidy and guarantee programs for low- and moderate-income families.

The bill in final form had attracted opposition from a variety of quarters. Civil rights and labor groups opposed a provision that would have given localities veto power over federal low income housing, effectively locking the program into the central cities. The Administration opposed the provision for mass transit operating subsidies, as well as new categorical programs to aid central cities, which went against the revenue-sharing approach of consolidated untied block grants.

Romney urges end to federal role.
HUD Secretary George Romney suggested Oct. 23 that all federal housing subsidy programs be abolished, or turned over to the states.

Romney told the Mortgage Bankers Association of America convention in San Francisco that "some aspects of subsidized housing are in crisis," the full dimensions of which had not yet been uncovered. He said drastic changes were needed to avoid another "$100 billion mistake," referring to the amount the federal government was committed to pay over 40 years under current programs.

Romney suggested the U.S. end subsidy programs for low and middle income families, "privatize" the Federal Housing Administration (FHA), and end subsidies for public housing. He proposed either a direct housing allowance to poor people or a transfer of federal housing funds to states, which would determine allocation among construction, preservation and various subsidy programs.

Romney had said Oct. 4 that federal grand juries were investigating evidence

of corruption in housing programs in 10 major cities: New York, Newark, N.J., Philadelphia, Detroit, Chicago, Boston, Washington, Columbia, S.C., Dallas and Los Angeles. HUD had also recommended an investigation in St. Louis.

HUD chaos charged—An internal HUD memorandum published Nov. 22 by the Washington Post charged that poor planning and management had contributed to massive inefficiencies and failures in various HUD programs, including home ownership subsidies, public housing, rehabilitation, model cities and urban renewal.

The memo, written by William Whitbeck, a former Romney special assistant, made the following points:

The dispersal of subsidized low income housing programs in suburban areas had not aided integration, since most of the tenants were already suburban residents and not inner-city dwellers.

New, tighter regulations of the "section 235" home ownership program had effectively stymied the program in "inner-city and middle-city" areas.

HUD had not gathered data on FHA loans in each city, blocking a successful analysis of scandals and defaults.

Although "Project Rehab" had successfully rehabilitated 50,000 housing units in 29 cities, management problems made it likely that "most if not all" the units would go into default.

HUD water and sewer grants had aided suburbs to attract middle class city residents, leading to increased residential segregation.

Operating subsidies to public housing projects were too low to prevent bankruptcy in some cities.

Whitbeck suggested that urban renewal programs return to a policy of massive clearance as the only realistic approach. He said the model cities program had had mixed results despite huge expenditures.

Congressional critique. The Congressional Joint Economic Committee issued a report Nov. 1 calling for an overhaul of federal housing programs, and suggesting the use of direct housing subsidy payments to poor families.

The report pointed to inflated costs

and lack of coordination in present programs, and charged that the total federal housing effort benefitted middle- and upper-income families (through homeowner tax benefits), contractors and investors far more than poor people.

As one solution, the committee suggested a $3.2-$4.1 billion program of grants to 6.8 million households with annual incomes below $7,500. The families would apply the grants to housing of their choice. HUD had begun such an experimental program in Kansas City and other areas.

The committee praised the apartment leasing program, under which local authorities rented private apartments and sublet them at lower rates to poor families. Fewer than 100,000 housing units were involved.

No St. Louis shutdown. The St. Louis Housing Authority's Board of Commissioners voted 5-0 Nov. 9 to close all conventional public housing projects in the city during 1973 for lack of adequate operating funds. The action, the first such move by any city, would leave 25,000 low-income persons homeless. In a less drastic move reported Dec. 9, the authority then voted to transfer operating control of St. Louis housing units to HUD. It took action on the ground that HUD had failed to provide funds to replace revenue losses incurred when rents were reduced for poor tenants in accordance with a federal law limiting public housing rents to 25% of a welfare recipient's income. (But the authority said Jan. 9, 1973 that it was cancelling the transfer of the units after HUD had approved a $3.7 million operating subsidy. The Office of Management and Budget had released a Congressionally appropriated $100 million operating subsidy fund Dec. 1, 1972 after several cities warned that their housing projects might go bankrupt.

Financing the Cities

Revenue-sharing bill passed. Congress completed action Oct. 13 on a compromise revenue sharing bill, as the Senate voted 59-19 to accept the conference committee report. President Nixon then signed the legislation Oct. 20.

The House had approved the measure Oct. 12 by a 265-110 vote, after defeating an amendment to delete a $2.5 billion annual limit on various social services programs by a 281-86 vote. The amendment had been proposed by New York representatives, since New York state would be the largest loser under the limit. The state, which had received $498 million in aid under the programs in the past fiscal year, and had expected to receive $855 million in the current year, would receive only $223 million under the new bill.

The bill would distribute $30.2 billion over five years in almost untied aid to states and localities.

Funds would be distributed within the states according to the Senate formula, with one-third going to state governments and two-thirds to localities, based on tax effort, population and per capita income. Large cities and rural areas were expected to benefit at the expense of more affluent suburbs.

The funds, which could not be used by localities to meet operating costs of education or general administration needs, could be spent on almost any capital project, or for operating expenses in the areas of public safety, environmental protection, transportation, health, recreation and libraries, social services for the poor or elderly or financial administration. There would be no restrictions on the state government share of the funds.

Cities and states would have to publicize their intentions for each year's allocation, and submit to Treasury Department audits.

The $2.5 billion social services authorization limit, compared with a $1.6 billion limit set by the Senate and none by the House, would curb a rapidly expanding program begun in 1962 to aid people currently, recently or potentially on welfare to become self-sufficient. Under previous law, the Department of Health, Education and Welfare (HEW) had provided unlimited funds on a 75% federal-25% state basis for a variety of services. Costs had totaled $1.5 billion for fiscal 1972, but had been expected to rise to $4.7 billion in fiscal 1973 without the new limit.

Under the compromise plan, the social services money would be distributed on a straight population basis. and would be retroactive to July 1. The money could be spent in any proportion on child care, family planning, aid to the retarded, foster care or treatment of narcotics or alcohol victims. Other programs could be covered, with a proviso that 90% of spending in such programs be for actual welfare clients.

Revenue sharing checks mailed. The first revenue sharing checks, totaling $2.65 billion, were mailed to 35,903 state and local governments by the Treasury Department Dec. 8.

The checks, which launched the five year, $30 billion federal program, were payments for the first half of 1972; July–December funds would be mailed in January 1973, officials said.

The District of Columbia received the highest per capita grant among the largest 100 cities. Its $23.8 million amounted to $15.80 a person. Under the allocation system, the District was considered a state, but one which was not required to share its funds with any other local government unit.

City chiefs meet. About 3,000 mayors and other city officials attended the annual convention of the National League of Cities Nov. 27–30, and called for an increased emphasis on urban problems by the Nixon Administration.

The delegates, representing nearly 15,000 municipalities, approved a resolution Nov. 30 asking the Administration and Congress not to use revenue sharing merely as a substitute for current federal grant programs, such as Model Cities. The meeting also approved a "sense of the convention statement" that Congress and the Administration had already committed themselves not to use revenue sharing for that purpose.

Other resolutions Nov. 30 asked for an end to Administration impounding of funds, and for appointment of a top-level presidential assistant "to secure priorities for the cities equal to that

which Dr. Henry Kissinger has achieved for international affairs."

California changes school tax. The California legislature completed final passage Dec. 1 on a tax reform measure designed to move the state toward compliance with a court ruling invalidating the previous school finance system.

The bill, backed by Gov. Ronald Reagan, would cut property taxes and allow tax credits to renters totaling $488 million a year. The state sales tax would go from 5% to 6%, bank and corporate taxes would go up 1.4% while local business inventory taxes would decline 20%. The provisions would result in a net increase of $332 million a year in education money.

Michigan fund reform ordered. The Michigan Supreme Court ruled Dec. 29 that the state's system of financing education for the 1970–1971 year, through property taxes and state aid, had been unconstitutional. While the court did not invalidate the current, similar system, it said it would accept a court challenge to any 1973–1974 system the legislature would devise, and said the new system would have to cease benefitting rich districts at the expense of poor ones.

School Integration

Nixon urges anti-busing bill. President Nixon asked Congress March 17, 1972 to approve legislation to deny courts the power to order busing of elementary schoolchildren to achieve racial integration. He proposed a moratorium on all new busing orders, a clear Congressional mandate on acceptable desegregation methods and a program to concentrate federal aid to education more effectively in poor districts in order to substitute "equality of educational opportunity" for racial balance as the primary national education goal.

Nixon began his March 17 message to Congress by saying that the dismantling of "the old dual-school system in those areas where it existed" was "substantially completed." Therefore, efforts to meet the "constitutional mandate" laid down in the 1954 Supreme Court's *Brown v. Board of Education* desegregation ruling, which Nixon defined as a requirement "that no child should be denied equal educational opportunity," should "now focus much more specifically on education: on assuring that the opportunity is not only equal but adequate, and that in those remaining cases in which desegregation has not yet been completed it be achieved with a greater sensitivity to educational needs."

Nixon approached the busing issue from that emphasis on education rather than desegregation:

"In the furor over busing, it has become all too easy to forget what busing is supposed to be designed to achieve: equality of educational opportunity for all Americans."

The President conceded that some opponents of busing were motivated by racial prejudice, but claimed that "most people, including large and increasing numbers of blacks and other minorities, oppose it for reasons that have little or nothing to do with race. It would compound an injustice to persist in massive busing simply because some people oppose it for the wrong reasons."

In many communities, Nixon said, busing was seen as "a symbol of helplessness, frustration and outrage," as parents were denied the right to choose their children's school, were forced to suffer inconvenience, and felt they were subjected to "social engineering on an abstract basis."

Among black parents, the President contended that the "principal emphasis" of the concern for quality education had shifted from desegregation, and now rested on "improving schools, on convenience, on the chance for parental involvement—in short, on the same concerns that motivate white parents—and in many communities, on securing a greater measure of control over schools that serve primarily minority-group communities."

In addition, Nixon charged that advocates of "system-wide racial balance" would condemn blacks to a permanent "minority status" in most schools, which would be "run by whites and dominated

by whites," while those black students in densely populated central cities could never be reached by busing plans in any case.

One of the "historical" factors leading courts to order large-scale busing, Nixon wrote, had been "community resistance" [in the South, which Nixon avoided naming in the message] against a unitary school system, which the courts "sometimes saw as delay or evasion." But "the past three years" had brought "phenomenal" progress toward unitary systems and toward a "new climate of acceptance of the basic constitutional doctrine."

Finally, Nixon implied that plans for massive busing imposed over community resistance would not be likely to achieve their objectives. The schools, he believed, should assume a more modest burden, since they could not by themselves bring about "the kind of multiracial society which the adult community has failed to achieve for itself," and might only risk imposing "lasting psychic injury" on children by trying.

Without Congressional intervention, the President warned, busing would continue to be ordered by some courts to a degree "far beyond what most people would consider reasonable" and beyond Supreme Court requirements. He cited a "maze of differing and sometimes inconsistent orders" which have caused "uncertainty" and "vastly unequal treatment among regions" and districts.

The President's legislative program consisted of two separate bills. The first, on which he requested immediate action, would impose a temporary freeze on all new busing orders by federal courts, "while the Congress considers alternative means of enforcing 14th Amendment rights." The second, an "Equal Educational Opportunities Act," would specify those alternative means, and would attempt through federal aid to improve education for poor and minority children.

Busing curbs passed. A compromise omnibus higher education-desegregation aid bill carrying mild anti-busing (Broomfield) provisions was passed by 63–15 Senate vote May 24 and 218–180 House vote June 8 and was signed by Nixon June 23.

The bill would stay all court ordered busing for integration until all appeals were exhausted or until Jan. 1, 1974. (The Supreme Court had ruled in 1969 that busing had to be implemented immediately when ordered by a federal district court.)

Federal funds could be used for busing only if requested by a community, and only if no risk to pupil health, safety or education was involved. Federal officials could not require or encourage local busing "unless constitutionally required."

The desegregation aid provision would authorize $2 billion over two years to school districts in the process of desegregation. Of these funds, 4% would be earmarked for bilingual programs, 3% for educational television and 5% for metropolitan area education plans, which could be implemented only if two thirds of the districts in an area approved them.

Busing curbs tested—In the first court tests of the antibusing amendments, stays of desegregation orders were denied for Oxnard, Calif., Augusta, Ga., Las Vegas, Nev., Nashville, Tenn. and Oklahoma City but granted for Chattanooga, Tenn.

The Ninth U.S. Circuit Court of Appeals in San Francisco rejected a plea Aug. 22 by the Oxnard school board and the Justice Department to suspend a busing plan begun in the 1971-72 school year. The court ruled that the newly adopted bill could not be applied retroactively, despite Justice Department arguments that the moratorium was intended to apply in all cases in which appeals had not been exhausted.

Supreme Court Justice Lewis F. Powell refused Sept. 1 to stay a busing plan for Augusta, on the grounds that the bill applied only to orders issued for the purpose of achieving racial balance. The Augusta plan, he wrote, had been ordered to correct unlawful segregation.

Justice William O. Douglas rejected a plea Sept. 12 by Las Vegas school officials, supported by Justice Department lawyers, to stay a busing plan in that city, "it not being shown that the conditions of the Broomfield Amendment of the Education Act have been met." The

schools involved in the plan, which clustered predominantly black and predominantly white schools, had remained closed during the appeal. Justice William Rehnquist had ruled in the Nashville and Oklahoma City cases that the amendment did not apply, according to the Washington Post Sept. 7.

In Chattanooga, U.S. District Court Judge Frank Wilson Jr. ordered a delay Aug. 11 of a busing order he had issued earlier for the lower grades, although leaving in effect a high school integration plan. Wilson said he did not think his order required "a racial balance," as specified in the bill, but approved the delay requested by the school board since he could not "ignore the popular use of the English language," which equated busing for desegregation with racial balance.

Antibusing bill dies. The Senate failed Oct. 12, for a third time, to end a filibuster by Northern liberals against a House-passed bill to limit school busing for integration. It put to rest for the session President Nixon's program to deal with school integration.

The bill would have prohibited federal courts and executive departments from ordering the assignment of elementary or secondary school students to any school other than the school within his district "closest or next closest" to his home, unless district lines had been drawn for deliberate segregation purposes. The bill would have prohibited all federally-ordered crosstown or interdistrict busing, although permitting school pairings.

Districts already operating under desegregation orders could have reopened their cases in the courts to conform with the bill's criteria.

Detroit area plan sought. U.S. District Court Judge Stephen J. Roth ruled March 28 that "relief of segregation in the public schools of the city of Detroit cannot be accomplished within the corporate geographical limits of the city." He rejected three proposed integration plans limited to Detroit city students, despite a March 23 plea by the

Justice Department for a delay of further action pending possible passage by Congress of President Nixon's proposed moratorium on court busing orders.

The ruling came under an integration suit originally brought by the National Association for the Advancement of Colored People. Roth had ruled in 1971 that Detroit segregation had been fostered by official actions in the past, although he acknowledged that the city had made attempts to eliminate segregation. He had ordered the Michigan State Board of Education to devise a Detroit metropolitan area school integration plan.

The state Board of Education submitted six different plans to the court Feb. 3, without expressing preference, ranging from a merger of 36 metropolitan school districts into six regions with equal black-white ratios, to a simple increase of funds and community control for black schools in Detroit.

The Justice Department entered the case after Nixon pledged March 16 that his Administration would seek to overturn court busing orders.

In rejecting the plans, Roth said school district lines were arbitrary, and could not be used to deny constitutional rights. He called it his "duty" under the 1954 *Brown* decision to "look beyond the limits of the Detroit school district for a solution."

Roth June 14 ordered massive busing to integrate Detroit city and suburban schools. But a three-judge panel of the U.S. Sixth Circuit Court of Appeals Aug. 24 issued an indefinite stay of the order.

Under Roth's suspended plan, which he based largely on an NAACP proposal, 310,000 of 780,000 pupils in Detroit and 53 suburban school districts would have been bused across Detroit city lines. Teachers also would have been reassigned to give each school a faculty and staff that was at least 10% black.

Roth wrote that under his order, "the greatest change would be in the direction of the buses," and set a general maximum of 40 minutes for a one-way ride. But he added that "transportation of kindergarten children for upwards of 45 minutes one way, does not appear unreasonable, harmful or unsafe in any way."

The appeals court panel ruled Dec. 8 that a city-suburb integration plan was necessary to assure equal rights for black schoolchildren in Detroit.

Court orders free Norfolk buses. The Supreme Court refused by an 8–0 vote May 15 to review a ruling by the 4th U.S. Circuit Court of Appeals in Richmond that Norfolk, Va. must provide free transportation of 24,000 children assigned to schools beyond walking distance under an integration plan. The court also voided a stay issued by the appeals court that plaintiffs said would have prevented implementation of the integration plan in the coming school year.

Norfolk had argued that it had never provided free school transportation, and that the court had intervened in budget decisions and imposed its views "as to what constitutes wise economic and social policy." The appeals court ruled that it would be "a futile gesture" and a "cruel hoax" to "compel the student to attend a distant school and then fail to provide him with the means to reach that school."

Nashville order approved. Memphis plan stayed. The 6th U.S. Circuit Court of Appeals in Cincinnati, in two separate rulings, May 30 upheld a lower court plan that required 49,000 Nashville area school children be bused for integration, but granted a stay June 5 to the Memphis Board of Education, which had been under a lower court order to begin a busing program in the fall.

In the Nashville case, the court upheld U.S. District Court Judge Clure Morton, who had ordered the Metropolitan County Board of Education of Nasvhille and Davidson County to implement the busing plan during the current school year. The board claimed it lacked funds for full implementation, and lacked taxing power to acquire the funds. The Justice Department had intervened in favor of the board's appeal, although the plan had originally been proposed by the Department of Health, Education and Welfare.

In the Memphis case, the court overruled U.S. District Court Judge Robert M. McRae Jr., who had denied a stay of a plan to begin busing 14,000 pupils in the fall. The Memphis Board of Education had argued that without a stay it would have had to commit itself to buy or lease buses before it knew the final disposition of the case.

The appeals court Aug. 29 ordered the Memphis board to put the plan into effect. Judge Anthony Celebrezze's majority opinion said the board had failed to prove that the 128 of 162 schools that were segregated were not "in any way the product of its past or present discriminatory conduct," which would be the only way the board could refute charges that it had "failed to eliminate its dual system," according to Celebreeze's interpretation of Supreme Court decisions.

Dissenting Judge Paul C. Weick said the court had "given scant consideration to the "constitutional rights" of "black and white children who do not want to be bused away from their neighborhood schools."

Richmond plan overturned. The 4th U.S. Circuit Court of Appeals in Richmond overturned a lower court order June 6 that would have merged the school districts of Richmond and two suburban counties and bused thousands of schoolchildren to achieve racial integration.

The court ruled by a 5-1 vote that U.S. District Court Judge Robert R. Merhige Jr. had interpreted the 14th Amendment in an "excessive" manner when he ruled that governmental actions had helped lead to an increasingly black central city and a ring of white suburbs, and that the resulting school segregation was unconstitutional whatever the cause. In "exceeding his power of intervention," the court said, Merhige had slighted the "principle of federalism incorporated in the 10th Amendment," which reserved powers to the states.

Judge James Braxton Craven Jr. wrote for the majority:

"Neither the record nor the opinion of the district court even suggests that there was ever a joint interaction between any two of the units involved (or by

higher state officers) for the purpose of keeping one unit relatively white by confining blacks to another. We think that the root causes of the concentration of blacks in the inner cities of America are simply not known, and that the district court could not realistically place on the counties the responsibility for the effect that inner city decay has had on the public schools of Richmond."

The court said the mere fact that the city school population was 70% black while the suburban school population was 90% white did not constitute a constitutional violation. Any county actions to enforce segregation had been "slight" compared to other "economic, political and social" factors. Furthermore, "school assignments cannot reverse the trend" of racial concentration.

In a dissent, Judge Harrison L. Winter cited "the sordid history of Virginia's and Richmond's attempts to circumvent, defeat and nullify" Supreme Court integration rulings.

Suburban Henrico and Chesterfield counties had been joined in their appeal of Merhige's ruling by the Justice Department after President Nixon set down new antibusing guidelines March 16.

Boston fund cutoff stayed. A Massachusetts Superior Court judge ordered the state Sept. 27 to grant $52 million in withheld school aid to Boston, but ordered the city to devise a school integration plan.

The state had found Boston in violation of a Massachusetts law which barred any school from having more than 50% minority students, and had cut off the funds in September when the Boston School Committee revoked a plan to integrate one school after both white and black parents protested.

The judge ordered the School Committee to draw up a temporary integration program by mid-November, and to make "maximum progress" toward racial balance by June 1973.

Atlanta order. A three-judge panel of the U.S. Fifth Circuit Court of Appeals ordered Atlanta's school Oct. 7 Board to implement an integration plan within seven weeks. Overturning two lower court rulings, the appeals panel termed Atlanta's system "virtually totally segregated." It told the board, "at a minimum," to pair or group "contiguous segregated schools," paying "special attention" to 20 schools "which have never been desegregated" and remained "all or virtually all white." Superintendent of Schools Ed Cook said the number of such schools had declined to 17.

Since the filing of a National Association for the Advancement of Colored People (NAACP) suit in 1958 that led to the ruling, Atlanta's schools had become over 75% black. The court said that 106 of 153 schools were at least 90% of one race, and most of them had always been so.

The U.S. district court in Atlanta had rejected an NAACP plan in June which the appeals court had ordered it to consider, which would have bused 33,000 of Atlanta's 95,000 pupils. The appeals court, in its latest ruling, said "the fear of white students' flight shall not be utilized as a factor in composing this plan," but cited as guidelines for Atlanta two recent decisions in Austin and Corpus Christi, Texas, that condoned some busing but barred cross-town busing until all other remedies were tried.

California bans forced busing. A state constitutional amendment against forced busing was approved by California voters Nov. 7.

The amendment, passed 4,905,247–2,877,596, banned involuntary pupil transfers for integration.

Integration gains denied. A study of school integration programs involving busing in six Northern cities, reported May 21, found no improvement in either academic achievement among black students or racial cooperation.

The study was conducted by Harvard University professor David J. Armor, and included programs in Boston, White Plains, N.Y., Ann Arbor, Mich., Riverside, Calif. and Hartford and New Haven, Conn. While no significant academic differences were found between black students bused and control groups which remained in ghetto schools, the

first group tended to show declines in self-esteem and in educational and job aspirations. Armor recommended, however, that voluntary busing programs be continued, since the bused students tended to get better opportunities for higher education.

Armor emphasized that his study involved only short-term effects, but wrote "it appears that integration increases racial identity and solidarity," and "at least in the case of black students, leads to increasing desires for separation."

30,000 black school jobs lost. A National Education Association (NEA) survey found that over 30,000 teaching jobs for blacks had been eliminated in 17 Southern and border states through desegregation and discrimination since 1954, it was reported May 19.

The proportion of teachers who were black declined in the region in 1954–70 from 21% to 19%, although the proportion of black students increased slightly. The percentage of existing or projected black teaching jobs displaced was lowest in Alabama, which the report attributed to court orders and continued segregation, and highest in Kentucky, Missouri and Delaware.

Southern segregation charged. Six civil rights organizations released a report May 23 charging that desegregation of urban schools in the South was "far from complete," and that resegregation was increasing with the complicity of all levels of government.

In a study of 43 Southern cities, the report found that at least a dozen were "operating under shockingly inadequate and outdated court orders and desegregation plans." Of 2,727 schools, over 1,000 were totally or nearly completely segregated, partly because of changing racial residence patterns fostered by "the Federal Housing Administration, local planning commissions and housing authorities, urban renewal, school boards, highways departments, realtors, and even transit companies."

The report found a trend toward disproportionate suspension of black students in integrated schools, and said policemen were too frequently stationed in schools, which "does not seem to have eliminated or significantly decreased the number of disciplinary problems."

The study was sponsored by the Alabama Council on Human Relations, the American Friends Service Committee, the Delta Ministry of the National Council of Churches, the NAACP Legal Defense Fund, the Southern Regional Council and the Washington Research Project.

Municipal Workers

Strikes mar school opening. More than 700,000 children were affected by strikes when the fall school term started in Philadelphia, Washington, and towns in Rhode Island, New York State, Michigan and Massachusetts.

Philadelphia teachers Sept. 29 ended an 18-day walkout of the 285,000-pupil school system, after negotiators for the Board of Education and 13,000 striking teachers reached an interim agreement to reopen the schools, at least until Dec. 31.

A two-week strike by the 3,500-member Washington Teachers Union ended Oct. 2 when the union accepted a two-year 12% salary increase and a no-reprisal pledge. The settlement depended on Congressional appropriations.

Indianapolis teachers returned to work Oct. 30 after a seven-day strike, when a Marion County Circuit Court judge agreed to arbitrate a settlement. School board president Kenneth T. Martz, however, resigned Nov. 14 after the teachers ratified the resulting 5% pay raise, saying the accord would force the district into deficit spending.

A month-long strike in the suburban Roosevelt, N.Y. school district ended when teachers ratified a three-year 19% increase Nov. 10.

Phila. police ratio extended. District Court Judge John P. Fullam issued a preliminary injunction July 8 continuing his order that the Philadelphia Police Department hire one black for each two whites hired. He extended the order to include promotions.

U.S. sues 2 cities. The Justice Department, citing provisions of the 1972 Equal Employment Opportunity Act, filed civil suits Aug. 7 against local government agencies in Montgomery, Ala. and Los Angeles charging them with racial discrimination in hiring for public jobs.

In the Montgomery suit, filed in U.S. district court in Montgomery, the Justice Department accused the city, its water department, sanitary sewer board and the city-county personnel board of giving some black workers lower-paying job classifications even though they performed the same work as higher-paid whites.

The Los Angeles Fire Department was accused of pursuing "policies and practices that discriminate against black, Mexican-American and Oriental applicants for employment."

War on Crime & Drugs

8 cities to get crime funds. The Nixon Administration announced Jan. 13 that eight major U.S. cities would each receive about $20 million over the next three years to help their police departments fight street crime.

The grants were described by Vice President Spiro T. Agnew and Attorney General John N. Mitchell at a press conference in Washington.

Agnew said the Administration hoped "to reduce street crimes and burglaries by 5% in two years and as much as 20% in five years in each of the cities." The effort was to be known as the High Impact Anti-Crime Program.

The cities to receive funds were Atlanta, Baltimore, Cleveland, Dallas, Denver, Newark, N.J., Portland, Ore. and St. Louis.

Each would receive $5 million in 1972, $10 million in 1973 and $5 million in 1974 for new and improved crime fighting efforts. The funds were to come from the Justice Department's Law Enforcement Assistance Administration.

Most of the funds were to help the cities improve new crime-fighting controls involving better radio-dispatch systems, increased use of helicopters, expanded public education campaigns and better training techniques for policemen.

Cities get aid vs. drugs. Myles J. Ambrose, head of the Justice Department's Drug Abuse Law Enforcement Office, March 25 named 33 cities in which special teams of federal, state and local narcotics policemen would concentrate their efforts to crack the pipeline that spread heroin across the U.S.

Ambrose said the number and makeup of the police teams would vary according to the city in which they were operating. He indicated that large metropolitan areas such as New York City, which was a major port of entry for heroin from abroad, might have as many as five teams operating at once.

In addition to New York City, eight other cities which had been designated earlier as regional headquarters for the program were also named target cities.

They were Atlanta, Chicago, Cleveland, Denver, Houston, Philadelphia, Kansas City, Mo. and Los Angeles.

The other cities: Albuquerque, N.M., Austin, Tex., Baltimore, Boston, Buffalo, Cincinnati, Columbus, Ohio, Dallas, Detroit, Indianapolis, Miami, Milwaukee, Newark, N.J., New Orleans, Phoenix, Pittsburgh, Portland, Ore., Rochester, N.Y., San Antonio, Tex., San Diego, San Francisco-Oakland, Calif., Seattle, St. Louis and the Washington-Maryland-Virginia area.

N.Y. high school drug use widespread. A New York commission on education reported Oct. 12 that nearly half of New York City's high school students were current "users of some psychoactive drug." The Fleischmann Commission put the figure of those in grades 10–12 using drugs at 45%.

The commission, which also looked into school drug use in other New York cities, concluded that the New York City problem was the most serious, affecting even lower grades. The commission estimated that 20% of those in grades seven through nine were also "currently users of some psychoactive drug."

The commission's estimates included users of marijuana and the so-called soft drugs in addition to users of heroin and other hard drugs. For purposes of the report, the commission defined users as "more than just weekenders" or occasional users.

The 496-page report said there were no accurate statistics on drug addiction and that most estimates were "underestimates." The panel said its figures did not include "hardcore addicts who have dropped out or been expelled" from school.

In Rochester, Buffalo, Syracuse, Albany and Yonkers—the state's five next largest cities—the commission estimated that 25% of the students in grades 10–12 and 10% of those in grades seven through nine were drug users.

Drug use was also found to be widespread in suburban areas. The commission estimated that 25% of students in the junior- and senior-high school grades were drug users. In rural areas, 10% of senior high school students were estimated to be using drugs.

The commission also reported that venereal disease among high school students had reached "epidemic" proportions.

Crime rate rise slowed. The Federal Bureau of Investigation (FBI) said in its annual crime survey, released Aug. 28, that the rate of serious crime reported to police rose more slowly in 1971 than in any previous year since 1965.

In a statement accompanying the bureau's report, Attorney General Richard G. Kleindienst said the general 1971 rate of increase was 7%. He said this marked "the third consecutive year that a tapering-off has been reported in the growth of crime."

The FBI report showed that the slowdown had resulted from a slower rise in the rate of crimes against property, and not from the rate of crimes of violence.

Property crimes, such as auto theft, larceny and burglary, rose 7% in 1971. Crimes of violence rose 11%.

Miami, which had 5,726 crimes for

every 100,000 persons, had the highest major crime rate of any metropolitan area listed in the report for the second year. The San Francisco area was second with 5,514, Los Angeles third with 5,443 and New York fourth with 5,307.

1973-74: Urban Woes Mount

Demographic Changes & Other Data

There appeared to be a continuing acceleration of urban problems as the mid-1970s approached. Although the direction of population migration shifted from the previous South-to-North trend to a North-to-South preponderance, the population of Northern urban areas continued to increase as the number of births outnumbered the number of deaths.

North-South shifts. The Census Bureau reported July 23, 1974 that population growth and migration patterns among states since the 1970 census were significantly different from previous trends, with some Southern states showing heavy net in-migration and the Northern states having moderately heavy out-migration.

Reporting on data for the April 1970–July 1973 period, the bureau said there was a net migration of 1,428,000 persons into the South and 751,000 into the West, while the Northeast lost 150,000 to migration and the North-Central area lost 298,000. (All states showed net population gains during the period because of the excess of births over deaths.)

Florida had the highest population increase, 888,000, with 782,000 attributable to migration. California showed a total in-

crease of 648,000; Texas, with a total gain of 600,000, was the only other state to gain more than 300,000. Arizona had the highest rate of total growth (16.1%) and migration growth (12.1%).

Of the states showing net migration losses, New York had the highest numerical loss (268,000), and Ohio showed the highest percentage loss (1.7%).

The report also noted a sharp decline in the number of births in all states compared with earlier periods, with the most noticeable declines in California and New York.

The bureau had reported May 30 that the basic indices of population growth had reached new lows in 1973. The crude birth rate—number of births per 1,000 population was 14.9, compared with 18.2 in 1970 and 15.6 in 1972.

A Census Bureau report on six non-Southern urban areas had showed July 29, 1973 that Southern-born black men living in those areas were more likely to be in the labor force and more likely to be married and living with their spouses than northern-born blacks living in the same area.

Robert Hill, research director of the National Urban League, said the report refuted the widely-held view that "blacks migrate from the rural South to the North to get on welfare."

The study, based on 1970 data, showed that in the New York City area, for example, about 65% of the black men born in New York were in the labor force. The figure rose to 78% for southern-born men who migrated by 1965 and to 82% for those who moved north after 1965.

In the Chicago area, the study found that 70% of southern-born men were married and living with their wives, compared with 51% of Illinois-born blacks.

School enrollment drops. The Census Bureau reported March 25, 1974 that elementary school enrollment in the 1973–74 school year had declined for the third straight year, a trend attributable to the declining birth rate.

Total elementary enrollment (first through eighth grades) was 31.5 million, compared with 32.2 million the previous year and the high of 34 million in 1970–71. Of the latest total, 28.2 million were in public schools and 3.3 million were in private schools.

Total enrollment at all grade levels, public and private, was 59.4 million, down from 60.2 million the previous year.

Study finds higher real crime rate. Surveys in 13 selected U.S. cities by the Law Enforcement Assistance Administration (LEAA) suggested that crime rates were at least twice as high as police statistics indicated. The LEAA data was made public in 1974 in studies whose goal was a more accurate picture of crime in the U.S. Conducted for the LEAA by the Census Bureau, each of the 13 surveys involved interviewing 22,000 residents and 2,000 businessmen about their experiences with different types of crime.

The first survey in eight so-called impact cities—where the LEAA made a concentrated effort to reduce street crime—was made public Jan. 27. Those cities were Denver, Portland, Ore., Baltimore, Cleveland, Atlanta, Dallas, Newark, N.J. and St. Louis. The second survey, released April 14, involved the nation's five largest cities: New York, Chicago, Los Angeles, Philadelphia and Detroit.

Growth curb trend reported. Despite questions of racial discrimination and other infringements on individual rights, the number of communities attempting to

limit population growth was rapidly increasing, according to a report published by the New York Times July 28, 1974.

Citing the trend as a significant reversal of the traditional American attitude of "bigger is better," the report said communities were becoming aware—and fearful—of overcrowded schools, potential water shortages, overloaded sewer systems and lack of open space.

A leading example was the northern California town of Petaluma (1970 population: 24,870) which for those reasons approved an ordinance in June 1973 limiting growth for each of the following five years to 500 new dwelling units. A federal district court Jan. 17 ruled the form of "rationing" invalid.

The report cited two Virginia counties near Washington which took different forms of action. Fairfax County adopted a 20-year program prohibiting all development that did not qualify under a point system based on need and feasibility. Loudon County had refused to approve a 4,200 unit "new town" despite the de-

Crime Victimization*

	Crimes of violence	Rape and attempted rape	Robbery	Assault	Ratio of unreported to reported crime
Detroit	68	3	32	33	2.7-1
Denver	67	3	17	46	2.9-1
Philadelphia	63	1	28	34	5.1-1
Portland	59	3	17	40	2.6-1
Baltimore	56	1	26	28	2.2-1
Chicago	56	3	26	27	2.8-1
Cleveland	54	2	24	28	2.4-1
Los Angeles	53	2	16	35	2.9-1
Atlanta	48	2	16	30	2.3-1
Dallas	43	2	10	31	2.6-1
Newark	42	1	29	12	1.4-1
St. Louis	42	1	16	25	1.5-1
New York	36	1	24	11	2.1-1

*Figures for crimes of violence, rape, robbery and assault were rates of victimization per 1,000 residents 12 years and older; rape was defined as "carnal knowledge through the use of force or the threat of force, including attempted rape;" statutory rape (without force) was excluded; robbery was "theft and attempted theft, directly from a person, of property or cash by force or threat of force, with or without a weapon;" assault was "unlawful physical attack by one person upon another."

veloper's promise to reimburse the county for installation of public services.

According to the report, the Department of Housing and Urban Development had found that 226 communities had imposed temporary or long-term moratoriums on such growth essentials as water and sewer connections, building permits and land subdivisions.

Other forms of growth limitation included restrictive zoning: large lot requirements and restrictions on multiple dwellings. Such practices had led to charges of bias against racial minorities and the poor.

Panel urges action vs. suburban bias—The U.S. Commission on Civil Rights said in a report released Aug. 12 that federal subsidies and state and local zoning reforms should be undertaken to break the "white nooses" of affluent suburbs surrounding increasingly black and poor central cities.

Accusing the Departments of Justice and Housing and Urban Development of failing to enforce existing fair housing laws, the report said the laws themselves were inadequate to insure access to suburban housing by racial minorities and the poor.

The commission urged that as a condition for receiving housing and community development grants, states should be required to establish metropolitan or statewide agencies with power to override local zoning ordinances and building codes which restricted housing availability.

As an incentive for neighborhood integration, the report recommended that property tax abatements, income tax deductions or direct payments be provided to families which would move to areas actively seeking housing integration.

At the enforcement level, the panel urged that companies receiving federal contracts be required to demonstrate the existence of adequate lower-income housing in suburbs where the company was located or intended to relocate.

Nixon Program

Urban affairs message. President Nixon told Congress March 8, 1973

that he was readying a "Better Communities" revenue sharing bill which would provide $2.3 billion in fiscal 1974 to cities and towns in place of categorical grant programs that the Administration had suspended for fiscal 1974.

The message, the fifth in a series of topical State of the Union addresses, promised a new housing bill to replace subsidized housing programs also suspended by the Administration.

Nixon pledged that no city would lose funds through substitution of revenue sharing for the categorical programs, which included Model Cities, urban renewal, water and sewer, open space, neighborhood facilities, rehabilitation loans and public facility loans. Unlike some of the categorical programs, revenue sharing would not require local matching funds, and could be spent by local governments for any community development purpose. Since the suspended programs emphasized aid to poorer neighborhoods, the effect of the new proposal might be to decrease assistance for the poor.

A similar urban revenue sharing proposal had died in the last Congress, largely because it was included in an omnibus housing bill with other, controversial provisions. But since the categorical programs would be suspended after July 1, Congress was under pressure to approve urban revenue sharing or leave the cities with no federal development funds.

On housing subsidy programs, Nixon pointed to "mounting evidence of basic defects," including "inequities," soaring costs and evidence that "the needy have not been the primary beneficiaries." He said some 300,000 more units would be built under the programs with funds already committed.

Nixon said "Americans today are better housed than ever before in our history," since 1.5 million low- and moderate income families benefitted from new housing aid in the past four years and an additional six million private units were built in the same period. He noted that the percentage of Americans in substandard housing had declined from 46% in 1940 to 18% in 1960 and 8% in 1970.

Among other proposals in the message were a previously announced request that up to $3.65 billion in highway trust fund money be diverted over the next three years to cities for mass transit improvements, and a measure to overhaul federal disaster assistance policies to "improve delivery," assure more equitable property loss financing and improve partnership with local governments and private citizens.

Radio message—In a March 4 radio speech announcing his urban program, President Nixon claimed that "the hour of crisis has passed" in American cities, and the quality of urban life had begun to improve. The remaining problems, he said, should be handled through local planning, rather than federal direction.

As evidence of urban improvement, Nixon noted that the crime rate was declining in "more than half of our major cities" and "civil disorders have declined." He said the cities' financial position had improved, air quality was in most cases improving, substandard housing had been cut by more than half since 1960, and "once again the business world is investing in our downtown areas."

Nixon criticized the "serious error of the past" in which "centralized planners" had designed "extravagant" programs that had turned the federal government "into a nationwide slumlord."

Nixon said he would submit a bill to provide $110 million "to help state and local governments build up their administrative skills and planning expertise." He said people must be given "a sense of control again," in "shaping the places where they live."

The President backed up his mass transit proposals by warning that cities would otherwise become "strangled in traffic, raked by noise" and "choked by pollution."

Nixon meets mayors—Twelve mayors met with Nixon and top aides in the White House March 6 to present their views on budget issues, but failed to obtain a commitment that the President would restore a $1 billion a year public service job program or approve a $250 million summer youth job project.

Mayor Roman S. Gribbs of Detroit, president of the National League of Cities, said Nixon promised to consider the summer program, but stuck to his position on other budget issues.

Urban aid bill submitted. President Nixon April 19 sent to Congress his proposed five-year "Better Communities" bill, which would replace categorical urban aid programs with a single, annual revenue-sharing allocation.

In a White House briefing on the bill, Housing and Urban Development (HUD) Secretary James T. Lynn confirmed fears of some critics of the revenue-sharing concept that it might eventually provide less than the specific grant programs. For the first year, however, the bill contained a "hold harmless" provision, which would insure that no locality could receive less in fiscal 1974 than it had averaged in specific grants in the years 1968–72.

Lynn said comprehensive figures were not available, but some large cities would receive less money later in the program. He contended, however, that the total annual amount was well above current spending levels.

Under the funding formula of the proposal, small cities and suburban counties would tend to gain at the expense of larger cities. A breakdown of communities to receive funds under the bill showed 268 urban areas which had received little or no aid in the categorical grant program, including 87 which were ineligible under the current law.

Other provisions, added largely to counter objections which had caused a similar bill to fail in the last Congress, included an allocation formula giving double weight to the incidence of poverty in communities and a requirement that citizens be given 60 days to comment on local plans for use of the funds.

State governments would also be given a larger role in community development, receiving 22% of the funds for distribution; the remainder would go directly to cities and counties.

Financial Problems

Fund share bias curb asked. The Treasury Department mailed about $2.5 billion in revenue sharing checks to 38,500 state and local governments Jan. 5, 1973. The Civil Rights Commission and private civil rights groups charged that the department's rules against discriminatory use of the funds were inadequate. The checks covered the second half of 1972. In a Jan. 5 memorandum reported Jan. 18, the commission said the Revenue Sharing Act had provided much weaker enforcement rules for violations of the non-discrimination clause than for violations of other sections, including record-keeping and wage rate rules.

Local governments were required by the act to take corrective action within 60 days of notification of most violations, but were given a "reasonable length of time" to correct civil rights violations, it was charged. If no corrective action was taken on most matters, all revenue sharing could be cut off from the government unit involved, while a civil rights violation could lead only to a cutoff of funds for the discriminating program.

The commission said the act did not prevent local governments from using revenue sharing to free local funds for discriminatory programs that would not be approved by the federal government.

The Leadership Conference on Civil Rights said the Treasury Department's interim enforcement regulations did not detail local government obligations to avoid or eliminate discrimination against individuals or communities, and did not provide for adequate violation detection machinery.

Fund-share flaws charged—State and local officials filed 3,600 requests for review of revenue sharing allocations to the Treasury Department's Office of Revenue Sharing by the Feb. 12 complaint deadline,

The large number of such requests, from nearly 10% of the local government units receiving checks, was seen by officials as a sign of the inadequate state of knowledge about government patterns, according to a New York Times survey reported Feb. 20. Indianapolis Mayor Richard W. Lugar said "revenue sharing may turn out to be a national civics lesson" since "it brings to the fore the structural difficulties of state and local governments."

The greatest number of complaints concerned federal computation of local tax figures, since tax effort was a major part of the allocation formula. According to the law, general revenue sharing could

not be used by local governments for education. Consequently, education taxes were not computed as part of the tax effort. But about 450 local units, including New York City, Baltimore, all counties in Maryland and Virginia and most in Connecticut, did not collect separate education taxes. These districts charged that too large a portion of their tax collections were written off by the Revenue Sharing office as education funding, leading the office to begin a re-evaluation of the formula.

Mayors start lobbying effort. The Nixon budget came under attack Feb. 3, 1973 from the National League of Cities and the U.S. Conference of Mayors. In a joint report on the budget, the groups criticized the "deep cuts" in domestic spending that, they said, "will be felt first and sharpest by minority groups and the poor, and, therefore, will hurt cities as a whole."

The report charged that the Administration had broken a promise to urban officials that revenue sharing, which was enacted in 1972, would not be a substitute for federal funds going into their areas from existing programs.

Mayor Joseph Alioto of San Francisco put it more bluntly Feb. 4. He said the Nixon Administration had "welshed" on the promise. He made the remark in New York while he and a dozen other mayors, who were members of a legislative action committee of the U.S. Conference of Mayors, met with Mayor John V. Lindsay of New York and made a public tour of several housing and water pollution control projects that would be adversely affected by reduced federal funding as projected in the Nixon budget.

The League's board of directors called for a "no-confrontation" policy in a March 4 statement. The mayors backed both general and special revenue sharing, and supported the concept of local control of spending, but warned that the cities could lose out during the transition without budget changes.

The statement said "we must recognize that the President is in a very strong position on the question of federal domestic spending and that sustained unanimity by the Congress against him is not very likely."

Members of the mayors' Legislative Action Committee appeared before Sen. Edmund S. Muskie's Senate Intergovernmental Relations Committee Feb. 21 to protest cutbacks in the Nixon Administration's budget and revenue-sharing proposals for urban aid.

The mayors disclosed that they were reversing their previous support for and activity on behalf of the Administration's revenue sharing proposal. Most of them, Seattle Mayor Wesley C. Uhlman told Muskie's panel, had "applauded" revenue sharing, "but it has not turned out to be the savior of the cities we thought it would be. Instead, it's a Trojan Horse, full of impoundments and cutbacks and broken promises."

Milwaukee Mayor Henry W. Maier said the mayors and their constituents had been victims of "a gigantic double-cross" by the Nixon Administration, since the President had explicitly promised that revenue sharing would be an addition to and not a substitute for the categorical aid grants.

New Orleans Mayor Moon Landrieu spoke of the mayors' "frustration, desperation, anguish and outrage" about the Administration's budget cutbacks and implications that revenue sharing could be used to fill the gaps. Figures were cited to show that their revenue sharing apportion would be much less than the aid lost from categorical funds impounded or reduced.

Landrieu complained that the proposed special revenue sharing fund would not be available until July 1974, while the "crippling cutbacks and reductions" in the budget could bring "the center city to its knees" before then.

Carter calls sharing a 'hoax'—Gov. Jimmy Carter (D, Ga.) charged Feb. 9 that revenue sharing had proved to be a "cruel hoax" for Georgia that especially affected the poor and powerless. His state's first-year share of revenue sharing funds was $36.6 million, he said, while $57 million was lost in child care and social rehabilitation programs and another $174 million was expected to be lost because of

Nixon's new budget and his impoundment of mandated funds.

N.J. school finance system invalid. The New Jersey Supreme Court April 3, 1973 upheld a lower-court ruling that the state's education financing system, based largely on the local property tax, violated the state constitution's mandate for a "thorough and efficient" education. Unlike rulings in other states, the case did not rest on federal constitutional rights, and would not be effected by the U.S. Supreme Court ruling against mandatory education financing reform.

Under the New Jersey system, only 28% of school costs were currently provided by the state, with 68% supplied by local governments through property taxes.

The court rejected the lower court finding that the system violated the equal protection clause of the federal Constitution, in light of the U.S. Supreme Court ruling, but said the counterpart clause in the New Jersey Constitution did apply, since the state's Constitution made education a right.

The court said the current system worked to the disadvantage of poor districts, and found that the quality of education depended on the amount of money spent for each child.

Oregon bars tax reform. Oregon voters May 1, 1973 reaffirmed a 1972 vote by deciding, by a 3–2 margin, to keep the local property tax as the major source of public school funds.

The vote rejected a proposal, backed by Gov. Tom McCall (R), education leaders and organized labor, to reduce local property taxes and have the state take over 95% of school operating costs. Construction and transportation costs would have remained a local responsibility.

To finance the plan, personal and corporate income taxes would have been increased, and the state would have imposed new taxes on business, real estate and profits.

Under the proposal, Oregon's spending range of about $600–$2,500 per pupil would have been narrowed over two years to $900-$1,200, and state funding would have increased from 21% to 95%.

Court orders sewer fund release. A federal district court in Washington May 8, 1973 ordered the Environmental Protection Agency (EPA) to make $6 billion available to states and cities for construction of sewage treatment plants, bringing federal funding up to the $11 billion authorized by Congress, over President Nixon's veto, in the 1972 Water Pollution Control Act.

Judge Oliver Gasch, ruling in a suit brought by New York City (later joined by Detroit), directed the EPA to allot $5 billion for fiscal 1973 and $6 billion for fiscal 1974. The agency had intended to allot $2 billion and $3 billion in the two years.

Although the ruling did not force the EPA to spend the additional funds, the agency would be compelled to consider applications up to the higher amounts. Under the terms of the act, state and local agencies were authorized to draw from a pool of federal funds for approved projects.

In his decision, Judge Gasch said he had "no choice" but to rule in favor of the fund release, noting that the language of the act "clearly indicated the intent of Congress to require the administrator to allot, at the appropriate times, the full sums authorized to be appropriated."

Gasch's ruling was upheld by the U.S. Court of Appeals in Washington Jan. 24, 1974.

Highway fund dispute resolved. A $20 billion highway bill, leading to eventual use of funds from the Highway Trust Fund for mass transit, was cleared by Congress Aug. 3. The Senate approved the bill by a 91-5 vote Aug. 1 and the House by a 382-34 vote Aug. 3. The President signed the bill Aug. 13, 1973.

The controversy over use of the road funds for mass transit projects was waged in the Senate-House conference for 10 weeks in 29 meetings. The Senate version called for spending trust fund money on mass transit over the three-year life of the bill. The House had rejected a similar feature. The compromise, reached July 19, would retain the exclusivity of the trust fund for road projects during fiscal 1974. States desiring to build mass transit in this period instead of roads would be required to return their federal highway funds to receive an equal amount of money from general tax revenues.

In fiscal 1975, urban areas would be permitted to use up to $20 million of the $800 million available from the highway trust fund to buy buses. In fiscal 1976, all or part of the $800 million earmarked for urban roads could be spent on bus or rail systems.

The bill also contained a provision authorizing $1 billion in federal grants for mass transit capital improvements, financed from general tax revenues. A tentative provision in the original Senate bill, to authorize $800 million over two years for mass transit operating subsidies, was eliminated by the conferees.

Bus aid bill vetoed—President Nixon Jan. 4, 1974, however, vetoed a bill that would have relaxed a curb on federal aid for purchase of local buses. The curb, contained in the 1973 highway act, barred grants to transit systems with charter services that competed with intercity or private bus companies.

The bill that Nixon let expire without his signature would have removed the curb on grants from general revenues but not on such funding from the Highway Trust Fund, which was the objection cited by Nixon in his veto. The bill "would discourage the use of highway funds for mass transit purposes," he said, and "thus undermine one of the central achievements" of the 1973 highway legislation.

President Nixon had sought passage of the bill. "Localities will have the flexibility they need to set their own transportation priorities," he noted in his signing statement Aug. 13. "The law will enable them at last to relieve congestion and pollution problems by developing more balanced transportation systems where it is appropriate rather than locking them into further highway expenditures which can sometimes make such problems even worse."

Transit aid rejected. The House of Representatives rejected by 221-181 vote July

30, 1974 a bill to provide $800 million in subsidies for operating urban mass-transit systems. Opponents considered the bill inflationary and a "big-city boondoggle." The opposition focused on the large share of the subsidies earmarked for New York City—$166.6 million.

Support for the bill also was diluted because of an overlapping bill prepared by the House Public Works Committee that would provide $20 billion over six years for transit operating subsidies and capital investment in buses and other equipment. The defeated bill, whose subsidies would come in the current fiscal year, was prepared by the House Banking and Currency Committee. A jurisdictional dispute between the two committees also was a factor in delay and eventual defeat of the first bill.

Early versions of the bill had been passed in 1973 by 53-33 Senate vote Sept. 10 and 210-205 House vote Oct. 3 after the program had been eliminated from the Federal Aid Highway Act. The measure then was approved by Senate-House conference committee Feb. 27, 1974 with new language in the face of Administration threats of a veto.

Transit grants—Earlier, several federal grants for urban mass transit were reported by the Wall Street Journal July 3-9. The awards by the Transportation Department were to cover 80% of project costs, with the remainder to come from local and state funds.

Chicago received $70 million for modernization of bus and rail systems, including new buses, new rapid transit stations and track replacement.

New York City received separate grants of $51.1 million and $33 million for bus purchases and subway improvement. The latter grant had previously been earmarked for highway construction.

Separate grants totaling $95.9 million went to the Philadelphia area for subway, streetcar and commuter-line improvements, construction of a downtown-airport rail link and a downtown bus-pedestrian mall.

Maryland received $60 million for a planned subway system in Baltimore and for new buses.

The San Francisco area received $13 million to cover cost increases in pre-viously-financed bus and ferryboat improvements and to purchase additional buses and other equipment.

N.Y.C. accused on U.S. funds. The Department of Health, Education and Welfare (HEW) found that the New York City school system had misused $28 million in federal funds in the years 1965-72 (reported March 21, 1974). The funds, intended for the education of poor children, had been granted under Title I of the Elementary and Secondary Education Act.

The HEW audit charged that the city had used the funds to replace state and local funds instead of supplementing them as required by law. All but $1 million had been used to support a currently-defunct special program in 10 schools providing small classes and extra services for disadvantaged students.

The remainder had been used for two programs in pupil testing and training of new local school board members, neither of which met Title I criteria.

State & local aides vs. federal cuts. State and local government officials cautioned Sept. 23, 1974 that Administration efforts to curb inflation by reducing domestic expenditures could prove counter-productive by forcing local governments to pay for the social and public service programs affected by federal budget cutbacks.

The warning was aimed at James T. Lynn, secretary of housing and urban development, and other Administration officials who had convened an anti-inflation meeting of over 60 governors, mayors, county officials, public employe labor union leaders and consumer advocates.

Mayor Joseph Alioto of San Francisco (D), president of the U.S. Conference of Mayors, told the group, "Too often, cutting the budget transfers rising expenditures to local governments" without reducing overall government spending.

"We cannot sanction the concept of bleeding out cities in hopes of achieving national economic health," New York Mayor Abraham Beame (D) said.

Housing & Urban Development

U.S. housing aid halted. Housing & Urban Development (HUD) Secretary George Romney said at a Jan. 8, 1973 meeting of the National Association of Home Builders in Houston that the Administration had ordered a freeze on all new applications for housing subsidies, public housing, and community development assistance. He said the freeze would be extended to the Model Cities and urban renewal programs during the 1974 fiscal year.

Despite the moratorium, Romney said, construction starts on low-income housing under the various HUD programs would continue for the next 18 months at an annual rate of 250,000 units, based on project commitments or approvals already made, and including projects "necessary to meet statutory and other specific program commitments." This was equal to the 1972 rate, but below the record 355,000 units begun in 1970.

At a news conference Jan. 8, Romney said the moratorium showed that the Administration was "adamant in its effort to halt inflation and to avoid tax increases at the federal level."

The announcement of the cutbacks, which had been rumored for two weeks, provoked strong opposition in Congress and among local officials, industry and public interest group leaders.

Rep. Wright Patman (D, Tex.), chairman of the House Banking and Currency Committee, said Jan. 8 the committee would do "everything in its power" to restore the programs. Rep. William A. Barrett (D, Pa.), chairman of the Committee's Housing Subcommittee, said the Administration "presumes to singlehandedly terminate the nation's existing housing and urban development programs," with "implications" he considered "grave."

Sen. John Sparkman (D,. Ala.), chairman of the Senate Banking Committee and its Housing and Urban Affairs Subcommittee said he would hold hearings to oppose HUD's "arbitrary exercise of executive power taken in violation of the intent of Congress and in complete disregard of the housing needs of the poor."

Subsidy suspensions upheld—The U.S. Court of Appeals for the District of Columbia ruled July 19, 1974 that HUD had been acting within its authority when it had suspended the subsidy programs for low- and middle-income housing. The ruling reversed a district court decision ordering HUD to resume processing fund applications under the programs.

While avoiding the question of impoundment of funds, the appeals court said HUD had "the discretion, or indeed the obligation," to suspend programs if it had been determined that the programs were not achieving the objectives intended by Congress.

Budgets. The fiscal 1974 budget was submitted to Congress Jan. 29, 1973. It called for a complete overhaul of all federal housing and urban development programs, previously announced by the Administration, with new commitments for most projects suspended.

The moratorium on new housing subsidies, public housing and community development aid was scheduled to be continued in fiscal 1974 although previous commitments would be carried out, allowing 270,000 subsidized units to be started in calendar 1973, compared with 250,000 in 1972.

The budget called for an urban development revenue sharing bill, to replace seven federal programs at a rate of $2.3 billion a year beginning in fiscal 1975. The programs would continue in the interim based on previously appropriated but unspent funds, and included $137.5 million in new urban renewal funds for earlier projects. The seven programs were urban renewal, model cities, open space, neighborhood facilities, water and sewer systems, rehabilitation loans and public facility loans.

Several other Housing and Urban Development Department (HUD) programs would end, including public facility grants for new communities and public housing modernization.

The budget for fiscal 1975 was submitted Feb. 4, 1974. HUD spending was budgeted at $5.6 billion, up from fiscal 1974's $5 billion.

Omnibus bill. Gerald R. Ford, who had succeeded Richard M. Nixon as President Aug. 9, 1974, signed an $11.1 billion housing and community development bill Aug. 22. The measure made broad revisions in the formulas for distributing federal aid. The compromise bill had been approved by 84-0 Senate vote Aug. 13 and by 377-21 House vote Aug. 15.

Most of the money ($8.6 billion over three years), as well as the major departure from previous programs, lay in provisions authorizing locally-administered block grants for community development to replace categorical aid plans such as Model Cities and urban renewal.

The funds would be allocated on the basis of population, degree of overcrowding and poverty (weighted double in the formula). During the three-year period, no community would receive less than the total previously granted under the categorical programs.

A separate provision established a $1.23 billion rent subsidy program for low-income families under which tenants would pay 15%–25% of gross income towards local fair market rentals, with the difference subsidized.

The bill also extended through fiscal 1976 two home ownership and rental assistance programs suspended in 1973, but with authorizations of only $75 million in new funds.

Among other features of the bill:

■ The Federal Housing Administration mortgage ceiling for single-family homes was increased from $33,000 to $45,000, and down payment requirements were reduced.

■ Rules governing real estate loans by savings and loan associations were eased, and the mortgage ceiling was raised from $45,000 to $55,000.

■ Annual funding of $40 million was authorized for the experimental program of cash housing allowances for the poor.

■ The conference version included a Senate-passed provision extending as a separate program the low-interest loans

for private rehabilitation of urban property.

■ The bill established minimum rent for public housing units at 5% of gross income, and specified that at least 20% of new public housing be reserved for families with incomes below 50% of the median income for an area.

Hamtramck black access ordered. U.S. District Court Judge Damon J. Keith April 3, 1973 ordered the City of Hamtramck, Mich. to start a program of public housing construction and active fair housing promotion to assure that 4,000 black residents displaced by urban renewal could find new homes within the city.

It was the first such ruling issued by a federal judge to compensate for past discrimination.

Keith ordered construction of 530 units of mostly low- and moderate-income housing, with some units reserved for the elderly, on acreage from which the former residents had been displaced. Relocated tenants would have first priority. In order to open an additional 530 units, Keith ordered city officials to accompany displaced residents seeking to buy houses and encourage owners to sell, and ordered anyone seeking to sell or lease housing to register the unit with a city agency.

Rights panel scores U.S. housing effort. The U.S. Civil Rights Commission, in a report Dec. 16, 1974, said that the Department of Housing and Urban Development (HUD) and six other agencies with fair-housing responsibilities had done a poor job in combating housing discrimination. The report said the positive actions taken by HUD and the other agencies had "generally been superficial or incomplete and have had little impact on the country's serious housing discrimination problem."

The other agencies cited were the Veterans Administration, the General Services Administration and four financial regulatory bodies—the Federal Reserve System, the Federal Home Loan Bank Board, the Office of the Comptroller of the Currency and the Federal Deposit Insurance Corp.

Welfare, Poverty & Jobs

Social services curbs eased. The Department of Health, Education and Welfare issued final rules April 26, 1973 on eligibility and payments for social services programs designed to get or keep people off welfare. The new regulations were generally less restrictive than curbs proposed Feb. 15.

In a key concession, HEW said it would continue to allow donations by private agencies to be used as part of a state's 25% matching funds for federal aid, but with safeguards to prevent donors from deriving benefits. Under the final rule, a donating agency could specify a particular activity as long as it was not the sponsor or operator of such a program.

HEW also retreated on the income-cutoff level for free social services, granting eligibility to families earning up to 150% of a state's standard for receipt of welfare payments. The February proposal had set a ceiling of 133.3% of a state's actual welfare payments, which in some states was less than the standard. Subsidized child care would be provided to families with incomes between 150% and 233.3% of a state's welfare standard, with recipients paying on a sliding scale to be determined by each state.

Among the rules retained from the February proposals: former welfare recipients could get social services aid for three months after leaving welfare rolls instead of two years, and potential recipients would be eligible for six months instead of five years; "block certifications," under which residence in designated poverty areas established eligibility for aid, would be eliminated; and payments for subsistence income maintenance and mental health services available under other programs would be stopped.

Although the new regulations were designed to meet a $2.5 billion annual spending ceiling for social services set by Congress, federal outlays would be held to as little as $1.6 billion, the Wall Street Journal reported April 27.

HEW Aug. 14 announced final rules affecting welfare eligibility requirements, restrictions on individual hearings and recovery of overpayments.

The rules would allow states to reinstate secret investigations of welfare applicants and recipients. Under current rules, states could make outside inquiries only with a welfare client's permission. Responding to complaints from welfare organizations that the new rule might lead to harassment and invasion of privacy, HEW included a regulation which "restates that constitutional rights are to be observed and protected."

Another rule would allow states to develop their own regulations for recovering overpayments, with a one-year retroactive limit which would also apply to correction of underpayments. Under old rules, overpayments were recoverable only if they involved fraud, an error caused by the recipient or if the recipient was found to have sufficient financial resources.

Other new rules would extend from 30 to 45 days the time in which states must decide on welfare applications, extend from 60 to 90 days the deadline for acting on hearings and reduce from 15 to 10 days the period of advance notice for reduction or elimination of benefits.

Job requirement upheld. The Supreme Court Jan. 14, 1974 upheld New York State's right to welfare plans requiring recipients to accept public service employment or face reduced benefits.

Hunger, poverty found worsening. The Senate Select Committee on Nutrition and Human Needs was told during hearings June 19-21, 1974 that the needy were getting hungrier and poorer and that government programs dealing with hunger were ineffective.

A report prepared for the committee by a panel of outside experts cited steeply rising food costs and inequities in federal food programs, particularly food stamps, as the major problems.

The panel noted that between December 1970 and March 1974, food stamp benefits for a family of four had increased 34% while the cost of foods in the Agriculture Department's "economy" food plan—the basis for food stamp allocations—had increased 42%.

The report said only about 15 million of

an estimated 37-50 million eligible persons were buying food stamps, and that many were not even aware of their eligibility. There were basic flaws in the program, according to the report, including an unfairly large monthly amount needed to purchase the stamps, the time-consuming "and frequently degrading" process of application and periodic recertification, and the exclusion of persons without kitchen facilities.

Poverty area unemployment. A report released by the Labor Department Aug. 29, 1974 showed that in 1973 the unemployment rate in metropolitan center poverty areas was almost twice that in non-metropolitan poverty areas: 9% vs. 4.7%. A "poverty area" was defined as a census tract in which at least one-fifth of the residents had incomes at or below the poverty level ($4,540 a year for a non-farm family of four).

The report also showed that 70% of the blacks living in poverty areas were in metropolitan centers. For blacks in all poverty areas, the unemployment rate was 10.8%, compared with 4.6% for whites. The rate for blacks outside the poverty areas was 4.7%, compared with 2.8% for whites.

Overall, the survey found 28,978,000 working-age persons living in poverty areas, with an unemployment rate of 6.5%.

Jobs program, jobless aid enacted. Congress cleared in the final days of the session a package of bills to authorize an emergency public service jobs program and to extend unemployment compensation coverage. President Ford signed the legislation Dec. 31, 1974.

A bill adopted Dec. 18 by a 346–58 House vote and Senate voice vote authorized $2.5 billion in fiscal 1975 for state and local governments to hire jobless workers for community service work in education, health, sanitation, day care, recreation and similar programs. The same bill extended jobless compensation to about 12 million workers not currently covered, primarily farm workers, domestics and state and local government workers. The extension was on a one-year basis and would provide eligibility for up to 26 weeks of compensation in areas of high unemployment.

A $500 million authorization in the bill was designed for acceleration of federal public works projects.

Companion legislation was prepared to provide an additional 13 weeks of emergency unemployment compensation benefits for unemployed workers who had exhausted their regular benefits. The Senate approved the final form of the bill by an 84–0 vote Dec. 16. The House cleared the bill for the President Dec. 19.

A bill to appropriate $4 billion in fiscal 1975 to fund the emergency programs was passed by both houses Dec. 19. More than $2 billion of it was allocated for the jobless compensation provisions. States and communities would receive $875 million for the public service jobs aspect. Another $125 million was channeled for stimulation of public works projects in depressed areas.

Conflict on NYC job plan. U.S. District Court Judge Morris E. Lasker July 25, 1975 overruled Labor Department objections and approved a New York City plan containing mandatory provisions to increase minority employment in the construction industry. But in a decision reported Aug. 10, a state supreme court justice ruled that the city had gone beyond its authority in imposing the mandatory standards.

The disputed plan had been formulated to replace the old "New York Plan" from which the city had withdrawn in 1973, citing unsatisfactory results.

The city's new plan required that contractors working on federally-aided municipal projects hire one minority on-the-job trainee for every four experienced workers on each project. In addition, long-term goals would require that the number of minority workers be increased so that their representation in the industry equaled their proportion of the city's population by July 1, 1978.

The Labor Department had withheld federal construction funds from the city on the ground that the city had implemented the new plan without federal approval. The city's suit to have the funds released led to Lasker's decision. The conflicting state court decision came in another suit filed by the industry and unions.

According to the Lasker ruling, the city had the authority to impose anti-discrimination rules more stringent than those approved in advance by the federal government. The ruling would also empower the city to require that contractors bidding on government-financed projects meet the same hiring standards on other operations, including private projects, during the life of the government contract.

Municipal Employes

Schools hit by teacher strikes. An agreement was reached Jan. 26, 1973 between negotiators for the Chicago school board and representatives of the 21,000-member Chicago Teachers Union on a $22.6 million pact to end a 12-day strike. The pact provided for a 2.5% pay increase raising starting pay to $9,797. The school year was shortened one week without loss of pay, and class size limitations were extended.

In Philadelphia, the local Federation of Teachers and the city's school board reached an agreement Feb. 27 to settle the 48-day teachers strike, the second longest in the nation's history.

According to Mayor Frank L. Rizzo Feb. 28, the settlement would cost the city $99.53 million over four years. Starting salaries would eventually rise to $10,000, with increments averaging $800 in succeeding years, in addition to annual increases of 4%-7% in current salary scales.

Classes had continued during the strike, staffed by newly hired teachers, substitutes and about one-fourth of the regular teachers, but over half the predominantly black student population did not attend.

The union's president, Frank Sullivan, and its chief negotiator, John A. Ryan, were released from jail on $1,000 bond Feb. 27, after spending 18 days in jail for defying a no-strike injunction.

Some 3,000 teachers began a walkout Jan. 22 in St. Louis in the face of a court injunction. Widespread student vandalism

was reported as the Board of Education tried to keep the schools open. The teachers voted Feb. 18 to settle for a contract offer of a $1,000 salary increase over 18 months. Members of the St. Louis Teachers Association and the St. Louis Teachers Union approved the pact. About 103,000 students had been involved.

About 3,200 non-teaching school personnel in Cleveland returned to work Feb. 5 after settlement of a five-day strike that had closed most schools for the city's 140,-000 students. Union leaders agreed to defer pay raises until the school board could contend with a $2 million deficit.

Teachers in New Haven, Conn. voted to ratify a new three-year contract March 20 after returning to work March 14, ending an eight-day walkout. Classes had continued during the strike, staffed by substitute teachers and supervisory personnel, but attendance and discipline were poor. There was no general increase for the current school year. A 3% raise and $400 annual increments were provided for 1973-74 and a 4% increase, plus the increments, for 1974-75.

The 1973-74 school year began with many teacher strikes.

The largest group affected was in Detroit, where a strike begun Sept. 4 by 10,-500 teachers closed classes for 280,000 pupils, although scattered attempts were made to operate with supervisory personnel. Salary increases—including cost-of-living raises were the main issue. The strike was settled and teachers returned to work Oct. 18 under an accord that included the Detroit school board's agreement to drop all damage claims against the union. Under a one-year contract, other issues—salary increases and class size—were submitted to arbitration. Court fines of $11,000 a day beginning Sept. 27 were not affected by the accord. The fines had been assessed after the union defied a court order to return to work.

Elsewhere in Michigan, strikes against all but two of the more than 30 districts affected had been settled by agreement or court order, it was reported Oct. 9.

Providence, R.I. teachers accepted a new contract Sept. 17, ending a nine-day walkout.

The school year's first strike had ended Aug. 21 after one day when teachers in

Houston returned to classes while negotiations continued. Strikes had been averted by new contracts in two New York districts. A five-year contract, said to be the longest for teachers in U.S. history, was accepted Sept. 4 in Port Washington, providing increases of 5.2% and 5.4% in the first two years and cost-of-living clauses in later years. Teachers in Rochester ratified a 4.1% pay increase Sept. 16.

All 100 public schools of Kansas City, Mo. were closed by a teacher strike March 26–April 29, 1974. A settlement approved in a vote by 1,700 teachers provided an immediate salary increase of 8%, with an additional 2% raise contingent upon voter approval of an additional tax levy.

U.S. sues cities on biased hirings. The Justice Department filed a civil suit in federal court in Boston Jan. 24, 1973, charging that the city of Boston, Boston Fire Commissioner James H. Kelly and the members of the Massachusetts Civil Service Commission had discriminated against blacks and Spanish-surnamed people in hiring new firemen.

Out of 2,100 firemen, only 16 were black and three had Spanish surnames, though these groups constituted 16% and 4% of the city's population, respectively. The department said the city had failed or refused to hire minority people on an equal basis with whites, and had used tests and qualifications that discriminated against minorities although they had "not been shown to be required by the needs of the fire department or predictive of successful job performance."

The department filed a similar suit in U.S. district court in Chicago March 15, charging that the city had discriminated against blacks and Spanish surnamed persons in hiring and promoting firemen. The department noted that only 4% of Chicago's 5,000 firemen were black and only .5% Puerto Rican or Mexican-American, although 32% of the city's people were black and 11% had Spanish surnames.

In separate civil suits that had been filed Aug. 14, 1973, the Justice Department accused the police departments of Buffalo and Chicago of discrimination against blacks, women and Spanish-surnamed persons in employment opportunities and conditions of employment.

The Chicago suit was the first brought by the Justice Department under the antibias regulations of the department's Law Enforcement Assistance Administration, which had made fund grants to the Chicago police.

Both suits charged that the proportion of minorities employed by the police was far below the minority percentages of the cities' population. The suits sought recruitment programs for minorities and women, hiring of applicants in sufficient numbers to offset past discrimination and compensation for those who had been unlawfully denied employment.

Federal Judge John Lewis Smith Jr. Dec. 18, 1974 ordered the Treasury Department's office of Revenue Sharing to stop making revenue-sharing payments to Chicago until the city took affirmative action to end racial discrimination in its police department. The action followed a finding Nov. 7 by Federal Judge Preston Marshall that the Chicago police department's hiring, promotion and personnel practices discriminated against blacks and women.

A spokesman for the Revenue Sharing Office said the $19.3 million quarterly check due to be mailed to the city Jan. 3, 1975, would be held because of Smith's order.

Meanwhile, Judge Marshall Dec. 16 accepted an interim hiring plan for the police department calling for 600 new employes. Of the 600 hired, 400 were to be from minority groups or women.

The Justice Department June 27, 1974 had obtained a consent decree that set quotas for minority hiring and that required a recruiting program that would emphasize that women were eligible.

The agreement provided a long-range goal of hiring racial minorities in proportion to their representation in the city's civilian labor force. To meet the goal, the city agreed that, beginning July 1, 50% of appointments as firefighters would be from black, Mexican-American and Asian-American applicants. The agreement also included a court injunction forbidding discrimination against employees already hired.

In two decisions reported Dec. 2, 1973, federal court judges in San Francisco ordered quota systems for the employment of minorities in the city's police and fire departments.

Concerning the police department, Judge Robert F. Peckham ordered that three minority persons (defined by Peckham as "blacks, Latinos and Asians) be hired for every two whites at the level of patrolman until minority representation reached 30%. A one-to-one ratio in appointments to the rank of sergeant was to be in effect until 30% of that rank were from minorities.

Peckham also enjoined the city's Civil Service Commission from using a hiring and promotion test which he said was discriminatory. He ordered future tests submitted to him for approval.

The city's fire department was ordered by Judge William T. Sweigert to fill half of more than 200 vacancies with members of racial minorities.

Jackson, Miss. and the U.S. Justice Department reached an agreement providing quotas for the increased placement of blacks on the municipal payroll and back pay up to $1,000 for currently-employed blacks who had been denied promotion opportunities, it was reported March 31, 1974.

Quotas in the plan set a five-year goal of a 40% black work force, approximately the same percentage as in the city's population. Currently, about 800 of the 3,000 workers were black, most in low-paying job classifications. The 40% figure would apply to both police and fire departments. It was agreed that at least one-third of city jobs would be filled by women.

The Justice Department, in a civil suit filed Oct. 17, 1974, charged Milwaukee's police and fire departments with bias in the hiring of women and minority groups. At the same time, a consent order was filed resolving the suit against the fire department and setting hiring goals for minorities.

Under the consent order, the fire department—which had six black men and no women among its 1,120 firefighters—agreed to recruit and hire blacks, persons with Spanish surnames and American In-

dians until the three groups made up 14% of the department's uniformed personnel. The department agreed to adopt a goal of making at least 40% of its appointments from among qualified applicants from the three minority groups.

The fire department also had to recruit and hire women in numbers reflecting their interest and ability to qualify.

The Justice Department filed suit against Tallahassee, Fla. Dec. 13, charging the city with discrimination against black job applicants and current black employes. Filed in U.S. District Court in Tallahassee, the suit was the first brought under the Revenue Sharing Act of 1972 as the result of a routine compliance review by the Justice Department.

The suit accused the city of discriminating against blacks in recruiting, job assignments, hiring and promotion. The department's compliance review and subsequent suit focused on 11 city departments, which had received some of the $1,054,264 in revenue-sharing funds given Tallahassee since 1972.

California bias charged. Four rights organizations filed a complaint March 13, 1973 with California's Fair Employment Practices Commission against the state's 28 largest cities, charging job bias against blacks and Spanish-surnamed people in police and fire departments.

The organizations said the two groups constituted 27% of the cities' population, but only 9% of the police and 5% of the firemen. They asked the commission to order population parity in the positions by 1977, to open up about 8,000 jobs.

Complainants were the National Association for the Advancement of Colored People, the League of United Latin-American Citizens, the American GI Forum and the Mexican-American Political Association.

NYC & Milwaukee firemen act. New York City firemen struck for 5½ hours Nov. 6, 1973. They returned to work when Richard J. Vizzini, president of the AFL-CIO Uniformed Firefighters Association, signed an agreement that provided for binding arbitration to end contract disputes that had precipitated the strike.

Vizzini Nov. 19 admitted that he had

falsified the results of a strike vote tabulated Oct. 29. The vote was 4,119 to 3,827 against a strike, but Vizzini had announced that the balloting was overwhelmingly in favor of a strike.

In Milwaukee, firemen ended a weeklong job action Nov. 10 and agreed to submit their contract dispute with the city to an independent fact-finding party. During the work slowdown, one-third to one-half of the firemen failed to report for duty because of sickness.

N.Y. transit pact. A new two-year transit pact for New York City was negotiated March 31, 1974, hours before a strike deadline. The pact, covering 37,000 bus and subway workers, most of them members of the AFL-CIO Transport Workers Union, called for a 6% wage increase immediately, a 3% increase Dec. 1 and a 5% increase April 1975. Cost-of-living increases also were to be added to the wage base July 1975 and Jan. 1, 1976.

San Francisco strike. San Francisco municipal workers struck in a wage dispute March 6–15, 1974. About 13,000 employes were involved in the strike, which closed hospital, sewage treatment and transit services.

The strike ended with agreement on an $11 million pay raise package which included an average pay increase of 5¼% and a fully paid dental plan. Mayor Joseph Alioto acted as a mediator in the dispute. Both sides had been in defiance of a state judge's order for the strikers to return to work and the police to arrest pickets.

Baltimore strikes. Baltimore municipal workers struck for two weeks and policemen for five days in new contract disputes in July 1974. The strikers, some 3,000 garbage collectors, park and highway workers and jail guards, settled July 15 for a 70¢ hourly wage increase over two years. The workers were members of the AFL-CIO American Federation of State, County and Municipal Employees (SCME). The striking policemen, some 500 of the city's 2,500-man force, were represented by another SCME local. Their walkout ended July 16 after

agreement on a two-year pact raising the starting salary from $8,761 to $10,000 by July, 1975 and the top minimum salary after five years on the force from $11,082 to $13,500 by mid-1975.

After the settlement, Police Commissioner Donald D. Pomerleau fired 91 police officers by July 18 and demoted 26 others.

School Desegregation

Bias fund cuts ordered. A federal judge in Washington ordered the Department of Health, Education and Welfare (HEW) Feb. 16, 1973 to begin action to cut off federal funds from school districts and state college systems that had not complied with desegregation requirements.

U.S. District Court Judge John H. Pratt had ruled in November 1972 that HEW had violated the law in refraining from any fund cutoffs since early 1970. Pratt set timetables for HEW action in several categories of cases, and ordered the department to submit detailed progress reports every six months to the NAACP Legal Defense and Educational Fund, which had filed the suit.

HEW was ordered to begin monitoring 640 districts under court desegregation orders "to the extent that resources permit" and report the findings to the court involved. But Pratt agreed that HEW could not cut off funds for "continuing" programs during enforcement proceedings, and could not require repayment of funds granted during the proceedings.

Joseph L. Rauh Jr., one of the plaintiff's lawyers, said about three million students were involved in the cases under the court's order. The systems were scattered in Pennsylvania and 16 Southern and Border states.

Pratt's order was upheld June 12 by the Circuit Court of Appeals for the District of Columbia.

Court blocks funds on teacher bias. The U.S. Court of Appeals ruled in Washington May 14, 1974 that HEW could not disburse funds to school systems with racially discriminatory teacher assignment policies. The ruling, which reversed a lower court decision, came in a suit to prevent grants totaling $20 million to systems in Baltimore, Detroit, Rochester, N.Y., Los Angeles and Richmond, Calif.

Citing Supreme Court rulings, the court said that faculties in schools receiving federal funds could not be "racially identifiable," and that the effects of racial discrimination must be removed immediately if federal funds were involved. HEW had decided the grants could be made if the school districts promised to end discriminatory practices in the future.

Desegregation aid cut. The Administration said March 1, 1973 that it would defer spending some $223.6 million of $270.6 million appropriated in fiscal 1973 to aid school districts undergoing desegregation.

An official of the Office of Education said most of the 336 districts applying for funds had filed unsatisfactory applications. The Office of Management and Budget had imposed a $50 million limit for the program in fiscal 1973, as an economy measure and because of the limited time available since the Emergency School Aid Act went into effect Feb. 1.

The withheld funds would be budgeted for programs in fiscal 1974, and $271 million budgeted for that year would be used for fiscal 1975. The Office of Education said about 130 districts still had funds available under the old Emergency School Assistance Program, designed for Southern and Border state districts.

Compromise school aid, bus curbs OKd. A conference committee version of a bill authorizing $25.2 billion over four years in aid to elementary and secondary schools and containing restrictions on busing of students was passed by 81-15 Senate vote July 24, 1973 and by 323-83 House vote July 31. President Ford signed it Aug. 21.

Busing provisions accepted by the conferees were generally closer to the more lenient Senate bill. The final version prohibited busing for desegregation beyond the school next closest to a student's home, except—as in the Senate bill—when courts determined that more extensive busing was necessary to protect

students' constitutional rights.

The final bill did not include a House provision that would have required the courts to reopen consideration of previous integration orders to bring them into compliance with the bill's restrictions. Under the compromise, parents or school districts could seek reopening of cases only if time or distance traveled would be harmful to students' health or would impair the educational process. A court, however, could terminate existing busing orders if it determined that a district was no longer violating students' rights and was not likely to do so in the future.

The conferees also accepted Senate amendments prohibiting busing across district lines unless boundaries were found to have been deliberately drawn to foster segregation and prohibiting implementation of integration orders after the beginning of a school year.

Busing curb defeated. In the final week of its 1974 session, Congress resolved a 2½-month dispute over an amendment prohibiting enforcement of federal anti-discrimination laws in school systems. The amendment, sponsored by Rep. Marjorie S. Holt (R, Md.), was attached to a bill making fiscal 1975-76 supplemental appropriations of $8,659,352,078, more than $5 billion of it for elementary and secondary education programs. Another $2.175 billion was for the community development grant program. The bill was cleared by Congress Dec. 16. President Ford signed it Dec. 27.

The House first approved the Holt amendment by a 220-169 vote Oct. 1. It was dropped in the Senate during the committee stage and rejected on the floor by a 43-36 vote Nov. 19 when it was offered by Sen. Jesse A. Helms (R, N.C.).

A House-Senate conference committee reinstated the amendment after discarding language prohibiting the Health, Education and Welfare Department (HEW) from requiring school districts to keep record files on the basis of race, sex, religion or national origin. As adopted by the conference, the Holt amendment read: "None of these funds shall be used to compel any school system as a condition for receiving grants and other benefits from the appropriations above, to classify teachers or students by race, religion, sex or national origin; or to assign teachers or students to schools, classes or courses for reasons of race, religion, sex or national origin." This was approved by the House by a 212–176 vote Dec. 4.

The Senate retained the amendment after adding 12 words: ". . . except as may be required to enforce non-discrimination provisions of federal law." The nullifying clause was sponsored by Senate Majority Leader Mike Mansfield (D, Mont.) and Minority Leader Hugh Scott (R, Pa.) and supported by HEW and the Justice Department. Sen. James B. Allen (D, Ala.) threatened to filibuster the revision Dec. 11 after his motion to table it was rejected 60–33. A motion to invoke cloture, or limit debate, was adopted Dec. 14 for only the 19th time in Senate history. The vote, requiring a two-thirds majority to carry, was 56–27. The Scott-Mansfield proposal then was approved 55–27.

The House reversed itself on the amendment by approving the nullified version by a 224–136 vote Dec. 16. Then the bill was cleared for the President's signature.

Although busing of students was not mentioned in the amendment, the provision was considered an antibusing stricture in the original version. Holt told the House Dec. 16 the busing issue was "going to destroy our school system" if Congress continued to sanction the "harassment" of local districts. Congress should "spell out what we want," she said, and not leave it up to the courts and HEW.

HEW had authority under the 1964 Civil Rights Act to enforce school desegregation and had exercised it by cutting off federal funds for non-complying school districts. Opponents of the Holt amendment considered it a subversion of the 1964 legislation.

Schools still segregated. In a report marking the 20th anniversary of the Supreme Court decision ordering an end to public school segregation, HEW reported May 17, 1974 that, based on data compiled in a late 1972 survey, 11.2% of black students attended schools where there were no white children. The report noted that segregation was clearly an urban problem: in 20 large Northern and

Southern cities, 25% of the black pupils attended all-black schools.

The survey also found that more than 71% of the public schools in the North had enrollments of more than half black. Comparable figures for other areas were 68% in border states and 53.7% in the South.

A private rights study group charged Sept. 5 that the federal government had failed to desegregate schools in Northern and Western states despite legal requirements that it do so.

In its report, the Center for National Policy Review said government efforts had been characterized by "bureaucratic caution, needless delays, administrative inefficiency and sloppy investigation."

The report charged that HEW had not made sufficient use of a weapon that had proved effective in integrating schools in Southern and Border states—the cutoff of federal funds to segregated districts.

In preparing the report, the center reviewed HEW files on 84 cases involving Northern and Western schools undertaken since 1964. Of these, the report said, 52 were still "open" as of July 1, 1973, and no enforcement of any kind had been undertaken in 37 of the 52 cases. The report noted that the average case remained unresolved for more than three years before the district involved was informed that it was violating the law.

According to the report, only four of the 84 districts investigated had been forced to undergo formal enforcement proceedings in which a fund cutoff was threatened.

The report included statistics which, while not perfectly analogous, showed the differences among regions in the progress of integration. In 1964, the report said, 98% of black students in 11 Southern states were in all-black schools; the figure had fallen to 9% by 1972. The latest figures for the North and West, however, showed 1.6 million of 2.8 million black students (57%) were in schools that were at least 80% black.

Responding to the report Sept. 6, HEW Secretary Caspar W. Weinberger said the cutoff of federal school funds was an extreme weapon which in some cases should be supplanted by "persuasion and discussion." He said there were instances in which fund cutoffs had increased the degree of segregation.

Weinberger denied that HEW was lax in enforcing the law, contending that delays were caused by the "very fierce" public opposition in many Northern cities. He said the public in the South had been "much more willing to accept desegregation."

Chicano school bias charged. The U.S. Commission on Civil Rights, in the final report of a study of Mexican-American (Chicano) education, said Feb. 4, 1974 that the five southwestern states with big Chicano populations had consistently failed to provide equal educational opportunities.

While placing much of the blame on local government and the states (Arizona, California, Colorado, New Mexico and Texas), the commission criticized the Department of Health, Education and Welfare for failing to cut off funds of school districts found to be discriminating against Chicanos.

Court rejects cross-district busing. The Supreme Court July 25, 1974 voided a plan to desegregate the predominately black Detroit school system by merging it with mostly white, neighboring districts. The 5–4 decision all but banned desegregation through the busing of children across school district lines.

Chief Justice Warren E. Burger, author of the court's majority opinion, was joined by Justices Harry A. Blackmun, Lewis F. Powell Jr. and William H. Rehnquist, all appointees of President Nixon, and Potter Stewart, named to the court by President Eisenhower.

In his opinion, Burger noted reasoning by lower courts that Detroit's schools, which were 70% black, would not be truly desegregated unless their racial composition reflected the racial composition of the whole metropolitan area. However, Burger challenged what he called the lower court's "analytical starting point"—that school boundary lines might be casually ignored and treated as mere administrative conveniences.

Such notions were contrary to the history of public education in the U.S., Burger wrote. "No single tradition in

public education is more deeply rooted than local control over the operation of schools; local autonomy has long been thought essential both to the maintenance of community concern and support for public schools and to quality of the educational process. . . . local control over the educational process affords citizens an opportunity to participate in the decision-making, permits the structuring of school programs to fit local needs and encourages experimentation, innovation and a healthy competition for educational excellence."

Moreover, Burger continued, consolidation of 54 historically independent school districts into one super district would give rise to an array of new problems concerning the financing and operation of the new district. In the absence of a complete restructuring of the laws of Michigan relating to school districts, the proposed interdistrict remedy would cause the federal district court to become "first, a de facto 'legislative authority' to resolve these complex questions, and then the 'school superintendent' for the entire area," Burger said.

"Disparate treatment of white and Negro students occurred within the Detroit school system and not elsewhere, and on the record the remedy must be limited to that system. The constitutional right of the Negro respondents residing in Detroit is to attend a unitary school system in that district. Unless petitioners drew the district lines in a discriminatory fashion or arranged for white students residing in the Detroit district to attend schools in Oakland and Macomb counties, they were under no constitutional duty to make provisions for Negro students to do so. . . . We conclude that the relief ordered by the district court and affirmed by the court of appeals was based upon an erroneous standard and was unsupported by record evidence that acts of the outlying districts affected the discrimination found to exist in the schools of Detroit."

In a dissent, Justice Thurgood Marshall charged that the court's answer to this problem was to "provide no remedy at all. . . , thereby guaranteeing that Negro children in Detroit will receive the same separate and inherently unequal education in the future as they have been unconstitutionally afforded in the past."

Failing to perceive any basis for the state's erection of school boundary lines as "absolute barriers" to the implementation of effective desegregation remedies, Marshall castigated the court majority for seeming to have "forgotten the district court's explicit finding that a Detroit-only decree . . . 'would not accomplish desegregation.' "

The state, not simply the Detroit board of education, bore the responsibility for curing the condition of segregation in the Detroit schools, he asserted. Marshall pointed out that the state, under the 14th Amendment, bore responsibility for the actions of its local agencies. Given that Michigan operated a "single, statewide system of education, Detroit's segregation could not be viewed "as the problem of an independent and separate entity," Marshall said.

The principle of merging city and suburban school districts to achieve racial balance had been upheld in the Detroit case by the 6th Circuit Court of Appeals in Cincinnati June 12, 1973.

Memphis busing begins. The first stage of a court-ordered desegregation plan for Memphis took effect Jan. 24, 1973 although only about half the whites assigned to the 45 affected schools attended classes the first two days of the program.

Some 13,000 of Memphis' 139,000 public school students were to be bused, in order to cut in half the number of black students in all-black schools. Previously, 88% of the blacks were in such schools, making Memphis the most segregated large school system in the South. The city was under court order to eliminate all-black schools by 1974, although 57% of the system's students were black.

The U.S. 6th Circuit Court of Appeals Dec. 4 upheld the Memphis busing plan. It rejected contentions of the National Association for the Advancement of Colored People that the plan left too many all-black schools.

Citing Supreme Court precedents, the court said there was a "necessity of tolerating some one-race schools because

minority groups concentrate in urban areas."

The court also upheld a lower court's finding that the city of Memphis had acted improperly by cutting its transportation budget in an attempt to avoid implementation of the busing order.

Prince Georges busing starts. A busing desegregation plan involving 33,000 students was implemented without serious incident Jan. 29, 1973 in Prince Georges County, Md., as a boycott threatened by white parents' groups seemed to falter.

The plan had been ordered in 1972 by U.S. District Court Judge Frank A. Kaufman, who ruled that the county school board had failed to meet its constitutional requirements to desegregate the 162,000-student system. One-fourth of the system's students were black, concentrated in communities bordering on Washington.

The U.S. 4th Circuit Court of Appeals upheld the ruling Jan. 23, over an appeal by the county government, Gov. Marvin Mandel and the Justice Department. Chief Judge Clement Haynsworth called the case "routine" and "the same kind of case we had in the cases to the south of here." All six justices of the Supreme Court present in Washington Jan. 26 refused a plea for a stay.

The plan increased the percentage of students being bused from 48 to 56.

Boston plan brings violence. Efforts to integrate Boston's public schools by means of busing resulted in repeated incidents of violence in 1974.

Earlier, a federal administrative law judge had ruled March 2, 1973 that the Boston School Committee had deliberately discriminated against black students by maintaining two largely segregated school systems.

HEW's Office for Civil Rights had brought the case, charging that Boston's school feeder patterns had concentrated blacks in high schools containing grades 9–12 and whited in the 10–12 grades schools. The judge rejected HEW's contention of deliberate discrimination against Puerto Rican pupils, since federal law did not require special education for Spanish-speaking pupils.

The state Supreme Court Oct. 29 upheld a plan to redraw Boston's school district lines to achieve racial balance by September 1974. The plan, involving large-scale busing, had been drawn to conform with a state law limiting the number of black students in any school to 50%.

U.S. Judge W. Arthur Garrity Jr. ruled June 21, 1974 that Boston had deliberately maintained segregated public schools, and he ordered that the state-devised racial balance plan be implemented in September. Ruling in a suit by black parents and the National Association for the Advancement of Colored People, Garrity said school officials had knowingly carried out a system segregating both teachers and students through special attendance and grading patterns. Garrity ruled that the plaintiffs were entitled to every legal means of relief, including busing, no matter how "distasteful."

Under the state plan, the number of black-majority schools would be reduced from 68 to 40. At least 6,000 pupils, black and white (out of 94,000) would be bused.

Scattered violence and boycotts of some schools marked the opening of Boston's schools Sept. 12 under the integration plan.

Trouble was focused in the predominantly white South Boston area. At South Boston High, a boycott proclaimed by white parents and fear of violence kept attendance Sept. 12–13 at fewer than 100 pupils out of the 1,500 expected to be enrolled. Buses carrying black students were stoned as they left the school on both days, although Mayor Kevin White had ordered police escorts after the first incidents Sept. 12. In another neighborhood, a bus carrying white students was stoned as it passed through a black area.

The busing plan was carried out without serious incident in most other areas of the city, and system-wide attendance was about 65% of normal.

Protests continued in South Boston on the third day of busing Sept. 16, with crowds of mostly young whites staging anti-busing marches.

The situation was generally calm by the next day as police lined the streets of South Boston to prevent demonstrations. But attendance at the boycotted high

school remained low (about 210 pupils), while city-wide attendance had risen to about 73%.

Occasional violence and boycotts continued during the next weeks, and Judge Garrity ordered Mayor White to use all potential help from local law enforcement agencies to quell the disorders. White's office announced Oct. 9 that 300 state police, 100 Metropolitan District Commission police and their supervisory personnel had been placed under the control of the city's police commissioner, Robert J. diGrazia. The police were made available by Gov. Francis Sargent following a request by White.

In issuing his order for a "gradual escalation" of force up to the point necessary to insure public safety and implementation of the desegregation order, Garrity rejected a petition by White asking for at least 125 U.S. marshals to augment Boston police, who the mayor said were stretched "razor thin" and whose presence in one ethnic enclave—predominantly Irish South Boston—was itself a contributing factor "to the incredible intensity of emotion." Use of federal marshals would be nothing more than a "symbol" that a federal court order was being enforced, Garrity said, adding that blacks being bused to South Boston were in "serious danger daily" and needed protection, not symbolism.

As incidents of violence continued, Gov. Sargent Oct. 15 ordered the mobilization of 450 National Guardsmen and urged President Ford to send federal troops to Boston.

President Ford declined to act on Sargent's request. Use of federal troops to deal with violence in Boston schools, Ford said Oct. 15, should be only as a "last resort." A request for U.S. troops would not be in order until Sargent had exhausted the full resources of the state, a White House statement indicated.

By Oct. 22, a general calm, punctuated by minor racial flare-ups, had returned to the Boston schools. Searches with metal detectors at two high schools in the Roxbury-South Boston area, the focal point of the controversy, had apparently prevented students from bringing weapons into the schools. (As the violence subsided, school attendance at all grade levels rose to a city-wide average of 75%

Oct. 18. However, attendance in the Roxbury-South Boston district hovered at 28% of a projected enrollment of 3,361.)

A referendum to end the independent Boston School Committee and replace it with a decentralized system of local advisory boards appointed by the city's mayor was defeated by Boston voters Nov. 5 by a recorded vote of 76,769 to 46,656. Mayor Kevin White had campaigned for passage of the measure, while a group of antibusing whites known by the acronym ROAR (Return Our Alienated Rights) had strongly opposed approval. The five-member School Committee, which was white and predominantly Irish-Catholic, had been the leader in the fight against forced busing and integration of Boston's schools.

Earlier, Judge Garrity had signed a final order Oct. 30 requiring the Committee to develop by Dec. 16 a city-wide school integration plan to replace the interim court-ordered program of busing for desegregation. In his order, Garrity urged the Committee to draft plans that would achieve desegregation with a minimum of busing and reassignment of students.

In defiance of an Oct. 31 order by Garrity to adopt a busing plan for citywide school desegregation for the fall of 1975, the School Committee, by a 3–2 vote Dec. 16, rejected a plan drawn up by the school system's attorneys and staff.

In disavowing the busing plan, John J. Kerrigan, chairman of the School Committee, said, "I can't in good conscience be an architect of a plan that would increase the bloodshed and hatred in the city of Boston." The other four members of the committee indicated full agreement with Kerrigan, but two voted to approve the citywide plan.

The program submitted to Garrity called for busing 35,000 pupils in all sections of the city. The city would be divided into six zones, each extending into the predominately black neighborhood of Roxbury. (The interim desegregation plan currently in effect mandated busing of 18,000 of the city's 82,000 students.)

Meanwhile, school system officials Dec. 17 decided to keep South Boston and Roxbury High Schools closed until Jan. 2, 1975. The schools had been closed Dec. 11 when a crowd of whites, angry over the stabbing of a white student by a black, trapped 135 black students in South Boston High School for four hours.

In reaction to the violence Judge Garrity Dec. 13 banned all gatherings of more than three persons within 100 yards of South Boston High School.

As tension escalated, demonstrations by pro- and anti-busing forces became more frequent and grew larger than during initial weeks of the busing plan. Supporters of the court-ordered program marched through downtown Boston Dec. 14, protesting the chaos that accompanied implementation of the plan. The crowd, estimated by police at 15,000–20,000 persons, contained contingents from Washington, Chicago, Newark and other areas of the nation. Opponents of forced busing mounted a counterdemonstration Dec. 15 in the Boston Common.

Integration of NYC school ordered. In what was said to be the first decision of its kind, a federal district court judge in New York Jan. 28, 1974 ordered federal, state and city housing authorities, along with city departments of education, police, parks and transportation, to cooperate in formulating plans to integrate a junior high school in the borough of Brooklyn. As of 1973, 43% of the school's pupils were black, 39% hispanic and 18% white.

Ruling in a suit filed by the National Association for the Advancement of Colored People, Judge Jack B. Weinstein ordered housing officials to provide a joint plan "to undo the racial imbalance" in publicly-supported housing in the area served by the school. Weinstein said all levels of government had failed to take "available steps" to reverse trends toward segregation in both housing and education, and concluded that "federal complicity in encouraging segregated schooling through its housing programs" was unconstitutional.

Noting that entrenched segregation at the school had discouraged white families from moving into the area's public housing, Weinstein said the plans should include "advertisements and inducements" directed at the white middle class to "stabilize" the district's population.

Weinstein ordered the city's transportation department to provide busing plans for short-term balancing of the school's enrollment; the police department was to submit plans for adequate protection of children in the area; and the parks department—whose facilities were heavily used by the school—was ordered to provide a separate plan.

When Weinstein issued his final ruling, however, the judge July 26 softened his Jan. 28 decision.

Weinstein gave the city's central school board and the district board until the beginning of the 1977 school year to raise the number of white students in the school to 70%, the overall percentage of white junior high pupils in the district. Currently, 18% of the one school's students were white.

To attain this proportion, Weinstein ordered that feeder patterns within the district be redrawn to reflect the racial make-up of the district as a whole. The junior high school would also be made a special "school for gifted children" to attract students from throughout the district.

Atlanta plan ordered. A U.S. district court in Atlanta ordered into effect April 4, 1973 a compromise integration plan that some civil rights attorneys had first accepted, then rejected.

The plan had been devised by the school board and the local chapter of the National Association for the Advancement of Colored People (NAACP), but then rejected by the NAACP national office and the NAACP Legal Defense and Educational Fund, an independent group whose attorneys had participated as counsel for the black plaintiffs in the long-standing desegregation suit.

Denver ordered to integrate. Federal Appeals Judge William E. Doyle April 8, 1974 ordered integration of the 70,000-student Denver school system for the 1974-75 school year, mostly by redrawing boundaries and pairing black, white and Mexican-American pupils to share classrooms on a half-day basis. An integration plan had been ordered drawn up by the Supreme Court in 1973.

Doyle rejected the school board's planned closing of 12 schools as a tactic "to avoid adoption of a desegregation

plan." He also ordered the merger of two high schools and implementation of bilingual programs in schools with large numbers of Mexican-American students.

The order provided that elementary schools have between 40% and 70% white enrollment and that white enrollment in secondary schools be between 50% and 60%.

Indianapolis busing ordered. U.S. District Judge S. Hugh Dillin July 20, 1973 found the State of Indiana guilty of maintaining segregated school systems and ordered the state legislature to devise a permanent integration plan for the Indianapolis metropolitan area. For the 1973-74 school year, Judge Dillin ordered an interim plan under which almost 6,000 black students from Indianapolis would be bused to 18 suburban districts.

Under the interim order, suburban districts were required to accept black students from the city in numbers equal to 5% of total enrollment. City schools were ordered to reassign pupils so that no school had less than 15% black enrollment. Dillin said schools in the metropolitan area should eventually reflect the 19.5% black enrollment in the area, but added that "perfect racial balance . . . is not required by law, and will not be ordered."

Dillin June 11 had rejected a plan submitted by the Indianapolis school board to integrate city schools without involving suburbs.

Knoxville plan upheld. The U.S. 6th Circuit Court of Appeals July 18, 1973 upheld a desegregation plan for the Knoxville, Tenn. schools calling for pairing of schools, adjustment of school zones and the closing of two schools—one all black and the other all white. The plan did not provide for busing.

The ruling affirmed a 1971 order by District Court Judge Robert L. Taylor, who had said busing of a large number of pupils "to obtain a certain percentage of black students in each school" was not required.

The plan, which placed 59% of the city's black students in nine schools that were 64% or more black, was upheld by the U.S. Supreme Court Jan. 21, 1974.

Topeka school bias cited. The Department of Health, Education and Welfare said Jan. 17, 1974 that racial discrimination still existed in the Topeka, Kan. school system, a defendant in the landmark 1954 Supreme Court decision outlawing segregation.

HEW had begun an investigation in December 1973 after being named a party in a new suit against the city. The department's latest action included an order for the city to submit corrective plans.

HEW said it had found that a "substantial number" of schools had disproportionate minority enrollments and that attendance zone transfers had impeded integration. Most minority junior high and elementary pupils, HEW said, attended schools with facilities generally inferior to those in the predominantly white schools.

Pasadena loses integration funds. The Department of Health, Education and Welfare told Pasadena, Calif. school officials April 11, 1974 that the district had failed to comply with a court-ordered desegregation plan, forcing the department to cut off the city's share of federal integration-aid funds, provided under the Emergency School Aid Act of 1971.

Montgomery busing rejected. U.S. District Court Judge Frank M. Johnson Jr. May 22, 1974 accepted an integration plan of the Montgomery County, Ala. school board that would, in general, allow elementary school pupils to attend neighborhood schools. Johnson rejected plans involving cross-city busing submitted by black groups and the federal government, ruling that while some schools would have high percentages of black students under the school board plan, all students would attend a "substantially desegregated school for a majority of their school careers."

1975: New York's Financial Impasse

City Rescued From Default

New York City was on the brink of bankruptcy several times during 1975—and was rescued from default by last-minute aid from the state government, from the city teachers' pension fund and, finally, from the reluctant Ford Administration.

The city's financial predicament had been in the making under several city administrations, according to many observers. A decade before New York's narrow escape from bankruptcy, William F. Buckley Jr. had warned that the city "is in dire financial condition as a result of mismanagement, extravagance and political cowardice." But Buckley then (Oct. 7, 1965) was a mayoral candidate, and many New Yorkers considered his warning nothing more than normal political disagreement with the policies of an administration he sought to displace.

By 1975, however, with financial disaster imminent, censure of the city's fiscal management, while not unanimous, had become widespread. Critics of the city administrations charged that New York had brought its troubles on itself by such allegedly "spendthrift" policies as: (a) providing record-high payments and costly services for welfare recipients, (b) building up an excessively large, overpaid bureaucracy, (c) subsidizing housing for middle- and high-income residents as well as the poor under programs that took previously tax-paying property off the tax rolls, and (d) financing

the tuition-free City University with open enrollment for all graduates of city high schools regardless of their academic standings.

New York City's financial plight became increasingly apparent in the spring of 1975:

City's financial woes discussed. New York City's financial straits were being widely discussed by April. Some observers said that the city might be forced to default on its debts and declare bankruptcy. "Legal insolvency certainly has been, and presumably still is, a very real threat. New York City, in effect, is broke," the Wall Street Journal reported April 4.

The city's financial problems were highlighted April 2 when Standard & Poor's Corp., one of the nation's foremost credit rating agencies, suspended its "A" rating on New York City bonds.

The action was taken, the firm said, because of the possible "inability or unwillingness of the major underwriting banks to continue to purchase the city's notes and bonds." Standard & Poor's had upgraded its ratings on the city's bonds from "BBB" meaning a medium-good investment, to "A" meaning a good investment, only 16 months earlier.

According to the Journal April 4, the city's publicly held debt totaled a staggering $14 billion. Because of the city's well-publicized flirtation with insolvency, officials had been forced to pay tax-free interest rates exceeding 10% in order to attract investors, further compounding the city's fiscal distress.

New York City's cash-flow problems were so bad that state officials April 3 loaned the city $400 million, representing an advance on payments of state revenue-sharing funds not due until late June, so that city welfare benefits could be paid. The loan obviated the need for city officials to attempt a $450 public offering of short-term notes in order to raise the cash needed to help meet payments totaling $3.6 billion due in 90 days.

In an effort to restore the city's financial credibility, Mayor Abraham Beame April 1 proposed a $12.8 billion "austerity" budget for fiscal 1976, beginning July 1. Despite some draconian economies, including plans to fire nearly 4,000 city workers and close 43 schools, three hospitals, and eight to ten libraries, Beame said the city still faced a $641.5 million deficit. (Beame earlier had trimmed the projected deficit by $135 million, bringing the total savings in the 1976 budget to $323.75 million.)

New York City's planned personnel cutbacks came at a time when the city's unemployment rate for March was 11.5%, a postwar record.

New York state, whose unemployment rate in March was 10.2%, was not in the best of financial health, either. Gov. Hugh Carey (D) told the legislature that New York's fiscal crisis, evidenced by the near collapse of the state-owned Urban Development Corp., demanded drastic action.

Loans rescue UDC. The rescue of the Urban Development Corp. (UDC) had taken place only days earlier. Gov. Carey had announced March 26 that 11 major New York commercial banks had agreed tentatively to lend UDC $140 million to complete its construction projects throughout the state. The UDC, the nation's largest builder of public housing, having defaulted on payment of $130 million in short-term debt Feb. 25, faced possible lawsuits that would have forced it into bankruptcy and put the other $1.1 billion of its bonded indebtedness in jeopardy.

Besides acting to prevent the collapse of the UDC, Carey also sought means to ensure completion of the remainder of the corporation's planned $1.6 billion program. To this end, Carey obtained passage by the state legislature Feb. 26 of a bill creating a new state agency, the New York State Project Finance Agency. The new agency was empowered to buy mortgages on UDC projects, thereby providing the UDC with cash to finish its building and pay its debts.

The new agency was to obtain money to purchase UDC mortgages through the sale of "moral obligation" bonds, the same fiscal device employed by the UDC. The new agency, unlike the UDC, would get its revenues from specific projects on which it had mortgages. The UDC had based its bonds on general revenues, a practice enabling it to apply earnings from strong projects to losses from weaker ones.

The banks' loan, which was contingent on the legislature's appropriating $80 million annually to service the UDC's bonded debt, was actually made to the Project Finance Agency, which in turn was to buy UDC mortgages.

The 11 banks were First National City, Chase Manhattan, Chemical, Manufacturers-Hanover Trust, Irving Trust, Morgan Guaranty, Marine Midland, National Bank of North America, U.S. Trust, Bankers Trust and Bank of New York.

Near UDC failure raises basic issues. Beyond its immediate effect on the U.S. housing bond market, the near collapse of the UDC raised questions about the fundamental safety of the "moral obligation" bond.

The "moral obligation" bond had been created in 1960 to circumvent New York State's need to hold voter referendums to gain approval of traditional "full faith and credit" bonds—ones guaranteed by the state. By issuing moral obligation bonds, a state agency could obtain funds to build its projects and later retire its indebtedness with revenue from its projects. The state's role, if it wished, was to appropriate money annually to replenish any deficit in the borrower's "debt service reserve fund."

The uncertainty over the soundness of the moral obligation bond was reflected in the nation's money markets. Michigan's Housing Development Authority tried to sell a $33 million bond issue but was forced to cut back to $25 million. An authority spokesman said underwriters blamed the "UDC situation." The New Jersey Housing Finance Agency experienced similar difficulties, said its acting director, William Johnson, who blamed investors' nervousness over "the New York problems" as the reason his agency had to sell short-term notes at interest rates from 7.4 to 7.9% instead of 6% as had been initially hoped.

The UDC's troubles not only brought into focus the potential dangers of the moral obligation bond but also the use of private capital markets to finance social benefits projects.

New York City's fiscal crisis deepens; Ford rebuffs plea for aid. Officials of New York City, which faced an immediate need for $1.5 billion by June 30 to meet its short-term debt obligations, sought assistance on many fronts for dealing with the city's fiscal crisis, but met rejection from President Ford, Republican leaders of the New York State Legislature, and New York commercial bankers.

President Ford May 14 rejected Mayor Abraham Beame's plea for $1 billion in aid in the form of a federally guaranteed, 90-day emergency loan. Such a loan, Ford said in a letter to Beame, a Democrat, would "provide no real solution" to the city's fiscal plight, "but would merely postpone, for that period, coming to grips with the problem." In meeting the city's immediate cash-flow shortage, Ford suggested that Beame redirect his request for emergency aid to New York State officials.

The President urged Beame to practice "fiscal responsibility" by curtailing "less essential services and subsidies" and transferring other activities to the state. Contending that the city was living beyond its means, Ford said, "We must stop promising more and more services without knowing how we will cover their costs."

Ford conceded that he was "deeply impressed" by the city's immediate cash needs and by Beame's efforts to reduce a projected $641.5 million budget deficit for fiscal 1976, but he said it was "also clear

that the city's basic critical financial condition is not new but has been a long time in the making without being squarely faced." "The adoption of sound budget policies would have a substantial and beneficial effect in both short- and long-term credit of the City of New York," Ford said.

Beame and Gov. Carey, also a Democrat, who had accompanied the mayor to a meeting in the White House with Ford May 13 to present the city's aid proposal, reacted angrily to Ford's statement. The President's response showed a "level of arrogance and disregard for New York that rivals the worst days of Richard Nixon and his gang of cutthroats," Carey told a political gathering May 14.

Beame, who was also present at the fund-raising dinner when news of Ford's rejection was received, said it was "incredible" that Ford "thinks more about the stockholders of Lockheed or Penn Central than the eight million people of our city. Instead of help, we got a lecture—a lecture that sounded more political than practical."

At the root of the issue dividing city and federal officials was disagreement over whether New York City faced a temporary cash-flow squeeze or a longer-range problem involving the city's basic creditworthiness. The Administration's position on bailing out New York City had been indicated May 10 when Treasury Secretary William E. Simon tentatively rejected the city's plea for aid, pending a final determination by Ford. Simon said he had concluded that "not only is the federal government's legal authority to provide financial assistance limited, but also that such assistance would not be appropriate." "The fundamental solution to the city's financial problems does not lie at the federal level," Simon said.

(At a press conference May 11, Beame termed Simon's arguments "specious" and "legal double talk," saying he would take his case to President Ford.)

In a further statement May 14, Simon said the city should regard Ford's response as a signal that "it take the extremely difficult political actions" required "to put its fiscal and financial house in order." In the past, Simon declared, New York City had "demonstrated an absence of fiscal responsibility."

Federal Reserve Board Chairman Arthur Burns echoed those sentiments May 14, telling a delegation of New York State congressmen that the city had lost its credibility. Burns said that until the city faced its problems directly by producing a balanced budget, there was little chance New York City could avert financial disaster, the Wall Street Journal reported May 15.

In discussing Ford's response May 14, Simon said the President had considered and rejected three options for meeting the city's immediate cash needs: advancing Medicaid and revenue-sharing payments due the city; seeking legislation to permit the Treasury to either buy city notes outright or guarantee their purchase; and allowing the Federal Reserve to assist the state.

Instead, Ford suggested that city officials seek "bridge loan legislation" from the state legislature allowing New York State to make first claims on city revenues in case of default.

Simon voiced fear that granting aid to one city in financial distress would create "extremely dangerous" precedents requiring that the federal government rescue other municipalities facing budget imbalances during the current recession. A federal official asked, "Where does this stop?" the Journal reported May 13. "We'd have Newark (N.J.) and Detroit and 10 or 12 other cities lined up here if we do this for New York," the official said.

The Administration's rebuff to city hopes for assistance spurred talks that New York City might be forced to default on its debt and plunge into insolvency. Simon acknowledged these fears May 16, but said the possible impact of such an action on the national economy would be "negligible." Earlier he had expressed concern about the possible "ripple effects" of a New York State default on the nation's credit market.

Albany leaders reject city plea—City officials heeded Ford's suggestion that they turn to the state legislature for help, but Republican leaders of the State Senate May 15 turned down Mayor Beame's request for a $640 million package of aid and taxes to finance the city's fiscal 1976 budget.

Approval of Beame's proposed aid package would be "totally imprudent and really a severe disservice to the long-range well-being of the city and its people," Senate Majority Leader Warren M. Anderson said.

The plan would "give the city a few more taxes to impose, a small increase in aid, and a set of magic mirrors to make everything—gimmicks, taxes, and all—look like the budget crisis was over, at least for a year," Anderson said.

"The city's real problem," he declared, lies not in its budget deficits, "but in the almost total loss it has suffered in investor confidence in its bonds and notes, both long-term and short-term." Anderson attributed this loss of investor confidence to a legacy of "trick or treat municipal budgetry."

The only way city officials could regain public confidence, Anderson continued, was to "balance the budget under existing revenue and aid structures." He called on the officials to restore "discipline, self-control and austerity" to the city's budget-making and spending policies. New York City "must stop trying to deliver more services than it can afford to give," Anderson declared.

In a later meeting with reporters, Anderson said of the city's aid requests: "I can only liken it to someone addicted to heroin. Do you really help him by giving him more?"

In a joint statement issued in response to the GOP refusal to aid the city, Beame and Gov. Carey said the spending cuts suggested by Anderson "will seriously jeopardize the social stability of eight million people and will . . . place the safety and health of the citizens at risk." The Ford Administration and Republican leaders in Albany were "driving a great city into default" by denying it aid, Beame and Carey charged.

Bankers refuse to buy city notes—Three New York commercial banks and one investment house refused May 19 to buy $280 million in city notes offered them without bidding by Comptroller Harrison J. Goldin. Officials of Morgan Guaranty Trust, First National City Bank, Chase Manhattan Bank and Salomon Brothers "told us there was no public market at this point," Goldin said.

New York City officials had astounded the bond market May 14 when, in the midst of seeking aid to refinance current debt obligations, and giving rise to constant speculation about default, they announced that $275 million in bond anticipation notes and $5 million five-month capital notes would be offered for sale.

Bond dealers noted that the market already was glutted with New York City notes: assuming the city could obtain the $1.5 billion needed to refinance its immediate obligations, the city's short-term debt would total $6 billion—45% of all the municipal short-term debt in the nation; the city's total debt would exceed $13 billion and debt service alone would approach $2 billion—one-sixth of the entire city budget.

Investor interest in other New York City securities was minimal. During the week ended May 16, the Times reported May 17, some city bonds traded at only two-thirds of their face value, and notes were selling sluggishly at discounts that raised their yields to 16.5%.

Goldin cancelled the planned auction May 17 when it appeared that the offering, scheduled for May 19, would attract few investors. Goldin said he would try to borrow the $280 million in a sale negotiated directly with lending institutions.

Proceeds from the note sale had been needed to refund $220 million in other notes expiring May 30 and to meet an employe payroll. Another $752 million was needed by June 11 to refinance four additional debt issues; another $249 million payment was due June 25 on a bond anticipation note issue; by June 27, the city was required to pay $2.7 million in interest on long-term indebtedness.

News of the bankers' refusal to buy city notes came hours after Mayor Beame asked the state legislature to grant a third delay in submitting the city's expense budget for fiscal 1976, projected at $12.8 billion.

Welfare rolls pass million mark. The number of persons on welfare in New York City passed the one million mark in May, James R. Dumpson, human resources administrator and social services commissioner, said May 31. Dumpson, who blamed the recession and federal economic policies for generating a "caseload of catastrophic proportions," said relief rolls had grown at an average of 6,000 persons a month in the first quarter of 1975. Of those recently added to the rolls, he noted, two-thirds were under age 18.

City's first rescue from default. New York City was spared from defaulting on $792 million in notes due June 11 when the New York State Legislature approved the creation of a new state agency, the Municipal Assistance Corp., designed to alleviate the city's immediate cash-flow crisis and oversee New York City's long-range borrowing policies.

Passage of the act, coming at dawn June 10, culminated several weeks of political and financial maneuverings aimed at solving the city's complex short-term and long-term fiscal problems.

The new agency's first task was to gradually refinance the city's current short-term indebtedness, totaling $3 billion, that was due for repayment by September. The corporation, dubbed "Big Mac," was empowered to offer long-term bonds to raise money needed to retire the city's short-term notes. As security for the 15-year bonds, investors would be offered the corporation's reserve fund, made up of money from the city's sales and stock transfer taxes. Nearly $1 billion a year would be earmarked for the reserve fund. The state also offered a "moral obligation" guarantee against default on the agency's bonds. Over the long-term, it was hoped that the corporation's management of the city's debt would restore investor confidence in New York's ability to pay its obligations. The fiscal crisis and constant talk of default had doomed the city's efforts to raise cash through public offerings, thereby severely limiting prospects for an orderly settlement of the city's immediate debts and the eventual reform of the budgetary process.

In return for Big Mac's help in managing its massive debt, New York officials agreed to turn over partial control of city finances to the state agency. The corporation could set a limit on the city's total short-term borrowing, currently estimated at about $6 billion. The city agreed to adopt an improved, state-approved system of accounting over a 10-year period and cease its much-criticized practice of using capital budget funds, intended for construction projects, to pay off its more immediate needs in the city expense budget.

The law also required the city to

provide the agency with periodic reports on municipal expenditures and operations. The mayor would have to certify that his annual budget proposals were "feasible" and in balance, and that conditions of the new law were being fulfilled.

If the city failed to live up to its obligations under the act, the agency could issue a "determination of noncompliance," notifying the state and the public that the city was not honoring the terms of its contract.

Five of the nine voting members of the corporation would be appointed by the governor, four by the mayor; another six non-voting members would be selected by state and city politicians.

City officials had been loath to accept the new state agency and relinquish partial control over the budget process. They contended that Big Mac's bonds should not be backed by prime city revenues unless the state agreed to assume control over some of New York's major cash-draining operations, such as the courts, welfare and the tuition-free university and college system.

Politicians had matched rhetoric with financial brinkmanship while the merits of the assistance plan were being debated. On May 30, when a teachers' payroll coincided with a deadline for short-term debt payments. Gov. Hugh Carey had announced that the state would advance the city $200 million in welfare funds to offset an expected $21.4 million shortfall in operating funds.

In an eleventh hour attempt to raise additional cash, the city council May 30 approved an 8% discount for prepayment of the city's real estate tax. An estimated $200 million was raised June 6 by this stopgap measure. The cash-flow crisis was postponed again June 9 when payment of a $35.9 million teachers' payroll was delayed for two weeks.

The city was forced to accede to the state plan, developed by an advisory panel created by Gov. Carey, after the panel informed city officials June 4 that the assistance plan was their only option for solving New York's fiscal problems. The banks would not roll over, or extend, $280 million in short-term notes with a maturation date of June 11 unless the state plan were adopted, investment banker Felix Rohatyn, a member of the advisory panel, told city officials.

With passage of the Municipal Assistance Act, however, New York won immediate pledges of aid from the group of 11 banks which had refused to lend the city any more money until its debt management problems were settled and its budgetary process reformed.

Shortly after Gov. Carey signed the bill into law June 10, the banks announced the notes would be rolled over for one year at 8% interest. A $100 million bridge loan for the city also was made available to the new state agency for 90 days at 5.75% interest.

The state also pledged to advance the city another $200 million from its education funds. The balance of the $792 million needed by June 11 would come from "various [city] sources," including pension fund investments, Beame said June 10.

Although creation of the new agency promised relief for the city's immediate financial crisis, Mayor Beame also had to reconcile a projected $641.5 million deficit in the city expense budget for fiscal 1976, beginning July 1, and the banks' demand for a balanced budget in fiscal 1976.

Beame had presented two budget proposals May 29 while Albany legislators debated the city's financial fate. The first, an $11.9 billion "crisis" budget, was based on the assumption the city would receive none of the state aid and additional taxes Beame had requested from the legislature. Payroll cutbacks in the crisis budget would require the dismissal of 67,347 city employes, Beame said.

In his alternative proposal, Beame offered a $12.678 billion budget with a $641.5 million deficit, requiring the dismissal of 38,000 city employes, whose layoffs had been announced previously.

The crisis budget presented a "humiliating prospect" for the city, Beame said, involving a $285 million cut in education funds and a 200,000 reduction in student admission to the city's higher education system; a $112.2 million slash in health care spending; a $50 million reduction in sanitation services; and a $185 million cutback in police funds and a reduction in street patrols.

A $120 million deficit was expected for the fiscal 1975 budget. As adopted in 1974, the budget totaled $11.1 billion, but because of declining revenues and rising costs, including higher debt service payments and welfare benefits, outlays for fiscal 1975 were expected to total $11.875 billion. A deficit, initially projected at $650 million, had been pared to $120 million because of service cutbacks and dismissals of 1,941 city employes.

Unions protest layoffs. Mayor Beame's proposal to lay off city employes to bring the budget into balance produced angry reactions from the unions representing municipal workers.

The leadership of the Patrolmen's Benevolent Association (PBA) and the Uniformed Firefighters Association (UFA) organized a "fear city" campaign, warning tourists and others to stay away from New York City because of unsafe fire conditions and crime and violence. As a part of the campaign, one million copies of a four-page pamphlet, entitled "Welcome to Fear City—A Survival Guide for Visitors to the City of New York," were to be distributed beginning June 13 at the city's airports, bus terminals and major hotels.

The campaign was immediately denounced by Mayor Beame as a "new low in irresponsibility." To halt the unions' campaign, the city obtained two court orders June 12 temporarily restraining distribution of the leaflets. The fear city campaign, the city said in its applications for the court orders, "endangers the safety and the security of the lives and property of the people" and "threatens the economic well-being of the city."

Ken McFeeley, president of the PBA, defended the campaign in a June 12 rally in front of New York City Hall: "The public is aware of the danger that massive layoffs of firemen and policemen will create. We have to alert everyone coming into New York to put pressure on them [city officials] to cancel these insane layoffs."

Leaders of the unions, who claimed not to have been served with the restraining orders, began handing out the fear city fliers at the city's John F. Kennedy Airport June 13. But they quickly halted the distribution when process servers appeared with the restraining orders.

The unions' position was subsequently upheld by U.S. District Court Judge Orrin G. Judd, who ruled June 14 that while the leaflet was "intemperate," it was "probably entitled to protection as an

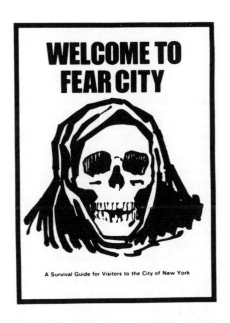

WELCOME TO FEAR CITY

A Survival Guide for Visitors to the City of New York

exercise of free speech." Despite the favorable ruling, the unions June 14 suspended their campaign.

The pamphlet, whose cover pictured a shrouded skull [see illustration], warned visitors in its introductory paragraph, "By the time you read this, the number of public safety personnel available to protect residents and visitors may already have been further reduced. Under these circumstances, the best advice we can give you is this: Until things change, stay away from New York City if you possibly can." Visitors who did come to the city, were urged to stay off the streets after 6 p.m.

Other protests against municipal layoffs were also organized. About 10,000 city workers rallied in front of First National City Bank's Wall Street headquarters June 4 to protest what they called the bank's "refusal" to help the city in its financial crisis. In a protest march organized and supervised by the city's Board of Education and the unions representing school workers, an estimated 25,000 persons demonstrated against cuts in the education budget June 9.

Economy Measures

Job cuts & state aid. Mayor Beame began a program of reducing city employment. When the job cuts helped induce the state legislature to aid New York City financially, Beame rehired some of the dismissed employes.

On June 30, despairing of aid for the fiscal year beginning July 1 from the Republican-dominated state legislature, Beame ordered the dismissal of 40,000 municipal workers, including large numbers of police, firemen, and sanitation workers. City officials said that during fiscal 1975, which ended June 30, 5,050 city workers had actually lost their jobs out of the 12,700 threatened with dismissal.

Sanitation men responded to the dismissal of nearly 3,000 of their number by launching a two-day wildcat strike that resulted in the accumulation of 58,000 tons of garbage on city streets. They were joined in the protest by policemen angered at the dismissal of more than 5,000 officers. Firemen, whose ranks were being cut by 1,700, also staged a "sick-in."

The protest actions ended after the state legislature voted July 3 to give the city $330 million in additional taxing authority to help fill an estimated budget gap of $641 million. (The price of the agreement exacted by Republican legislators was Democratic approval of $190 million in educational aid that mainly helped upstate Republican areas.)

The amount was far less than Beame had requested, but the action enabled him to rehire more than 5,000 of the 19,000 city workers scheduled for immediate dismissal, officials said July 7. Nearly $50 million in budget cuts for education and health agencies also was restored because of the new taxing powers granted the city.

However, differing reports of job and budget restorations emanated from city hall during the next two weeks and on July 23, officials admitted they had no idea how many municipal workers had been cut from the payroll as a result of austerity measures.

After an exhaustive audit, the city's Office of Management and Budget reported July 29 that 13,668 municipal employes—10,271 full-time workers and 2,795 part-time workers—had been dismissed from city jobs in the two-month-long economy drive.

Bank executives and other key investors also were dismayed by Beame's proposal to raise another $32 million through "nui-

sance taxes" in an effort to restore more city jobs.

As pressure from MAC and investors mounted, Beame dropped his nuisance-tax proposal, ordered an end to shortened "summer hours" for municipal employes, and agreed to consider a wage freeze, pay cuts and more layoffs.

In a gesture symbolic of the new hard-line stand at city hall, the city council July 25, at Beame's urging, raised the round-trip fare on the Staten Island ferry from 10¢ to 25¢. The increase was the first since 1898, when Staten Island joined Manhattan and three other boroughs in an enlarged city government system.

Austerity plan includes pay freeze. As New York City's financial problems deepened, Mayor Beame July 31 disclosed new austerity measures, designed, he said, "to overcome a crisis of confidence in our fiscal integrity."

The economy package, which was expected to amount to $500 million in an expense budget of $12.08 billion for fiscal 1976, was announced after four days of negotiations among city officials, members of the Municipal Assistance Corp., and municipal union leaders. The plan called for a wage freeze for all unionized city workers and indefinite deferral of a 6% wage rise due July 1; a wage freeze for managerial level employes at July 1973 levels; a $32 million cutback in the budget of the city university system in lieu of imposing tuition fees; a $375 million reduction in the city's capital budget; the consolidation and elimination of several city departments; 15¢ increases in mass transit fares to 50¢; toll increases for most bridges and tunnels; a 25% hike in commuter railroad fares; and the promised elimination of "give-away and frills" in future collective bargaining.

The wage freeze was accepted voluntarily by union leaders representing more than 50% of the city's unionized work force, but representatives of the police, firemen, and teachers rejected the plan and threatened a court test of the mayor's right to impose the wage freeze.

In announcing the "slashing economies," Beame said, "There is nothing that I have done in public life that has been more bitter." He acknowledged, however, that even these extreme actions might not prevent the city from defaulting on a $792 million payment of principal plus interest due Aug. 22 on short-term notes, or help MAC sell long-term bonds to retire the city's other short-term debt obligations.

MAC had sold $1 billion in city bonds, the largest tax-exempt offering in the history of capital markets, to underwriters June 11 to meet New York's cash-flow needs and prevent the city from defaulting on an earlier $792 million payment for notes that had come due. A second $1 billion sale had been scheduled Aug. 7, but the plan collapsed when the dollar price of the initial issue plunged about 10% in public trading July 21. Efforts to obtain federal guarantees for the remaining offerings failed July 25 when Treasury Secretary William E. Simon rebuffed the request from MAC member Felix Rohatyn.

With its rescue effort impaired by lack of investor confidence and the unwillingness of banks to make further interim, or bridge, loans to the city, MAC officials had brought increasing pressure on city officials to implement sweeping new austerity measures and overhaul the city's accounting procedures.

MAC members expressed satisfaction July 31 with Beame's program for drastic budget cuts and wage freezes, but also urged him to implement a thorough-going reform of the city's budget practices.

Beame refused during secret negotiations July 30, claiming the agency was trying to "humiliate" him by inserting itself as a "shadow government" in his Administration.

In its public demands, issued July 31, MAC called on the mayor to set a three-year spending ceiling on the city budget, limit tax increases over the same period, and accept supervision of the city's finances by a "skilled management apparatus."

Beame was forced to compromise with the state agency on crucial points when banks and other major lenders indicated that even tougher measures than those announced July 31 were needed to restore investor confidence in the city's willingness to control expenditures.

Beame Aug. 2 announced the appointment of Richard R. Shinn, president of the Metropolitan Life Insurance Co., as chairman of the new mayor's management council. Formation of the advisory group, to be dominated by businessmen, was intended to restore the financial community's confidence in the Beame Administration while thwarting MAC's bid to assume de facto control of New York's budget, city officials said.

Beame also agreed Aug. 6 to set "stringent ceilings" for the next three years on city expenses subject to his control.

City gets fresh credit. New York City's economy moves were rewarded Aug. 7 when MAC officials announced that they had concluded a $960 million financing arrangement that would enable the city to pay its August bills. The package was concluded when state officials and trustees of pension funds for the city's teachers, police, and firemen agreed to join banks in the purchase of MAC bonds. The state also agreed to make a $120 million advance directly to the city.

As a sign of the financial community's revitalized faith in the city, the banks agreed Aug. 8 to renew all of their city notes (totaling $550 million) falling due between October and June 1976 at a lower-than-usual interest rate of 7.5%. (When notes had been renewed in March, the city had paid about 8%.)

"We've achieved our monthly miracle," Felix Rohatyn, MAC's chief financial negotiator, said Aug. 8. His optimism was short-lived, however.

The $960 million package called for the sale of $275 million in bonds to individual investors. In subsequent days, MAC was able to sell less than half of that amount to the public. The deal was sealed only after the city's 11 major banks agreed to buy up a large portion of the bonds and the remainder was offered to the public again at 11% interest, a record for tax-exempt issues.

Analysts agreed that the specter of default had caused the bond market to collapse, according to the Times Aug. 17. In light of fears that default seemed likely and even inevitable, a MAC official said that plans to offer a final $1 billion bond issue during September was like "rearranging the deck chairs on the Titanic," the Times reported.

Gov. Carey, who had been in close, but private, contact with MAC officials throughout this period, became actively involved in the city's dilemma Aug. 20 when he charged that the city's actual total deficit was $2.8 billion, accumulated from past and present budgets.

Most of the deficit, $2 billion, resulted from unsound budgetary practices of past years, Carey said, adding that the information came from MAC's auditing committee. Carey called on Beame to take more drastic steps to give MAC a "fighting chance" to sell its bonds.

"The governor was compelled to emerge from his off-the-record activity because the mayor refuses to take the lead in establishing the city's credibility," a Democratic Party leader told the Times Aug. 21.

The political confrontation heightened Aug. 21 when Beame angrily rejected Carey's estimate of the city deficit and barred any further cuts in "vital life-support services." However, he was forced to retreat from that position the next day when MAC officials told the governor and the mayor that no cash could be raised to meet the city's September needs until the crisis of confidence in the city's management was resolved.

The governor, the mayor and MAC officials carried on constant negotiations during this final phase of the city's fiscal crisis, and each party to the talks offered a rescue plan.

Beame vowed Aug. 23 to freeze taxes and institute further management reforms if the state would advance the city $800 million. His plan was rejected.

Carey's plan, which was announced jointly with Beame Aug. 26 to minimize their political estrangement, called for the creation of a three-member panel, consisting of the governor, the mayor and the state controller, to oversee the city's finances.

Implementation of Carey's plan, which also would raise MAC's borrowing authority, create a state controller's post to monitor New York City's fiscal affairs, and make up to $1 billion in state appropriations available to the city, required legislative approval.

The plan collapsed almost immediately when the city's three major banks rejected a provision requiring that they purchase $1 billion in MAC bonds 12 months hence if the issue could not be sold to investors.

While final negotiations proceeded, city, state and MAC officials announced

jointly Aug. 29 that the city's actual budget deficit for fiscal 1976 now was estimated at $3.3 billion, rather than $641 million as previously forecast.

Terming the deficit "shocking," Rohatyn warned that default was a "good possibility" by Sept. 5 when the city faced a $150 million payroll.

MAC officials Sept. 2 outlined details of their complex legislative proposal to restructure city finances and raise cash for a three-month period. The program, whose features resembled a measure finally passed by the legislature, won quick support from Carey and the banks.

Beame was initially resistant, terming the plan "onerous for the city." "I do not think the plan need include a takeover of the city by the state," he said.

Beame finally endorsed the plan Sept. 4 after meeting with Carey and state officials who pointed out that Beame's only alternative was default.

New York City's pension payments already were straining the municipal expense budget, according to the New York Times Sept. 4. The $897 million earmarked for the city's retirement system in the current budget represented a 35% increase over the previous year's budget allocation. This meant that 13.8% of the newly estimated municipal tax yield ($6.483 billion) was being set aside for pension payments, compared with less than 10% in the 1974–1975 budget. The city's pension contribution was expected to exceed $1 billion by 1977.

New York City's retirement system was made up of five pension funds supporting 99,000 already retired former employes and 338,000 active members. City payments were constitutionally protected by labor contract guarantees; by state law, any retrenchment in the program could apply only to future members of the retirement system.

Payouts to the 99,000 retirees for the fiscal year ended June 30 totaled $558 million, 250% more than the amount paid in the 1968–1969 fiscal year.

Teachers' strike. Among developments jeopardizing the city's economy efforts was a strike of public school teachers beginning Sept. 9. The city and the United Federation of Teachers settled the strike Sept. 16.

The union vote on the new two-year

agreement, 10,651 in favor, 6,695 against, revealed considerable dissatisfaction. There also was public dissatisfaction, reflected by many of the city's locally elected community school boards, with a provision of the new agreement that would shorten the school day by 45 minutes twice each week. This would give the teachers preparation periods without the necessity of having other teachers cover their classes.

As part of the agreement, two customary 45-minute preparation periods per week during the regular class day were being "waived" by the union. This would put that time into the teaching sector and eliminate the replacement requirement.

The class-size maximums of the old contract were to be retained, partly as a result of the cost reductions from the above provisions. More teachers were to be hired; 2,400 of the 4,500 teachers recently laid off because of budget cuts were to be rehired. The unpaid salaries of the teachers while on strike, and any penalties incurred under the state's Taylor law, which forbade strikes by public employes, also would go toward the rehiring.

The teachers were to get a $300 cost-of-living adjustment and "longevity" increments of $1,500 annually for those with over 15 years' service, $750 for those with 10–15 years. The funds, however, were to come, if possible, from a sum that had been frozen by city wage controls. The city's fiscal crisis was an overshadowing factor of the entire strike situation, even in settlement. Union President Albert Shanker told his complaining members, in urging acceptance of the agreement, "A strike is a weapon you use against a boss that has money. This boss has no money."

State Attempts 2nd Rescue From Default

$2.3 billion state aid program. In a last-ditch effort to save New York City from financial collapse, the state legislature Sept. 9 passed a $2.3 billion aid bill that also set stringent financial curbs on the city and gave control of city revenues to a state-appointed board of fiscal managers.

Final approval came after an all-night debate during a special legislative session.

Gov. Hugh Carey, who had worked hard for the passage of the bill, widely described by legislators as a state "gamble" on behalf of the city, signed the measure early Sept. 9. "We have begun a major effort to save a city and secure a state," Carey said.

All major state officials conceded that the effort by the state, which had tried to avoid being drawn into the city's fiscal and political morass, was a risky one,

Under chief provisions of the aid package, the state would advance $250 million directly to the city, and $500 million to the Municipal Assistance Corp. MAC had succeeded in averting default through August because it was able to sell nearly $2 billion in bonds, thereby easing the city's repayment pressures by converting mounting short-term obligations to long-term debt.

MAC's authority as the city's fiscal arbiter widened, however, when the financial community questioned Beame's resolve to make the difficult political decisions implicit in budget cutbacks. The latest crisis, requiring direct state intervention, was precipitated by investors' refusal late in August to purchase any more MAC bonds,

Carey and the legislature were spurred to act by MAC officials when the banks refused to participate in another patchwork rescue plan to raise the $2 billion needed through November without assurances that meaningful cuts would be made in the city budget and that the state would take a more active role in monitoring city fiscal practices.

These conditions were met in the new assistance legislation. The law's offer of $2.3 billion to meet the city's projected cash needs through December was regarded as only a temporary answer to the city's fiscal plight. Politicians and financial analysts agreed that the ultimate solution of the city's deep-rooted financial problem demanded an end to budgetary gimmickry and a restructuring of the city's fiscal management so that investor confidence could be restored and the city could regain access to commercial money markets with saleable bonds.

The key to Carey's legislative program, which was devised chiefly by MAC officials, was the creation of the Emergency Financial Control Board, a seven-member, state-appointed panel authorized to act in a receivership capacity by carrying out budgetary reforms, enforcing state-mandated austerity measures, and controlling the flow of city revenues.

Under the law, all city revenues would be deposited daily beginning Nov. 1 in the control board's bank account and disbursements would be made in accordance with a three-year financial plan that the city was directed to draw up for itself and its independent agencies. The control board would oversee implementation of the city plan and set payment priorities.

In signing the new bill, Carey described the control board's function. "The board is like the one who gives out the chips at the casino," he said. "You go to the window and get your chips and play the game."

Carey was chairman of the new panel, whose other members were Mayor Beame, State Controller Arthur Levitt, City Controller Harrison J. Goldin, and three other persons named by the governor with the advice and consent of the state senate.

Carey Sept. 11 appointed William M. Ellinghaus, president of New York Telephone Co. and former president of the MAC panel; Albert V. Casey, chairman and president of American Airlines; and David I. Margolies, president of Colt Industries Inc. Investment banker Felix Rohatyn, chairman of MAC's finance committee, was named president of MAC, which would continue to act as the city's chief vehicle for raising cash. The new legislation also increased the amount of state-backed bonds MAC could issue on the city's behalf from $3 billion to $5 billion.

The act authorized State Controller Levitt to appoint a special deputy for New York City who would function as the control board's operating director and monitor the city's compliance with the legislation. Sidney Schwartz of Levitt's staff was named to the post Sept. 18.

The plan's success would be measured at year's end when the city's ability to raise the projected $3.7 billion needed through June 30, 1976 would be tested through direct borrowing in the market.

In the event that the latest retrenching and refinancing plan proved inadequate and New York City could not meet its cash needs, the law also established procedures for default:

■ Creditors would be required to give 30 days' notice before taking legal action.

■ Once a suit was filed, action against the city would be stayed 90 days.

■ The city and the control board would be authorized to submit a repayment plan to the state courts and seek relief in federal court under the federal bankruptcy law.

The legislation made a state law of the one-year wage freeze, imposed by Mayor Beame in June over the protests of municipal workers. The control board also was given the power to extend the freeze for the duration of the city's fiscal crisis.

The law also imposed penalties against public officials who violated "any valid order of the board" or refused to heed its directives. The governor or the mayor could suspend or remove from office any city official who issued false, incomplete, or misleading information; criminal charges also could be lodged.

Details of the aid package—The state's $750 million in appropriations to the city through direct and indirect aid would be financed by note sales. An equal amount, $750 million, would be invested in MAC bonds by state and city pension funds. The balance of the $2.3 billion program would be financed by commercial banks, the state insurance fund, and city sinking funds. Prepayment of city real-estate taxes also would ease the projected $900 million budget shortfall for September.

The provision directing State Controller Levitt, as sole trustee for the two state pension funds, to purchase MAC bonds aroused heated controversy. (The law was passed over the objections of Levitt, a Democrat with a reputation for fiscal rectitude.)

The law also declared MAC bonds to be legal and prudent investments and absolved trustees of culpability in the event the funds lost money as a result of their MAC investments.

The two state pension funds that were directed to purchase $225 million of MAC bonds (1.6% of their funds' total assets) challenged the law as unconstitutional and were upheld by a lower state court. However, a higher court reversed that decision Sept. 22, declaring that investments in the MAC bonds would not violate pension safeguards.

The suit had been filed on behalf of the Civil Service Employes Association, representing 230,000 state and local government workers, and the Police Conference of New York Inc., representing 45,000 upstate police officers.

Prior to passage of the special assistance act, four of the city's municipal unions had agreed to purchase $100 million in MAC bonds to overcome a cash shortfall anticipated Sept. 6 when city welfare benefits and payrolls came due.

Legislative debate—Gov. Carey had underlined the seriousness of the city's latest fiscal crisis Sept. 5 in a message to the legislature. New York City was faced with "unparalleled disaster," he said, because of its inability to pay its debts and operating expenses.

Because the "doors to the capital markets have been closed to [the city] directly and indirectly," Carey said, referring to investors' refusal to purchase either city or MAC securities, "New York City's financial failure threatens to paralyze government functions, endangering the health, safety and welfare of the more than 12 million persons in the city and region."

Emphasizing the dire consequences he said would result from the city's default, Carey said it "holds the prospect of inestimable harm for an indefinite time, not only to New York City, but to the state and nation as well."

Carey's arguments and the support of a few key Republicans carried the measure through the reluctant legislature. The aid package was approved on an 80-70 vote in the Democratic-controlled Assembly and on a 33-26 vote in the Republican-controlled Senate.

However, the debate was acrimonious and often partisan. State and city politicians of the last 15 years were castigated, including Vice President Nelson Rockefeller, who had been governor from 1959-1974. Assembly Majority Leader Albert H. Blumenthal (D, Manhattan) termed Rockefeller the "godfather of the mess." A Republican assemblyman responded by denouncing Beame, who in his last appeal for state aid had told the legislature that city finances were under control. "If he had been a Republican, there would have been charges of a coverup," the assemblyman charged. A Democrat replied, "The banks never blew the whistle, either."

Many Republicans from upstate rural areas indicated they thought New York was beyond help and default was inevitable. Proponents of the aid bill warned that if New York defaulted, the municipal bond market also would be closed to other cities. "It's the city of New York today, It may be Buffalo tomorrow," a Buffalo representative said.

Others opposed to the legislation downgraded the possible "ripple effect" on other urban areas if New York defaulted. They stressed the grave risks posed to state in the rescue plan. "The ripple exists more in this room than anywhere else. There isn't going to be any ripple effect unless we drag in the state and then there will be a tidal wave effect," an upstate Republican legislator said.

The turning point in the debate came late Sept. 8 when Senate Majority Leader Warren Anderson (R) returned from an 11th-hour mission to Washington where he had sought assistance from the Ford Administration in rescuing the city.

Anderson said he got "no commitments that are cashable" from Washington, but said federal officials showed a "growing awareness" of the state and city problems. This evidence of concern caused Anderson to announce his support for Carey's bill. (Anderson also was under heavy pressure from the banks to back the aid bill.) Nine other Republican senators, all from the New York area, joined Anderson in voting for the measure (two Democrats opposed the bill) and gave the margin of victory in the Senate.

State pays record interest cost, credit rater warns of jeopardy—Doubts that the state would succeed in its efforts to rescue New York City were expressed in the investment community Sept. 10 when the state was forced to pay a record 8.7% interest costs on three new notes totaling $755 million. That was an "unprecedented charge on a short-term loan secured by a state's full faith and credit," according to the Wall Street Journal Sept. 11.

The added interest penalty, 1.5 percentage points higher than what the state would pay under normal conditions, would cost New York $10 million, State

Controller Levitt said Sept 10. In early July, before its commitments to New York City had deepened, the state had paid only 5.23% on a similar issue. The previous high for state short-term notes was 6.75% in 1970 when tight money made borrowing expensive, according to the New York Times Sept. 10.

A portion of the proceeds from the note sale would be used to begin meeting New York City's debt. The sale was crucial to funding the aid package, officials said.

Standard & Poor's Corp., one of the nation's chief investment rating services, warned Sept. 15 that any further state aid to the city would jeopardize its AA credit rating. Commenting on the report, Gov. Carey said the statement "supports precisely" his position that no more state aid was possible and that the federal government must provide some help.

The state had made "heroic attempts" to stave off default for the city and its latest efforts "appear now to be within its financial capabilities," Standard & Poor's said in its publication for bond dealers and investors. However, the report added, "any additional efforts most certainly will strain the state's resources, have a compromising effect on its fiscal integrity and jeopardize its AA high-grade credit rating."

The AA rating was the second highest category in Standard & Poor's system. A downgrading of the rating would make securities less desirable to investors and raise the state's borrowing costs.

State rescue plan falters. The New York State Court of Appeals ruled Sept. 29 that a key portion of the emergency state legislation enacted to save New York City from default on its debts was unconstitutional.

In its 6–1 decision, the state's highest court struck down a provision requiring the investment of $725 million from state and city pension funds in MAC bonds.

Although the suit was filed by the Civil Service Employes Association and the Police Conference of New York, which contested the order to purchase $125 million in MAC bonds with their pension funds, the court decision invalidated the law's entire pension financing provision in the $2.3 billion aid package voted by the legislature.

The court did not flatly prohibit use of pension funds in financing the legislature's rescue plan, but it ruled that the pension trustees could not be compelled to make the investments in MAC bonds. In its majority opinion, the court stated that the legislature could not order State Controller Arthur Levitt, the sole trustee for the pension funds which had filed suit, to invest "mindlessly in whatever securities they direct, good, indifferent, or bad."

The ruling did not bar Levitt from deciding voluntarily to invest the pension funds in MAC bonds; however, Levitt had long been opposed to using state pension funds to ease the city's fiscal crisis.

After several days of negotiations, a compromise was announced Oct. 2. Levitt agreed to use $250 million from two state pension funds to purchase short-term notes issued by the state, rather than long-term bonds issued by MAC.

Prospective underwriters for a planned special issue of $500 million in state notes, also intended to raise funds to ease the city's cash-flow problems, informed Gov. Carey that there was virtually no market for the state notes, the New York Times reported Oct. 1. The market already was glutted with city and state offerings, the underwriters said, and investor confidence in New York offerings was continuing to erode.

According to the Times Oct. 2, $300 million in state notes, part of a $755 million offering to underwriters made shortly after the legislative rescue plan was enacted, remained unsold. These issues currently were trading at discounts that would give investors an "unbelievable" return of 20.956%, the Times reported.

There was evidence that investor resistance was spreading to even the most solid state issues. The Times reported Oct. 1 that bankers had told the state Housing Finance Agency, which regularly borrowed about $100 million a month, that the credit market was closed to it for the foreseeable future.

The agency had a good credit rating and revenue flow, according to the Times, but was caught in what State Controller Levitt called the "irrational emotional" reaction of potential investors against all New York State offerings, regardless of quality. An earlier default on notes issued by the state Urban Development Corp.

also had tainted the HFA's fiscal reputation, state officials said.

State officials were described as angered Oct. 2 because the state's fiscal condition was essentially healthy. Unlike the city, the state had not accumulated a huge budget deficit, did not roll over (or extend) its short-term debt, and generally had been able to finance expenditures out of revenues.

Moody's Investors Service, one of the nation's two major credit-rating agencies, Oct. 2 confirmed the worsening market conditions by downgrading its ratings for state and city securities. The action would make the issues more difficult to market and raise borrowing costs. Commenting Oct. 3, MAC Chairman Felix Rohatyn said he felt Moody's action reflected "the fact there is no market left" for state notes rather than judgment on their worth.

Moody's also withdrew altogether its ratings on the state's tax- and revenue-anticipation notes—short-term notes that Levitt had agreed only that day to purchase with pension funds. The state constitutional provision giving bondholders a first claim on revenues did not apply to short-term borrowing, Moody's noted.

Ratings for state bonds were lowered from Aa, Moody's second highest category, to A-1, its third highest.

Ratings for city bonds were reduced from Moody's fourth highest category, A, to its seventh highest, Ba, indicating investors could expect only a "very moderate" protection of their interest and principal. The court ruling barring use of pension funds in MAC investments and the city's inability to market its securities were cited as reasons for the move.

In earlier action, on Sept. 26, Moody's had withdrawn its rating altogether for the state Housing Finance Agency and the state Medical Care Facilities Finance Agency. On Oct. 3, Moody's lowered its ratings on three additional types of city securities, as well as offerings made by the City Educational Construction Fund, a state agency only recently rescued from default by an infusion of city money.

The educational construction fund was an independent agency created by the state legislature to build schools in New York City. The city prevented a default by the state agency, which needed $81 million to retire debt maturing Sept. 25, by advancing funds that day from operating funds currently being provided out of proceeds of MAC bond sales. The financing move was not a goodwill gesture, however; payment of the money was mandated under a rent-lease agreement between the city and state agency.

Simon on default, federal aid. Treasury Secretary William E. Simon Sept. 16 declared that the nation's financial markets were "capable of handling a [New York City] default with no more than moderate and relatively short-lived disruption."

In a letter to Sen. Hubert H. Humphrey (D, Minn.), chairman of the Joint Economic Committee of Congress, which was studying New York City's fiscal crisis, Simon said, "We don't believe default would undermine fundamental confidence in restrictive credit policies." Reiterating his opposition to direct federal aid for New York City, Simon said, "There is serious risk that the capital and credit markets would react adversely" if the federal government were to "act to prevent a default."

Simon said that because bankers, brokers, and private investors now anticipated a city default and had acted on those expectations, "We would expect only a moderate degree of further [market] adjustments" if default actually occurred. "We don't believe any other issuer [of bonds] would default as a direct consequence of a default by New York City," Simon said.

Simon shifted his position significantly after bankers warned Administration officials that New York State's financial future might be in jeopardy because of its inability to sell issues in the credit markets.

Although he continued to oppose direct federal aid to New York City, Simon said Oct. 4 that the "psychological effects" of continued predictions of default "can make an impact" and could have a "domino effect" on the markets generally.

Simon proposed a three-point plan for averting default:

■ He urged the banks currently holding more than $1 billion in New York City's short-term notes to declare a moratorium on interest payments. He also asked the banks to agree to "stretch out" the city's short-term notes into obligations maturing in two–four years so that the city could delay repayment. Simon said his proposals were based on the assumption the Emergency Financial Control Board, created by the state legislature to reorganize the city's finances, could produce a "credible" cost-cutting plan that would bring the city's deficit-swollen budget back into balance.

■ Simon also proposed a temporary increase in the state sales tax, currently 4% (city residents also paid another 4% in city sales tax). He proposed that part of the additional revenue be loaned to the city and the remainder revert to the state.

■ Simon said the federal government should undertake an immediate study of its proper financing role in such areas as welfare, with the ultimate aim of relieving "legitimate" city problems.

There was little immediate reaction to Simon's proposals. Felix Rohatyn, MAC's chairman, said Oct. 4 that most of the city's maturing short-term debt was not held by banks, but rather by individuals, funds, and institutions. Banks already had agreed to refinance the $550 million of short-term notes they held that would fall due between Sept. 1 and June 30, 1976; the city's total short-term obligations maturing over this period were $4 billion, Rohatyn said.

Ellmore C. Patterson, chairman of Morgan Guaranty Trust Co., told the Wall Street Journal Oct. 6 that "Everyone should be reminded that the [New York] banks have already extended $600–$700 million of city notes at concessionary interest rates," and were committed to rolling over another $106 million of notes as part of the $2.3 billion emergency aid package voted by the state legislature.

In testimony Oct. 9 before the Senate Banking Committee, Simon was questioned by Sen. John Tower (R, Tex.), an opponent of aid, as to what would be the "least obnoxious" type of assistance legislation Congress could enact.

Simon replied that the plan should "not create a new federal bureaucracy" with power to supervise local budgetary affairs; the plan should be "narrow and restricted, administered by the secretary of Treasury," who would have to be satisfied that "a program is in place" to restore budgetary balance; and thirdly,

"the financial terms should be so punitive that no other city will be tempted to turn down the same road."

Simon contended that the city had not yet succeeded in its fiscal reform efforts, and that "substantial additional expenditure cuts are required." He was supported in this view by Sen. William Proxmire (D, Wis.), chairman of the banking committee.

Simon said New York City's financial problems had not been the crucial factor in causing the recent rise in interest rates for municipal bonds. That came about "primarily because of inflation and the growing federal usurpation of the supply of credit in the country" to finance the federal deficit, Simon said.

"New York City's difficulties have been the major factor in the uncertainty" afflicting the municipal bond market and "have intensified investor concern with quality," Simon said. But he added, "New York's financial crisis did not create the other problems besetting the market and an end to that crisis will not make them go away."

Impact of default on banks feared. A confidential study by federal bank regulators indicated that 100 of the nation's 14,-000 banks would be in serious financial difficulty if New York City defaulted on its debt obligations, the New York Times reported Sept. 26.

The conclusions were based on a survey by the Federal Deposit Insurance Corp. of the 9,000 U.S. banks that were not members of the Federal Reserve system. The findings indicated that 60 small- and medium-sized banks would be in a precarious financial position because they held New York City securities equivalent to at least 50% of their total capital. (Another 200 non-Federal Reserve banks owned city securities equivalent to between 20% and 50% of their capital.)

Based on these findings, federal officials also concluded that 40 of the 5,000 banks within the Federal Reserve system would face similar problems in the event of a default.

James E. Smith, comptroller of the currency, had predicted earlier that only 10–15 banks, mostly within New York state, would be in jeopardy from a New York City default.

Bank officials and financial analysts expressed mild relief at the FDIC's findings because they had feared that many more banks would be affected by a default. Commenting on the report, an FDIC spokesman did not minimize the impact of default on the nation's banking system, but said, "It's a problem of the kind of magnitude that can be handled by the normal procedures of the banking system."

He admitted, however, that the FDIC survey did not measure bank holdings of debt issues by New York state and its agencies, nor the possible ripple effects a default would have on the finances of state and local governments.

Federal bank regulators underscored their belief that default would have a limited and manageable impact on the nation's banking system in testimony Oct. 8 before a subcommittee of the House Government Operations Committee.

FDIC Chairman Frank Wille saw "serious" consequences from default for 271 banks in 34 states that were supervised by the FDIC because they held New York City securities equal to at least 20% of their net worth.

Another 56 banks in 18 states held New York City debt issues equal to at least 50% of their total capital, Wille said. He added, however, that they were expected to be able to absorb the impact of default because they were well capitalized and "conservatively managed."

According to Wille, the effects of default would be "limited" unless default also spread to other debt issuers, in which case, he said, the consequences would be "significantly more serious."

Smith emphasized that federal officials believed that the liquidity problems caused by default could be limited "to avoid serious dislocations" in the nation's banking system. He based this view, Smith said, on the fact that those banks with the heaviest investments in New York City debt had less than 1% of the nation's total banking assets.

Insolvency was a "distinct possibility" for nine national banks in the event of default because of their large-scale purchases of city securities, Smith said. These banks, whose combined assets totaled nearly $900 million, would face "substantial" capital losses if default occurred, Smith said.

Another 18 national banks with assets totaling $737 million "appear capable of

absorbing initially the write-down of New York City obligations," Smith said, "but most would be left seriously undercapitalized" and would need to recapitalize to survive or face take overs by healthier banks.

Smith said that another 22 banks, with assets of $2.25 billion, could absorb a write-down but would need additional capitalization.

Charles Partee of the Federal Reserve Board also testified at the subcommittee hearings. Although he joined in reassuring legislators that the nation did not face a "major financial disaster" if default occurred, Partee indicated a growing concern among Federal Reserve officials regarding the national repercussions of default.

The Federal Reserve did not begin to worry about the national impact of default "until very recently when New York State and various other governmental units [were] caught up in widening investor concerns," Partee said.

One sign of this growing concern was the change in Federal Reserve Board Chairman Arthur F. Burns's position regarding aid for New York City.

According to the Wall Street Journal Aug. 15, Burns had given private assurances to city officials that the Federal Reserve's resources would be made available to prevent default. Burns had denied the report, according to the Journal, in order to maintain public pressure on the city to continue its cost-cutting drive.

Burns said Aug. 23 that the Federal Reserve, in its role as lender of last resort, would make loans available through the "discount window" to banks whose liquidity positions were threatened by heavy investment in bonds issued by the Municipal Assistance Corp. He emphasized, however, that the Federal Reserve would not provide "direct or indirect assistance to the city" by buying city- or MAC-issued securities and would not pressure commercial banks to make further investments or offer guarantees against default.

In a letter Sept. 11 to Sen. Hubert Humphrey (D, Minn.), chairman of the Joint Economic Committee, Burns said that the federal government's three bank regulatory agencies—the Federal Reserve, the FDIC, and the comptroller of the currency's office—had prepared a contingency plan to insulate the nation's banking system from the effects of default.

Included in the plan was a provision giving banks a six-month grace period before requiring them to write down New York City securities. This would make time available "for the market for such securities to stabilize and to permit the issuer [New York City] to develop a fiscal program that may eliminate default," Burns said in the letter.

He also confirmed that in the event of default, the Federal Reserve would lend money to any bank "in a basically sound position," even if it were not a member of the Federal Reserve system, to ease a "temporary liquidity problem" caused by default.

Burns indicated his growing concern about the city's problems Oct. 2 in testimony before the House Budget Committee.

He warned that if New York City's "financial crisis is not resolved, it could injure the recovery process underway in our national economy."

Burns appeared to shift his position again Oct. 8 when he testified before the Joint Economic Committee, where support for legislation to aid the city was growing. Although he stopped short of personally endorsing federal aid to New York City, Burns said that if Congress were inclined to bail out the city, "I wish you would do it quickly."

He reiterated his view that the fiscal crisis could jeopardize the economic recovery and said a default could "produce serious strains in securities markets" by closing some state and local governments out of the bond market or forcing them to pay "excessive" borrowing costs.

"I still believe," Burns said, "that the damage stemming from a prospective default by New York City is likely to be short-lived," but he added that default by New York state could trigger a serious national recession and cause a "domino effect" of municipal defaults.

Other cities affected—Other cities were reported to be suffering from the "ripple effect" of New York's troubles.

A delegation of 15 big-city mayors, led by Mayor Moon Landrieu (D) of New Orleans, chairman of the U.S. Conference of Mayors, met with President Ford Sept. 24 to tell him that the threat of default already was being felt in their areas. The group, which included Mayor Beame, asked Ford to support legislation that would provide either federally guaranteed municipal bonds or federal emergency loans to cities on the brink of default. They received a cool response from Ford, spokesmen said.

Speaking for the group, Mayor Coleman Young of Detroit said that "New York's problems are symptomatic of a national urban crisis that has been overlooked in Washington." Young noted that his city was paying an interest rate of about 9.9% on its tax-exempt bonds, "which we consider extortion," despite efforts to reduce a budget deficit. (Young said 5,000 of the city's 25,000 municipal workers had been laid off in an effort to pare expenditures.)

In Congressional testimony earlier Sept. 24, Mayor William H. McNichols of Denver said, "Every city in the nation is like a tenant in the same building. If somebody says the third floor is going to collapse, you can't say that's not going to bother me because I'm on the second floor."

Henry M. Maier (D), mayor of Milwaukee and a member of the delegation that met with Ford, said Oct. 19 that his city, which had the highest possible credit rating (AAA), had seen its interest costs on municipal bonds rise from 5.8% in April to 7% "or higher."

Members of the Democratic Governors Committee also agreed that New York City's financial crisis was a national problem that required a federal solution.

Gov. Richard Kneip of South Dakota said Oct. 9, "The fallout effect hits us in an increase between 1% to 3% on the cost of borrowed money. If anyone thinks the New York situation doesn't affect South Dakota, they're wrong."

Gov. Michael Dukakis of Massachusetts noted that the state's housing finance agency credit problems already were costing Massachusett's taxpayers $2 billion. This meant that "half of our federal revenue-sharing money has been eaten up right there," Dukakis said.

Carla Hills, secretary of housing and urban development, took exception Oct. 26 to the Administration position on the impact of default, saying New York City's financial difficulties already had adversely affected the federal government's new subsidized housing program.

Hills said that because state and local housing authorities were encountering problems selling bonds to finance their portion of the construction project, the Administration would find it "very tough" to meet its goal of building 240,000 new subsidized units by June 30, 1976.

International repercussions seen— Chancellor Helmut Schmidt of West Germany, who was visiting the U.S., Oct. 2 characterized New York City's fiscal crisis as one with "international" implications.

Meeting privately with President Ford, Schmidt, according to the New York Times Oct. 3, warned that a default by New York City would have a "domino effect," striking at other world financial centers, such as Zurich and Frankfurt. Schmidt cited the "enormous impact" of two bank failures in 1974, involving the Herstatt Bank of Cologne and the Franklin National Bank of New York.

Three of the U.S.' leading bankers testified before the Senate Banking Committee Oct. 18 that default would have an adverse effect on international money markets, and could exert a downward pull on general economic activity.

Walter B. Wriston, chairman of First National City Bank, David Rockefeller, chairman of Chase Manhattan Bank, and Ellmore C. Patterson, chairman of Morgan Guaranty Trust Co., said they had expressed the same warning to President Ford in a private meeting.

(Rockefeller also contended that the continuing threat of default had contributed to the dollar's recent decline in value.)

The bankers urged the committee to enact legislation easing the city's fiscal crisis. They were joined in that call for immediate federal aid by four other prominent bankers, including A. W. Clausen, president of Bank of America.

The New York Times said Nov. 7 that concern over the potential consequences of default had spread among foreign bankers and could result in the withdrawal of foreign funds from New York banks if default occurred.

These conclusions were based on interviews with bankers from 10 countries and a survey of 281 participants at a foreign exchange conference sponsored by the American Bankers Association.

According to the survey, conducted by the ABA, 68% of 118 foreign bankers responding believed default would have a major negative impact on international financial markets; 46% of the 92 U.S. bankers who responded shared that concern, and 20% expressed uncertainty.

(A contrasting opinion was expressed Nov. 3 by Federal Reserve Chairman Burns who said the European financiers he had telephoned "were not really concerned" about the impact of default.)

Aid to City Debated, Situation Analyzed

Ford vs. federal aid. President Ford reaffirmed at a nationally televised news conference Oct. 9 his opposition to a federal solution to New York City's financial crisis. But he did not say he would veto legislation to help the city if Congress sent it to him.

He would consider it, as he always considered legislation passed by Congress, he said. But he stressed that he wanted to look at the "fine print" on any such bill. "I just am very reluctant to say anything other than 'No' until I see the fine print, until I see what New York City has done" to resolve its fiscal problems.

Ford said that no legislative proposal offered so far "seems to fill the bill" and none before Congress at the moment "would justify approval by myself." He indicated that he considered the prospect of Congressional action unlikely. "I find no substantial sentiment for any legislation of one kind or another in Congress to bail out New York City," he observed.

In restating his opposition to federal involvement, Ford said, "I do not think it's a healthy thing for the federal government to bail out a city—and I mean any city—that has handled its fiscal affairs as irresponsibly over a long period of time as New York has."

Ford touched on the subject of New York City's fiscal crisis again during visits to Knoxville Oct. 7 and Detroit Oct. 10. "People who vote in New York City," he said at his Detroit news conference, "ought to elect the kind of people to public office who will handle their local taxes and the money that comes from the federal government properly." In Knoxville, he agreed with some of his aides that the impact of a financial default by New York City would be "containable." For one thing, he said, New York State's problem was different and "I can't believe a state with all that wealth can't meet that problem."

Rockefeller urges swift U.S. aid—Vice President Nelson Rockefeller urged Congress Oct. 12 to extend aid to the beleaguered city as soon as city officials indicated their intention to return to a balanced operating budget.

Rockefeller said he believed federal help was necessary to bridge the "difficult period" between adoption of the fiscal reform plan and the "restoration of investor confidence in the city's full financial viability by June 30, 1978."

Rockefeller urged Congress to act quickly to "avoid a catastrophe." "Time is of the essence," he said, "and the resolution of this immediate New York City situation is crucial."

His remarks were delivered at a Columbus Day dinner in New York City. Rockefeller, a former governor of New York, was the first Administration official to publicly support direct federal aid for the city.

Chase Manhattan Bank of New York, whose chairman was David Rockefeller, a brother of the Vice President, had spoken out Sept. 27 "as a corporate citizen" to urge Congress to intervene in the New York City crisis.

"We feel from both a local and national perspective that temporary federal support for New York City is of the highest priority," Dennis Longwell, president of Chase, said in a letter to the Joint Economic Committee of Congress.

"Throughout the country, the capital market for municipal securities is in turmoil. It can safely be assumed that any failure by either New York state or city to meet maturing obligations will further erode the national market for municipal securities and cause vital government programs at the state, county and local level

to go unfunded through the nation," the letter said.

Study analyses city's fiscal plight. In an analysis of New York City's fiscal crisis, the Congressional Budget Office concluded that default was a near certainty by December unless additional state or new federal aid were provided to the city.

The "underlying problems facing New York, as well as a number of other large, aging cities, can be dealt with effectively only by the states or by the federal government," the report stated. The study, which was released Oct. 10, had been requested by Rep. Thomas Ashley (D, Ohio), chairman of the House Banking Committee's Subcommittee on Economic Stabilization.

The nonpartisan budget office, established by Congress to analyze any problem that might require federal expenditures, made no recommendations in its report, but it noted, "There is probably little New York City could do on its own that could restore investor confidence to the point that the city could soon re-enter the municipal bond market."

Attempts to force stringent economies on the city in an effort to bring the budget quickly into balance would be self-defeating, according to the report. If drastic manpower cutbacks were made to reduce city expenditures, the report said, about half of the city's current $726 million deficit would be transferred to the federal government because laid-off workers would be unable to pay taxes and would become eligible for unemployment assistance.

If balancing the budget entailed substantial cutbacks in public services and large tax increases, the study said, the exodus of middle- and upper-income persons and industrial establishments would accelerate, and further erode the city's shrinking tax base.

The report suggested that the federal government assume the city's share of welfare benefits and "related services to the poor." "Unless one is willing to consider policies that would redistribute the low-income populations concentrated in central cities among suburban and rural jurisdictions, or policies that would radically equalize incomes, the main alternative left for addressing the cities' problems is to relieve the city of some major portions of its current fiscal responsibility," the study stated.

Because New York City was composed of five counties, the report noted, the city's $12 billion expense budget included payments for services and employes ordinarily borne by county governments. If New York City's expenditures were limited only to those also paid by other cities, the report concluded that their outlays were similar; San Francisco, Baltimore, Newark and Boston actually spent more per capita than New York did when these adjustments were made. The report also noted that Baltimore, Newark and Philadelphia employed more municipal workers per capita than New York.

"With respect to the salaries paid public employes," the study said, "New York is generous but not the most generous of large cities" when New York's high cost of living was taken into account. However, the report added, "what little evidence there is seems to indicate that New York City provides its employes with considerably more in the way of fringe benefits—pensions, health insurance, etc.—than is offered the employes of other large cities."

In analyzing the city's fiscal problems, the report did not exonerate city or state

Cities' Expenditures Compared

New York City's expenses are adjusted in the figures compared below to reflect the additional outlays made by the city as a five-county governmental entity. In other localities, many of these expenses are borne by state or county governments. Expenditures noted below for standard city functions are for elementary and secondary education, police, fire, sanitation, parks, highways, general and financial administration.

	Per Capita Expenditures		City Employes per 10,000 Population	
	All present city functions	Standard city functions only	All present city functions	Standard city functions only
New York	$1,224	$435	517.1	242.9
Boston	858	441	378.0	219.2
Chicago	267	383	140.0	208.4
Newark	692	449	391.1	258.2
Los Angeles	242	408	162.2	206.2
Philadelphia	415	395	163.8	255.7
San Francisco	751	488	312.5	224.6
New Orleans	241	260	177.3	217.5
St. Louis	310	360	241.9	214.2
Denver	473	375	237.0	219.3
Baltimore	806	470	434.1	260.1
Detroit	357	396	194.8	202

Source: Congressional Budget Office

officials or the financial community. "One cannot ignore the city's questionable accounting procedures and loose fiscal management in relation to the current crisis," the study said. "These procedures masked the fact the New York officials were failing to make the difficult choices that were required if the city's expense budget was to be truly balanced, as required by law.

"The fault does not rest with the city alone. Many of the 'gimmicks' which allowed the budget to appear balanced were tolerated or even suggested by state officials and were certainly not secrets to the banking community. These 'gimmicks' produced small deficits which were allowed to accumulate and grow, producing a problem of large and unmanageable proportions."

Cost-cutting in uniformed services. Municipal-government experts said that the modernization of New York City's uniformed services—police, fire, and sanitation—was vital to the success of the city's drive to reform its budgetary practices and cut costs because the combined budgets of the three services for the current fiscal year totaled more than $1.2 billion, 9.8% of the city's entire $12.3 billion expense budget, the New York Times reported Oct. 14.

Salaries accounted for a large part of the service budgets, according to the Times, which noted that 95% of the Fire Department's $380 million operating budget was allocated for salaries.

Despite a wage freeze implemented in July, salaries of the city's police, firemen, and sanitationmen were "generally among the highest paid in the nation when compared with . . . salaries in the country's nine other largest cities," the Times reported. Its salary study was based on data from the U.S. Census Bureau and individual cities.

In addition to the wage freeze, city officials had tried to cut costs by laying off thousands of police, firemen, and sanitationmen, and by refusing to hire new recruits.

According to the Times, since spring, when the city's fiscal problems had become apparent, the Police Department's ranks had been reduced by 3,000 because of dismissals and attrition; the Fire Department had lost 900 men; and the sanitation department's force had been cut by 1,400.

Because of these personnel cuts, New York City, which had been a leader in the ratio of police, firemen and sanitationmen to its population, now ranked fifth among the nation's 10 largest cities.

City funds rescue state agency. New York City's Board of Estimate Oct. 13 rescued a state agency from default when the board narrowly approved the transfer of $20 million in city funds to the state

Housing Finance Agency (HFA). The state agency faced default Oct. 15 when $90 million was needed to redeem its notes and those of a subsidiary, the state Medical Care Facilities Finance Agency.

The agencies had been unable to borrow funds in the private credit market. The state—itself short of cash and experiencing a credit backlash because of its efforts to save the city from default—could provide the funds only if they were appropriated by a special legislative session.

State officials looking for other sources

Uniformed Services In 10 Leading Cities

A—Total force   B—Number of residents per 1 uniformed serviceman   C—Salary range

	Police			Fire			Sanitation		
	A	B	C	A	B	C	A	B	C
New York Population 7,646,818	26,836	285	$12,900–$16,470	11,800	648	$11,944–$15,650	8,670	882	$12,049–$15,731
Chicago Population 3,172,929	13,146	241	12,024–18,000	3,012	1,053	12,024–18,000	3,500	906	13,104–14,664
Los Angeles Population 2,746,854	7,440	369	13,572–18,816	1,716	1,600	13,560–17,796	1,222	2,247	11,592–13,656
Philadelphia Population 1,861,719	8,200	227	13,441–14,022	2,500	744	13,441–14,022	3,550	524	9,539–12,646
Detroit Population 1,386,817	5,562	249	12,924–17,292	733	1,891	12,924–17,292	1,630	850	12,084–12,896
Houston Population 1,320,018	2,558	516	11,544–12,744–	2,266	583	7,314–9,334	1,025	1,288	11,044–12,244
Baltimore Population 877,800	3,420	257	10,000–13,500	1,997	440	7,030–11,045	1,404	625	10,000–13,500
Dallas Population 815,866	1,975	413	10,332–12,120	1,405	581	5,762–8,840	1,545	528	10,332–12,120
Washington Population 734,000	4,645	158	11,600–16,705	1,373	535	8,923–12,792	758	968	11,600–16,705
Cleveland Population 678,615	2,222	305	13,118–14,618	1,199	566	9,277–11,690	833	815	13,118–14,618

Source: U.S. Census Bureau and Individual Cities

of money found three special state funds which had cash reserves as well as the legal authority to purchase HFA bonds. It was agreed that $70 million from these funds would be used to buy HFA bonds. Cash also was available in other special state funds but they were prohibited by law from investing in HFA bonds because the bonds were backed only by the state's "moral obligation" of repayment. Investments by these funds were limited to "full faith and credit" obligations—state bonds and notes backed by the state's power to levy taxes.

In a complex solution to the problem, state officials agreed Oct. 9 that one of these special funds with a limited investment capability would purchase $20 million in fully-guaranteed state bond-anticipation notes. State Controller Arthur Levitt then would channel the proceeds from the sale to New York City as an advance on an environmental bond issue due in 1976 to pay for sewer facilities.

The Board of Estimate was asked to transfer the $20 million to the Riverbay Corp., parent company for Co-op City, a large housing development in the Bronx. Riverbay had built five schools in the complex with the aid of a special $20 million mortgage from the HFA, repayable when the city paid Riverbay for the schools. Riverbay agreed to transfer the city's payment to the HFA, which would repay its creditors.

The Board of Estimate posed the only stumbling block to completion of the eight-way transfer of funds because rent-striking tenants at Co-op City lobbied with the board members to win concessions from the state in their dispute over Co-op City costs. Three board members supporting the striking tenants blocked a vote on the transfer issue Oct. 10.

Final approval, on a 12–10 vote, came Oct. 13 only after a city official asked, "How can we go to the state and Washington and ask them to help us avoid default if we don't use the tools in our hands to help a state agency avoid default at no added cost to the city?"

Municipal bond market weakens. New York City's fiscal crisis and its possible default on its debt obligations had generated speculation and controversy

about the "ripple effect" on other city and state governments seeking to borrow money in the nation's capital markets.

Herbert Elish, MAC's executive director, was sharply critical of Treasury Secretary William E. Simon, who had said that a default by New York City would have only a "tolerable and temporary effect" on credit markets.

Noting chaotic trading conditions and sharp price drops in the municipal bond market, Elish termed Simon's position "extraordinary," the Wall Street Journal reported Oct. 1. According to Elish, the likelihood of the city's financial collapse had made borrowing more difficult and more expensive for many cities and states, even those with excellent credit ratings and few fiscal problems.

The turmoil in the municipal bond market was especially evident Sept. 30, according to the Washington Post. A number of governmental entities, such as the Virginia Public Schools Authority, withdrew offerings rather than pay interest rates they considered excessive.

Because of its proximity to New York, Connecticut's bonds fell in price despite bearing the highest available credit rating. "We have buyers that will not buy anything in the Northeast, period," a dealer from a major municipal bond firm said.

Borrowing difficulties facing cities in New York state were especially acute. Buffalo, a financially-troubled upstate city, Oct. 1 was unable to attract any purchasers for a $17.5 million bond anticipation note offering. On another offering of $6.5 million in notes, only one competitive bid was submitted and the city was forced to pay 10.5% interest.

The problem, however, was not confined to New York's deficit-ridden large cities. New Castle, a small town in affluent Westchester County, which adjoined New York City, was unable to sell a $1.5 million note issue, and finally placed the offering with a local bank at 10.7% interest, the New York Times reported Oct. 2.

According to the Journal Oct. 1, New York's credit difficulties also had spread to California, which had been unable to sell about $14 million of a $50 million bond issue, rated AAA, although it boosted the bonds' yield by .2 percentage points.

The impact of New York's problems was also felt in Georgia. Underwriters for a $10 million state bond issue said Sept. 5 they were able to market the bonds only by selling them at a loss. New York's problem "has had an unsettling effect on the entire capital market," a Georgia banker said. "Prices are lower and interest rates are higher."

The Securities Industry Association, regarded as the most influential association of Wall Street firms, also concluded that New York City's financial problems had been a factor "in pushing up the borrowing costs of all major U.S. cities," the Times reported Sept. 4. The group noted that Philadelphia had paid 2 percentage points more in interest than the rate paid on a similar offering by Chelsea, Mass., a much smaller city. Both bonds were A-rated. Detroit also had been penalized, paying 2.5 percentage points more than Johnson City, Tenn. on similar offerings. Both bonds were rated Baa.

A Pittsburgh banker told the Journal Sept. 12: "There has been a substantial pullback from all kinds of municipal credits by individuals and investors who just are concerned about the unknown. I think the New York situation has had a tremendous effect not only on the municipal market but on other markets as well and on the thinking of monetary authorities." (According to the Times Sept. 4, recent weaknesses in corporate bonds also were attributed to New York's credit problems.)

Other bankers concurred in that assessment. The affluent St. Louis suburbs "already are paying more" on their borrowing because of New York's effect on lenders' confidence, a Missouri bank official said.

According to a California banker Sept. 12, the threat posed by New York City's possible default "is of such magnitude to impact negatively on financial markets nationwide. Municipalities in general already have to pay more for their money. And default would raise questions about the soundness of all municipal financing and would be a severe jolt to all financial markets."

A dealer in tax-exempt securities told Business Week Oct. 13, "New York is like a disease that is contaminating all issuers.

There is total panic in the credit markets. The city has taken the state down with it, and if the state goes, others will follow."

Default Again Averted

Teachers' fund saves city. New York City escaped default by less than an hour Oct. 17 when the city teachers' union reversed an earlier decision and agreed to use $150 million in pension funds to purchase Municipal Assistance Corp. bonds.

The teachers' purchase was essential to complete the rescue plan enacted by the state legislature. According to law, state appropriations totaling $750 million, $250 million of which was due Oct. 17, could not be turned over to the city unless there were sufficient proceeds from the sale of MAC bonds to meet the city's remaining cash needs through Nov. 30. According to MAC officials, they needed $1.15 billion from non-state sources to meet this "threshold" and required an affirmative vote from trustees of the teachers' union retirement system on a commitment to purchase MAC bonds.

The city's cash needs on Oct. 17 totaled $477 million, but it had $34 million on hand. Officials expected to receive $250 million in a state loan, financed by the sale of state short-term notes to state pension funds; $33 million from the city's sinking funds; and $107 million from the purchase of MAC bonds by city pension funds, the "bulk" of which would be provided by the teachers. (Banks earlier agreed to "roll over," or refinance $59 million in city notes that would mature Oct. 17.)

One of the two obstacles to completion of the elaborate state plan was overcome Oct. 13 when the State Court of Appeals upheld State Controller Arthur Levitt's right to sell the state notes to state pension funds.

The court challenge to the note-sale plan was brought by the Police Conference of New York, which also had contested the MAC bond directive. The group charged that the note-sale plan would leave their pension fund with excessive investments in New York state securities. The Police Conference also questioned whether Levitt could represent the interests of three divergent groups. A spokesman for the group said, "As controller of the state, he [Levitt] sells state securities. As trustee of the retirement system, he's supposed to protect our money by making prudent investments. And he also sits on the Emergency Financial Control Board, which is trying to save New York City."

The teachers' union posed the other major obstacle to completion of the state rescue plan. Soon after the legislation was enacted, trustees for the retirement system had voted an "expression of intent" to purchase $200 million of MAC bonds, as directed in the legislation.

When the state court ruled that the law ordering these investments was unconstitutional, lawyers for MAC sought another vote from the trustees, reaffirming their initial decision. (A small portion of MAC bonds already had been purchased by the pension fund.)

In the interim, however, the Emergency Financial Control Board, which had been created by the legislature to manage city finances, had rejected a teachers' union contract settling a seven-day strike at the opening of the school year.

The control board voted Oct. 7 to return the contract for renegotiation and seek what Gov. Carey called a three-year "wage deferral" for the teachers.

Talks continued at the teachers' pension fund meetings, where city officials sought swift approval of the MAC investments. The trustees' resistance mounted, however, reflecting the decision of union president Albert Shanker to use the pension fund commitment as a lever in contract negotiations. No votes were taken on the investment issue until Oct. 16 and the public remained unaware of the imminent threat of default until that date.

Two negative votes, opposing the investment in MAC bonds, were taken at an all-night meeting beginning Oct. 16.

After 14 hours of negotiations and a private meeting between Gov. Carey and Shanker, the trustees reversed their position and approved the pension purchase. Carey and Shanker denied that the union had won any concessions in its contract talks in return for the investment pledge.

Shanker's announcement of the union decision was made less than an hour before the close of the banking day. Holders of $453.1 million of New York City notes maturing that day had been waiting since morning to redeem their notes. In order to allow completion of the MAC bond sale and redemption of the city notes, the state superintendent of banks ordered Manufacturers Hanover Trust Co., the paying agency for the city notes, to remain open late into the night. The Federal Reserve Bank of New York also kept its facilities open to expedite the last-minute arrangements.

New York City's near-default provided a foretaste of what actual default might entail. As tension and uncertainty mounted Oct. 17 and it appeared that the city would not meet its expenses for the day, City Controller Harrison J. Goldin directed the sanitation department to halt its scheduled distribution of paychecks. Irving Trust Co. refused to cash city payroll checks drawn on other banks. City officials also obtained a court order outlining the city's payment priorities in the event of default—leading the list were vital public services, followed by city payrolls, followed by payments to holders of city debts.

In a telegram sent to President Ford after default was averted, Gov. Carey said: "New York, by exhausting all of its resources, can meet its obligations until Dec. 1. After then, the welfare of our citizens rests in the hands of the federal government. I seek your cooperation and leadership."

Carey told reporters, "We need not a bail out, not a hand out, but the recognition that we are part of this country, and that we are suffering because of the economic distress in this country."

White House Press Secretary Ron Nessen said later that Ford remained opposed to federal assistance for New York, believing that if officials implemented stringent cost-cutting reforms, the city could regain its fiscal health. "This is not a natural disaster or an act of God," Nessen said. "It is a self-inflicted act by the people who have been running New York."

Congress cool to NY plea. Following the close shave with default Oct. 17, Gov. Carey and Mayor Beame intensified efforts to win Congressional passage of a loan guarantee. But their Congressional hearers were generally unsympathetic.

During a hearing before a subcommittee of the House Banking Committee Oct. 21, Rep. Richard Kelly (R, Fla.) accused Beame of "buying elections for years and years" by offering services the city could not afford. "You want the people of Zephyrhills [Fla.] to pay your bills," Kelly said.

Rep. Carroll Hubbard Jr. (D, Ky.) told Beame to raise money by charging tuition at the city university system and imposing tolls in city bridges. In western Kentucky, Hubbard said, "If we want to go to college and we can't pay tuition, we work. If we build bridges, we have tolls," he said.

Rep. Richard J. Schulze, a Pennsylvania Republican, reported that he had held workshops in his district on the New York City aid issue during the Congressional recess "and the response has been 30 to 40 to one against assisting New York."

Rep. Thomas B. Rees, a Los Angeles Democrat, supported Beame's request for a loan guarantee. "If we can bail out Lockheed and half the world," Rees said, "probably we can do something to help New York."

(Sen. Hubert H. Humphrey [D, Minn.] also linked the foreign aid question with the Administration's steadfast refusal to permit aid for New York City. Humphrey reacted in anger Oct. 24 to the Administration's request for $60 million in emergency aid to Zaire, which was encountering financial difficulties, including the possible default on loans, because of a drop in copper export earnings. Zaire should not get "one damn dime" until New York was helped, Humphrey said.)

Carey, who had served six terms in Congress before becoming governor, received a friendlier reception from the same subcommittee when he testified Oct. 21. However, opponents of the aid legislation, remained adamant in their views.

Hubbard told Carey that the "people of Kentucky are about as interested in New York City's financial dilemma as the people of New York are in Louisville's forced-busing problem."

Control Board approves austerity plan. The Emergency Financial Control Board Oct. 20 approved a three-year austerity plan for the city that would erase an expected $724 million deficit in the city's expenditure budget and require layoffs of "thousands" of municipal employes.

City officials had been directed by the state legislature to prepare a new budget and submit the plan to the control board as a condition for obtaining the $2.3 billion in state emergency aid voted earlier by the lawmakers.

Mayor Abraham Beame's fiscal plan, which was submitted Oct. 15, generally was accepted by the board members, but they added provisions for a monitoring system to measure the city's compliance with the cost-cutting plan.

The board also directed Mayor Beame to reduce the city's separate capital budget $390 million more than city officials had proposed, lowering the amount of total funds available for construction projects to $3.6 billion over the three-year period.

The austerity plan was described by one board member as, at best, a "Dunkirk" strategy, providing a large-scale retreat for the sake of the city's fiscal survival, the New York Times reported Oct. 21.

Few details of the plan were made public. Methods for implementing many of the budget reduction goals had not yet been determined, according to the Times.

The control board made several key assumptions in approving the new budget regarding the availability of credit and cash during the life of the austerity plan. "Success of the plan rests" on the availability of $6 billion in "federally-guaranteed, taxable notes bearing 8.5% annual interest," the board said. (Sentiment in Congress on the aid issue was running against the city. Rep. Thomas P. O'Neill Jr. [D, Mass.], majority leader of the House, warned Oct. 22 that "if there were a vote today, I would have to say that New York would not prevail.")

In approving the budget cutbacks, the board also assumed that the state would make advances of various state-aid funds in the 4th quarter of the city's fiscal year, ending March 31, 1976. In fiscal 1975, state advances to the city totaled $785 million, according to the board.

A chief aim in reducing the estimated $724 million deficit in the city's three-year expenditure budget was a drastic reduction in the city's payroll. Kenneth S. Axelson, the city's deputy mayor for financial affairs, said that "thousands" of layoffs would be required under the new plan in addition to the 21,000 city workers already dismissed as a result of the continuing fiscal crisis. The austerity budget also included a wage freeze for municipal workers at current levels for the duration of the fiscal plan.

(Axelson, a senior vice-president and director of the J. C. Penney department-store chain, had been named to the post by Mayor Beame Sept. 12.)

Ford Rejects Federal Rescue

'Bailout' barred. President Ford Oct. 29 vowed to veto any bill passed by Congress that would prevent New York City's default by providing a federal guarantee of funds for the city. Ford's remarks barring a federal "bailout" were delivered in a televised speech at the National Press Club in Washington.

Ford charged that the "so-called solution" to New York City's fiscal crisis offered in various Congressional aid bills was only a "mirage." Its chief beneficiaries would be the politicians and bankers responsible for New York City's financial disarray, Ford said. A bailout would set a dangerous precedent, promising "immediate rewards and eventual rescue for every other city that follows the tragic example of our largest city," he added.

As a "fair and sensible" alternative to the Congressional rescue plans, Ford asked Congress to modify the federal bankruptcy law so that the federal courts would have "sufficient authority to preside over an orderly reorganization of New York's financial affairs, should that become necessary."

President Ford did not flatly predict the city's default if federal aid were denied, but nearly all observers agreed that his stiffened opposition to rescue plans being developed in Congress made default a near certainty.

Ford said his bankruptcy plan would "provide a breathing space" for the city to make repayment arrangements with its creditors. While this compromise was being worked out in the court, the President said, "essential government functions" could continue. He promised that

"in the event of default, the federal government will work with the court to assure that police and fire and other essential services for the protection of life and property in New York are maintained."

Under questioning, Ford declined to disclose the "means or methods" the Administration would employ to maintain essential city services in the post-default period.

The legislation Ford said he would send to Congress would add a Chapter 16 to the federal Bankruptcy Act. As outlined by Ford, the proposed modification in federal law would allow the city, "with state approval," to file a petition with the U.S. District Court in New York under Chapter 16, stating that it was "unable to pay its debts as they mature." The city's petition would be "accompanied by a proposed way to work out an adjustment of its debt with its creditors," Ford said. The legislation also would require that New York City present a "program for placing the fiscal affairs of the city on a sound basis," he added.

The court would be authorized to accept jurisdiction of the case, and issue an automatic stay of creditors' suits, the President said. This injunction, he noted, would prevent the city's remaining operating funds from being tied up in lengthy litigation.

Ford said his proposed changes in the bankruptcy law would provide the city with a short-term source of funds while undergoing fiscal reorganization. The legislation would empower the court to authorize the sale of debt certificates, secured by future city revenue.

Ford was asked why investors would purchase these city securities when they had refused to buy tax-anticipation bonds issued on the city's behalf by the Municipal Assistance Corp. Ford replied that holders of debt certificates would have the "highest priority on any revenues that come into the city," including revenue sharing or other federal funds.

Ford discounted warnings by public officials and financial analysts that a default by New York City would be a "catastrophe for the U.S. and perhaps the world." A federal bailout of the city posed a "greater risk," Ford responded, providing a federal blank check that insured no long-run solution to the city's problems.

According to the President, default would not result in "large or long-standing repercussions" in the nation's financial markets, and the municipal bond market in particular. Credit markets, Ford said, "have already made substantial adjustments in anticipation of possible default." He added that New York City's record of "financial mismanagement" was "unique among municipalities throughout the U.S." State and local governments with "clean records of fiscal responsibility" would have no difficulty in borrowing money if New York City defaulted, Ford said.

Ford had harsh words for New York's politicians and bankers, who had intensified their lobbying efforts in Congress after the city had its closest escape from default Oct. 17.

Ford accused them of "fear mongering" and spreading "scare talk." Citing their lobbying efforts, Ford said attempts had been made to "frighten" the public and Congress into the "panicky support of patently bad policy." "The people of this country will not be stampeded," Ford said. "They will not panic when a few desperate New York officials and bankers try to scare New York's mortgage payments out of them."

Ford said these politicians and bankers, not city residents, would be the chief beneficiaries of the various "bailout" plans under consideration in Congress, all of which involved the federal guarantee of funds for New York City.

A federal guarantee, Ford said, would reduce rather than increase "the prospect that the city's budget will ever be balanced." A federal guarantee, he said, would allow New York City officials to "escape responsibility for their past follies" and to "be further excused from making the hard decisions required now to restore the city's fiscal integrity."

The "secondary beneficiaries" of a federal guarantee, according to Ford, would be the "large investors and financial institutions who purchased these securities anticipating a high rate of tax-free return." In short, Ford said, a federal guarantee of funds would "encourage the continuation of 'politics as usual' in New

York, which is precisely not the way to solve the problem."

Ford criticized New York City's high wages and pensions paid municipal workers, its tuition-free university system, its city-run hospital system, and welfare administration. According to Ford, New York City was suffering from an "insidious disease . . . brought on by years and years of higher spending, higher deficits, more inflation, and more borrowing to pay for higher spending, higher deficits, and so on and so on." "Larger and larger doses" of federal aid were not the proper treatment for New York's sickness, Ford said.

There was no "painless cure," he warned. New York city officials "must either increase revenues or cut expenditures or devise some combination that will bring them to a sound financial position." Why, Ford asked, should taxpayers "support advantages in New York that they have not been able to afford for their communities?"

Citing New York City's fiscal plight as a "lesson," Ford warned that the nation could not "go on spending more than we have, providing more benefits and services than we can pay for." "When that day of reckoning comes" for the federal government, Ford said, "who will bail out the United States?"

Text of Ford's speech:

New York City, where one out of every 25 Americans lives, through whose Golden Door untold millions have entered this land of liberty, faces a financial showdown.

The time has come for straight talk—to these eight million Americans and to the other 206 million Americans to whom I owe the duty of stating my convictions and my conclusions, and to you, whose job it is to carry them throughout the world as well as the United States.

The time has come to sort facts and figures from fiction and fear-mongering in this terribly complex situation. The time has come to say what solutions will work and which should be cast aside.

And the time has come for all Americans to consider how the problems of New York and the hard decisions they demand foreshadow and focus upon potential problems for all government—federal, state and local—problems which demand equally hard decisions for them.

One week ago New York City tottered on the brink of financial default which was deferred only at the eleventh hour.

The next day Mayor Beame testified here in Washington that the financial resources of the city and the state of New York were exhausted. Gov. Carey agreed.

They said, it's now up to Washington. And unless the federal government intervenes, New York City within a short time will no longer be able to pay its bills.

The message was clear: responsibility for New York City's financial problems is being left on the front doorstep of the federal government—unwanted and abandoned by its real parents.

Many explanations have been offered about what led New York City deeper and deeper into this quagmire.

Some contend it was long-range economic factors such as the flight to the suburbs of the city's more affluent citizens, the migration to the city of poorer people, and the departure of industry.

Others argued that the big metropolitan city has become obsolescent, that decay and pollution have brought a deterioration in the quality of urban life, and New York's downfall could not be prevented.

Let's face one simple fact: most other cities in America have faced these very same challenges, and they are still financially healthy today. They have not been luckier than New York; they simply have been better managed.

There is an old saying: "The harder you try, the luckier you get." And I kind of like that definition of "luck."

During the last decade, the officials of New York City have allowed its budget to triple. No city can expect to remain solvent if it allows its expenses to increase by an average of 12% every year, while its tax revenues are increasing by only 4%-5% per year.

As Al Smith, a great Governor of New York who came from the sidewalks of New York City, used to say: "Let's look at the record."

The record shows that New York City's wages and salaries are the highest in the United States. A sanitation worker with three year's experience now receives a base salary of nearly $15,000 a year. Fringe benefits and retirement costs average more than 50% of base pay. There are four-week paid vacations and unlimited sick leave after only one year on the job.

The record shows that in most cities, municipal employees have to pay 50% or more of the cost of their pensions. New York City is the only major city in the country that picks up the entire burden.

The record shows that when New York's municipal employes retire they often retire much earlier than in most cities and at pensions considerably higher than sound retirement plans permit.

The record shows New York City has 18 municipal hospitals; yet, on an average day, 25% of the hospital beds are empty. Meanwhile, the city spends millions more to pay the hospital expenses of those who use private hospitals.

The record shows New York City operates one of the largest universities in the world, free of tuition for any high school graduate, rich or poor, who wants to attend.

As for New York's much-discussed welfare burden, the record shows more than one current welfare recipient in 10 may be legally ineligible for welfare assistance.

Certainly I do not blame all the good people of New York City for their generous instincts or for their present plight. I do blame those who have misled the people of New York about the inevitable consequences of what they are doing or were doing over the last 10 years.

The consequences have been:

■ A steady stream of unbalanced budgets.

■ Massive growth in the city's debt.

■ Extraordinary increases in public employe contracts.

■ And total disregard of independent experts who warned again and again that the city was courting disaster.

There can be no doubt where the real responsibility lies. And when New York City now asks the rest of the country to guarantee its bills, it can be no surprise than many other Americans ask why.

Why, they ask, should they support advantages in New York that they have not been able to afford for their own communities?

Why, they ask, should all the working people of this country be forced to rescue those who bankrolled New York City's policies for so long—the large investors and big banks?

In my judgment, no one has yet given these questions a satisfactory answer.

Instead, Americans are being told that unless the rest of the country bails out New York, there will be catastrophe for the United States and perhaps for the world.

Is this scare story true?

Of course there are risks that default could cause temporary fluctuations in the financial markets. But these markets have already made a substantial adjustment in anticipation of a possible default by New York City.

Claims are made that because of New York City's troubles, other municipalities will have grave difficulty selling their bonds. I know that this troubles many thoughtful citizens.

But, the New York City record of bad financial management is unique among municipalities throughout the United States. Other communities have a solid reputation for living within their means. In recent days and weeks, other local governments have gone to investors with clean records of fiscal responsibility and have had no difficulty raising funds.

The greater risk is that any attempt to provide a federal blank check for the leaders of New York City would insure that no long-run solution to the city's problems will ever occur.

I can understand the concern of many citizens in New York and elsewhere. I understand because I'm also concerned.

What I cannot understand—and what nobody should condone—is the blatant attempt in some quarters to frighten the American people and their representatives in Congress into panicky support of patently bad policy. The people of this country will not be stampeded; they will not panic when a few desperate New York officials and bankers try to scare New York's mortgage payments out of them.

We've heard enough scare talk.

What we need now is a calm, rational decision as to what is the right solution—the solution that is best for the people of New York and best for all Americans.

To be effective, the right solution must meet three basic tests:

■ It must maintain essential public services for the people of New York City. It must protect the innocent victims of this tragedy. There must be policemen on the beat, firemen in the station, nurses in the emergency wards.

■ Second, the solution must assure that New York City can and will achieve and maintain a balanced budget in the years ahead.

■ And third, the right solution must guarantee that neither New York City nor any other American city ever becomes a ward of the federal government.

Let me digress a minute to remind you that under

our constitutional system, both the cities and the federal government were the creatures of the states. The states delegated certain of their sovereign powers—the power to tax, police powers and the like—to local units of self-government. And they can take these rowers back if they are abused.

The states also relinquished certain sovereign powers to the federal government—some altogether and some to be shared. In return the federal government has certain obligations to the states.

I see a serious threat to the legal relationships among our federal, state and local governments in any Congressional action which could lead to disruption of this traditional balance. Our largest city is no different in this respect than our smallest town. If Mayor Beame doesn't want Gov. Carey to run his city, does he want the President of the United States to be acting Mayor of New York City?

What is the solution to New York's dilemma? There are at least eight different proposals under consideration by the Congress intended to prevent default. They are all variations of one basic theme: that the federal government should, or would, guarantee the availability of the funds to New York City.

I can tell you—and tell you now—that I am prepared to veto any bill that has as its purpose a federal bailout of New York City to prevent a default.

I am fundamentally opposed to this so-called solution, and I'll tell you why.

Basically, it's a mirage. By giving a federal guarantee we would be reducing rather than increasing the prospect that the city's budget will ever be balanced. New York City's officials have proved in the past that they will not face up to the city's massive network of pressure groups as long as any other alternative is available. If they can scare the whole country into providing that alternative now, why shouldn't they be confident they can scare us again into providing it three years from now? In short, it encourages the continuation of "politics as usual" in New York—which is precisely not the way to solve the problem.

Such a step would set a terrible precedent for the rest of the nation. It would promise immediate rewards and eventual rescue to every other city that follows the tragic example of our largest city. What restraint would be left on the spending of other local and state governments once it becomes clear that there is a federal rescue squad that will always arrive in the nick of time?

Finally, we must all recognize who the primary beneficiaries of a federal guarantee program would be. The beneficiaries would not be those who live and work in New York City because the really essential public services must and will continue.

The primary beneficiary would be the New York officials who would thus escape responsibility for their past folly and be further excused from making the hard decisions required now to restore the city's fiscal integrity.

The secondary beneficiary would be the large investors and financial institutions who purchased these securities anticipating a high rate of tax-free return.

Does this mean there is no solution? Not at all. There is a fair and sensible way to resolve this issue, and this is the way to do it.

If the city is unable to act to provide a means of meeting its obligations, a new law is required to assure an orderly and fair means of handling the situation.

As you know, the Constitution empowers the Congress to enact uniform bankruptcy laws. Therefore, I will submit to the Congress special legislation providing the federal courts with sufficient authority to preside over an orderly reorganization of New York City's financial affairs—should that become necessary.

How would this work? The city, with state approval, would file a petition with the federal district court in New York under a proposed new Chapter XVI of the Bankruptcy Act. The petition would state that New York City is unable to pay its debts as they mature and would be accompanied by a proposed way to work out an adjustment of its debts with its creditors.

The federal court would then be authorized to accept jurisdiction of the case. There would be an automatic stay of suits by creditors so that the essential functions of the city would not be disrupted.

It would provide a breathing space for an orderly plan to be developed so that the city could work out arrangements with its creditors.

While New York City works out a compromise with its creditors the essential governmental functions of the city would continue.

In the event of default, the federal government will work with the court to assure that police and fire and other essential services for the protection of life and property in New York are maintained.

The proposed legislation will include provision that as a condition of New York City petitioning the court, the city must not only file a good faith plan for payments to its creditors but must also present a program for placing the fiscal affairs of the city on a sound basis.

In order to meet the short-term needs of New York City the court would be empowered to authorize debt certificates which would be paid out of future revenues ahead of other creditors.

Thus, the legislation I am proposing will do three essential things.

First, it will prevent, in the event of default, all New York City funds from being tied up in lawsuits.

Second, it will provide the conditions for an orderly plan to be developed for payments to New York City's creditors over the long term.

Third, it will provide a way for new borrowing to be secured by pledging future revenues.

I don't want anybody misled. This proposed legislation will not, by itself, put the affairs of New York City in order. Some hard measures must be taken by the officials of New York City and New York State. They must either increase revenues or cut expenditures or devise some combination that will bring them to a sound financial position. Careful examination has convinced me that these measures are neither beyond the realm of possibility nor beyond the demands of reason. If they are taken, New York City will, with the assistance of the legislation I am proposing, be able to restore itself as a fully solvent operation.

To summarize, the approach I am recommending is this: if New York fails to act in its own behalf, orderly proceedings would then be supervised by a federal court.

The ones who would be most affected by this course of action would be those who are now fighting, tooth and nail to protect their authority and to protect their investments: New York City's officials and the city's creditors. The creditors will not be wiped out; how much they will be hurt will depend upon the future conduct of the city's leaders.

For the people of New York, this plan will mean that essential services will continue. There may be some temporary inconveniences, but that will be true of any solution that is adopted.

For the financial community, the default may bring some temporary difficulties but the repercussions should not be large or long-standing.

Finally, for the people of the United States, this

means that they will not be asked to assume a burden that is not of their own making and should not become their responsibility. This is a fair and sensible way to proceed.

There is a profound lesson for all Americans in the financial experience of our biggest and our richest city.

Though we are the richest nation, the richest nation in the world, there is a practical limit to our public bounty, just as there is to New York City's.

Other cities, other states as well as the federal government are not immune to the insidious disease from which New York is suffering. This sickness is brought on by years and years of higher spending, higher deficits, more inflation and more borrowing to pay for higher spending, higher deficits and so on and so on and so on. It's a progressive disease and there is no painless cure.

Those who have been treating New York's financial sickness have been prescribing larger and larger doses of the same political stimulants that has proved so popular and successful in Washington for so many years.

None of us can point a completely guiltless finger at New York City. None of us should now derive comfort or pleasure from New York's anguish. But neither can we let that contagion spread.

As we work with the wonderful people of New York to overcome their difficulties—and they will—we must never forget what brought this great center of human civilization to the brink.

If we go on spending more than we have, providing more benefits and more services than we can pay for, then a day of reckoning will come to Washington and the whole country just as it has to New York City.

An so, let me conclude with one question of my own:

When that day of reckoning comes, who will bail out the United States of America?

Reaction to Ford's speech—New York's leading Democratic officials as well as some Republican politicians denounced President Ford's proposals for dealing with New York City's fiscal crisis. Eight prominent bankers and financial executives also criticized the President's statements. Ford was commended by Congressional opponents of aid for New York City.

Gov. Hugh Carey complained that the "Ford formula deliberately unravels every step we've taken to solve our own problems." The proposed bankruptcy law, Carey said, would destroy investor confidence. "Who would risk his funds knowing that the government could avoid repayment simply by slipping into bankruptcy?" Carey asked.

Carey also contended that Ford was playing politics with New York's problems. The President's "simplistic, self-defeating plan" was "designed more to appease the Republican Party's Reagan wing than to help New Yorkers." "Evidently when he speaks of the conduct of

past officials in New York State," Carey added, Ford was "unmindful" of Vice President Nelson Rockefeller, who was governor of New York from 1959–73.

Mayor Beame said Ford's statement represented a "default of Presidential leadership."

Carey later called for a citywide demonstration to reply to Ford and focus the city's appeal for federal aid. Declaring he would "fight back," Carey told an AFL-CIO gathering in upstate New York Oct. 30 that "it isn't fair when the President of the United States hauls off and kicks the people of the city of New York in the groin."

Carey delivered a statewide radio-TV address Nov. 1 as a rebuttal to Ford. Carey denied that New York sought a "bailout" from the federal government. "The bill we seek," Carey said, "will impose on New York City the obligation to pay its bills in full, and to put its fiscal house in order."

Carey refuted Ford's claim that federal rescue legislation for the city would prove costly to taxpayers. "It is the Ford bankruptcy plan that would cost the cities, states and taxpayers of this nation billions of dollars," Carey countered.

Listing the "real costs" of bankruptcy to the nation's taxpayers, Carey said the threat of default already had made municipal borrowing more expensive. "That will be the wave of the future if New York defaults," he warned.

If the city defaulted, Carey continued, the holders of the city's $14 billion in outstanding debt would lose $6 billion in the value of those notes and bonds, a figure he said was "conservative." "That money will be written off on tax returns," Carey said, "and that means $2 billion less in federal tax payments."

Another "real cost" of bankruptcy, Carey said, would be the expense needed to maintain "essential city services" while the city was undergoing court reorganization. "The only source for that money is the federal treasury," he said, adding "When businesses owed money by New York City go under—businesses located in communities such as Grand Rapids, Mich.—who will pay the cost of unemployment and welfare?"

According to Carey, the fourth cost of Ford's proposal would be the "tremors and collapses in local governments around

America, including agencies of New York State." "It is the people of those localities who will pay to pick up those pieces," he said. "That is why the U.S. Conference of Mayors, the National League of Cities, the National Association of Counties, and the County and Municipal Financial Officers Association all overwhelmingly support local guarantees," he said.

Carey conceded that "some of what Mr. Ford said was exactly right. There is a history of reckless fiscal policy in New York going back years, perhaps decades." But Carey said the blame for fiscal irresponsibility could be shared by many persons:

- "City officials and interest groups;
- "Banks that did not ask the hard questions;
- "A state legislature and hand-picked Vice President that specifically authorized every fringe and pension benefit and every unwise borrowing Mr. Ford now attacks so righteously;
- "And presidents who diverted tens of billions of dollars to foreign dictatorships and senseless war, and who plunged our economy into its worst crisis in 40 years."

"Contrary to the deliberate impression left by Mr. Ford," Carey said, "New York has imposed on itself painful and unprecedented budget-cutting. The state has taken the financial power out of the city's hand." Because of a bipartisan effort in the state legislature, Carey said, "We have shaped a control board run by state officials and business people who are determined to rebuild fiscal integrity."

"That board has ordered reform of the city's books. It's presided over the cutting of 30,000 jobs from the city's payroll—and within three years, that payroll must be cut by 70,000 jobs. The transit and commuter fare's been raised to one of the highest of any city. Wages have been frozen for every city worker. The city university's budget has been cut by $30 million—the equivalent of imposing tuition. The capital budget's been reduced $800 million, and all housing programs have been suspended."

Carey noted that New Yorkers' appeal for federal assistance faced a "skeptical, hostile" Congress and public. He alluded to the antagonism that New York City aroused throughout the country, sentiment that many analysts believed clouded the issue of default and federal aid.

"Our city," he said, "is often abrasive and arrogant, sometimes cold and unfeeling, always challenging. For a lot of reasons, it has incurred the scorn of some of our countrymen; because of our pace and tone of voice, because of the colors of our skins and the accents in which we speak, and our tradition as a magnet for the disaffected, the dispossessed.

"What we're hoping to buy" from Congress, Carey said, "is time to finish the job we've started. "We don't want to be bailed out. We don't want to be a ward of the federal government."

"I ask Mr. Ford not to work against us to make New York bankrupt," Carey said. "I cannot believe that the spector of temporary political gain will lead him into driving a city into bankruptcy and risking the loss of taxpayers' dollars." "If the financial structure of government is shaken," Carey added, "Mr. Ford will be accountable to all the people."

Mayor Beame reiterated many of Carey's points in an address Nov. 5 before the National Press Club in Washington. "New York asks nothing of the American taxpayer except the opportunity to set its fiscal house in order," Beame said in his appeal for passage of a federal loan guarantee by Congress.

Beame contended that there were "ample precedents" for such a request in the current federal budget where $200 billion in guarantees covered "everything from the Washington Metro [subway system] to the construction of a chemical plant in Yugoslavia."

Noting that federal taxes generated by New York City totaled $19 billion, while all forms of federal spending in the city totaled $8 billion, Beame said the city wanted "to remain a giver, not a getter."

Beame warned that if New York defaulted, "there will be nothing abstract" about its impact on the rest of the nation.

"A default by the city would jeopardize payment on the more than $1 billion in goods and services contracted for by the city with firms in all parts of the nation. Heavy equipment from Chicago, Fort Wayne and Springfield, Ohio; blankets from Alabama; moving stairs from Indiana; electronic gear from Florida and Illinois; sanitary equipment from Virginia and Wisconsin; construction machinery from Baton Route; and chemicals from Maryland, and Delaware—all these areas will be affected.

"In addition, fully 30% of the pension checks for retired city employees are mailed to addresses outside New York City. They represent an annual contribution of $180 million to the economy of communities beyond the city limits. Florida residents alone receive $23 million annually in New York City pension checks.

"Contrary to the President's assertion that New York officials and banks stand to lose the most from a default, the Bank of America cited a survey which estimated that two-thirds of the city's securities are held by 160,000 individual investors around the country who could be financially crippled by a default.

Beame was especially critical of the tone of Ford's remarks about New York City's fiscal crisis, accusing the President of adopting a simplistic, "bumper-sticker philosophy." "He has used the city of New York as a foil for political slogans from Belgrade [Yugoslavia] to San Francisco and back. This has triggered hatred, disunity, and confusion," Beame said. (On a state visit to Yugoslavia in early August, Ford had made a derisive comment to the mayor of Belgrade about New York City officials' handling of financial affairs.)

Beame contrasted Ford's statement about New York with a statement made in April when the President said: "Our purpose is not to point the finger of blame; but to build upon our many successes; to repair damage where we find it; to recover our balance; to move ahead as a united people."

Beame noted that "generous statement was made when Saigon—not New York— was threatened with collapse, and the President was seeking a billion dollars from Congress in emergency aid. How can he explain to millions of Americans who live in New York why he will not raise his voice with equal concern for their city?"

Carey took his appeal for aid to the West Coast. He held a news conference in Los Angeles Nov. 7 and also met with a business group in San Francisco. Three New York Congressmen also were carrying the city's message to Chicago, Los Angeles, and Denver, the New York Times reported Nov. 6.

Mayor William D. Schaefer (D) of Baltimore was critical of President Ford's proposal that the city reorganize its fiscal situation in bankruptcy court. Commenting Oct. 30, Schaefer said, "This brinkmanship by the President is unwise." Although Baltimore projected a budget surplus because of stringent cost-cutting, Schaefer said, "with the accumulating problems of major cities, including the burden of caring for the aged and the

poor, New York's emergency could happen to anybody, and city."

Sen. John G. Tower (R, Tex.) supported Ford's position saying, "It would be wrong to bail out the city. To do so would encourage financial irresponsibility."

Several members of Congress reported that their constituents were vehemently opposed to aid for New York City, the Times reported Oct. 29. House Speaker Carl Albert (D, Okla.), who favored legislation to "save" the city, said his mail was running 8-to-1 against aiding the city. Rep. Charles A. Thone (R, Neb.) said that at a recent gathering of 60 Nebraskans visiting their state's Congressional delegation, none favored "bailing out New York."

The eight bankers and financial executives who criticized Ford's plan were part of a group of 10, representing a wide cross section of the financial community, who were queried by the New York Times Oct. 30. An official of Bankers Trust Co. said that "contrary to what the President said, default is a very serious matter and should be avoided." However, Walter B. Wriston, chairman of First National City Corp., termed Ford's bankruptcy proposal a "responsible fall-back position."

The Times of London warned Oct. 30 that the effects of default "on the financial systems of the world and on the recovery of the American economy could be of the most serious kind." In an editorial entitled, "Whom the Gods Wish to Destroy," the newspaper described President Ford's decision barring federal aid to the city as an "act of monumental folly." "With his personal and political roots in a community like Grand Rapids, Mich., the President perhaps is not able to comprehend the impact which the default of New York will have," the editorial said.

Two newspapers in Charleston, S.C., the News-Courier and the Evening Post, announced that of their 7,867 readers responding to a poll about helping New York City, 7,604 opposed federal aid, the Times reported.

But three polls taken shortly after Ford's speech indicated that a majority of those surveyed disagreed with Ford and supported federal aid for New York City. Analysts believed Ford's hard-line speech may have been the catalyst in changing public opinion because an earlier survey, made prior to Ford's speech, indicated that opponents of aid outnumbered supporters.

According to a Gallup poll, conducted Oct. 17–20 in 300 localities across the nation, 49% of those surveyed opposed making federal funds available "to help New York City get out of its financial difficulties"; 42% expressed support for the idea and 9% had no opinion. (The margin of error on this poll, published Nov. 1, was 3% either way.) Sympathy for the city was highest among Easterners, big-city residents, professional and business persons, young adults, and Democrats.

When asked the "cause of New York City's overspending," 39% said "mismanagement" and 18% cited the city's heavy welfare burden; 77% of the 1,358 adults questioned by Gallup pollsters said they had been following the New York City story.

A later poll by the New York Times and CBS News, published Nov. 5, indicated a change in public attitudes. Of the 778 persons interviewed Nov. 1–2 in the nationwide telephone survey, 55% favored federal funds for New York City; 33% said no; and 12% had no opinion. (This poll had a 4% margin of error.)

More than 68% of those surveyed said New York City's problems were similar to other cities. By a margin of 2 to 1, those responding also said default would have an "important effect" on the national economy—67% of this group favored federal aid for the city. (Eighty per cent of those rejecting the national importance of default also rejected federal aid for the city.)

Of those queried about about Ford's policy on New York City, 39% had no opinion and the remainder were equally divided between approval and disapproval; more specifically, 34% said Ford was exercising "good financial judgment" and 33% felt he was "playing politics" with the aid issue.

A Harris poll, conducted Nov. 2–4 and published Nov. 6, found that 69% of the 1,549 persons surveyed favored federal loan guarantees for the city if New York officials balanced the city budget and if federal support did not cost taxpayers

outside of the city any money; 18% opposed federal assistance.

By a wide margin, 82% to 18%, those responding believed "New York City has been at fault for not living within its means, spending more money than it takes in." Also by a large margin, those surveyed felt New York City was only the first of many cities that would eventually face financial troubles.

An NBC News poll, also conducted after the President's speech and published Nov. 6, showed similar findings: of the 1,066 persons surveyed across the country, 52% favored federal action to help New York City; 69% said default would hurt the economy (19% saw no impact); and 51% believed New Yorkers were victims of circumstances (35% thought the city had brought on its own problems and 13% were uncertain).

Ford scores N.Y. on political tour.
President Ford spoke against a federal bailout of New York City during political visits to Los Angeles, San Francisco and Milwaukee Oct. 29–30. The President addressed Republican fund-raising events in each city.

Championing fiscal prudence, Ford cautioned that the federal budget must be balanced if the nation was to avoid "what is happening in New York City," as he put it in Los Angeles Oct. 29. "The only thing wrong with this country," he said, "is that too many things have gotten out of balance—including too many budgets."

In a television interview in Los Angeles the next day, Ford blamed New York's fiscal crisis on years of "mismanagement by public officials." But he sought to exonerate from blame Vice President Nelson A. Rockefeller, who was governor of New York from 1959 to 1973. "There is no history of the state being involved" in the city's fiscal problems, he said, and the primary responsibility for the crisis rested with "locally elected officials."

The President rejected in the interview suggestions that some persons of modest means would be among those who would suffer most from a default of the city. Ford said the major investors were bankers who "took a gamble on a tax-free investment" and who "should have known that the circumstances weren't as good as they might have been told they were." Ford said the small investors would not lose their money "if the city is properly led."

He said there was not enough support in Congress to override a veto of legislation to aid the city prior to default. "The only choice is my proposal," he observed. In his San Francisco appearance Oct. 30, Ford erroneously gave the city credit for having rebuilt after the 1906 earthquake from its own resources. "The reconstruction of San Francisco was not a federal bailout," he asserted. "It was a local undertaking." Actually, San Francisco received substantial federal financial aid at the time and a large part of the financing of reconstruction came from New York City banks.

In Milwaukee later Oct. 30, Ford told his fellow Republicans he would "never allow the doors of the United States Treasury to be flung open to every city with a note in its pocket."

Default called national threat. Some observers held that a default by New York City would threaten the national economy. In an analysis released Nov. 1 of New York City's fiscal plight, the Joint Economic Committee of Congress warned that default could impair the national recovery from recession by increasing the number of jobless workers by 300,000 and reducing the "real" gross national product 1% over the 12-month period ending in December 1976.

According to the study, default also would make bank lending practices more conservative, raise all interest rates, and because of these increased borrowing costs, force a cutback in state and local government spending, which accounted for 15% of the total gross national product.

The study was critical of New York City's failure to recognize and respond adequately to the financial dilemma posed by rising expenditures and declining revenues. But the report also disagreed with President Ford's assertion that there were sufficient resources in the city and state to prevent bankruptcy.

The federal government had three choices, according to the report: "doing nothing, helping New York after default, and preventing one."

Nonintervention was not a "realistically viable option," the study contended, because the post-default consequences of trying to match spending levels with existing revenue were too grave. "Payrolls will be missed, massive layoffs will be required, and public assistance checks would have to be stopped," the report warned.

A default-with-aid plan, providing federal loan guarantees or a direct loan, possibly could avert serious cutbacks in essential city services, the study said. The report added, however, that there were legal barriers to the sale of new securities by recently bankrupt issuers, and that actual default might affect the entire municipal bond market.

Federal efforts to avert bankruptcy also had drawbacks, the study said. Holders of city debt issues would avoid the possibly adverse consequences of default, but city residents would bear the entire burden of budget-cutting measures. A rescue plan also "could weaken the resolve of city and state officials to make tough decisions" needed to resolve fiscal problems, the study added.

The report made no explicit recommendations but said "the central issue that Congress must examine is whether to provide a source of credit before or after default."

Business leaders and bankers fear default—The nation's largest commercial bank, California's Bank of America, declared Nov. 1 that "default, in the national interest, should be averted. New York would be punished by it surely, but the punishment cannot be localized. The entire nation would suffer. And that price is too high to pay for making New York City an object lesson in municipal profligacy."

Commenting on Ford's proposal that New York City declare bankruptcy, the bank said that allowing default to occur would prove more costly to taxpayers than preventing default from happening.

"The burden on the federal government through emergency loans, increased welfare payments, and other support services will swell correspondingly—weakening and further inflating the federal deficit," the bank said.

The bank also challenged Ford's assertion that a chief beneficiary of a federal "bailout" of New York City would be the banks and other large investors holding city securities. According to the Bank of America, two-thirds ($4.9 billion) of the city's outstanding bonds were held by 160,000 small investors and individuals. (According to the Federal Reserve, commercial banks held about $3 billion of the city's bonds.)

Charles F. Luce, chairman of New York City's Consolidated Edison Co., sent a telegram to President Ford Nov. 4, warning that the utility also would collapse if the city defaulted. Luce said the utility "could not survive for long if it continued to serve a bankrupt city, and continued to pay taxes but was not itself paid by the city."

"We should not be placed in a position where our choices are either to disconnect essential utility service to the city and state, or to withhold taxes we annually pay the city and state, or to slip ourselves into insolvency," Luce said.

Luce sent the telegram asking Ford to reconsider his promised veto of aid legislation after Federal Reserve Chairman Arthur Burns told the Senate Banking Committee Nov. 4 that a city default would not set off a chain reaction.

Crisis drives up municipal bond costs. States and cities could be forced to pay $130 million–$180 million more a year in interest rates on long-term municipal securities* because of New York City's fiscal crisis and the resulting loss of investor confidence in municipal bonds, according to a study released Nov. 7.

The report, prepared by two experts in municipal financing, Ronald W. Forbes and John E. Peterson, concluded that interest costs to state and local governments had risen dramatically since July, when the dimensions of New York City's fiscal plight began to be publicized. At the same time, the study noted, the Municipal Assistance Corp., a state agency created to refinance New York City's burgeoning debt, first encountered difficulties in selling bonds on the city's behalf.

If the "present deteriorated condition of investor confidence" continued, the study said, annual borrowing costs on long-term debt issued by state and local governments could climb to $180 million. The report added that since bonds currently on the market would be outstanding for many years, the long-term impact of New York City's crisis could raise interest rates $800 million–$1.5 billion. (If MAC-issued bonds were included in these calculations, the study said, total "lifetime costs" could swell $1.1 billion–$1.8 billion.)

The loss of investor confidence also had affected short-term borrowing rates, according to the study. Added interest costs for these municipal securities ranged from $200 million–$300 million.

The study found that weakness in the municipal bond market, caused by New York City's credit problems, was not evenly distributed among state and local governments. The mid-Atlantic region was hardest hit by the loss of investor confidence; its added borrowing costs were estimated at .55%. The North Central region, however, was paying only about .08% more in interest.

Examples cited in the report were Pennsylvania, whose bond interest costs had climbed $8.2 million, and North Dakota, whose added interest costs had risen $25,-000. (In computing these increases in debt service, the states' borrowing costs for the 3rd quarter were measured against borrowing costs in the previous six quarters. The increase then was projected to show the average annual increase in debt service over the life of bonds now on the market.)

The impact of New York City's fiscal crisis was not limited to higher interest rates, the report added. More than $1.2 billion in long-term borrowing by states and localities had been canceled or postponed since May because governments had been unable to market their bonds or had refused to pay the added borrowing costs.

In a report Oct. 29 on the national impact of New York City's financial troubles, the Los Angeles Times cited several instances of municipal bond postponements. In Buffalo, the city controller reported that the "entire 1975–1976 capital program had been put right on the back burner until the bond market settles down." Spokesmen for Illinois and Portland, Ore. also reported postponement of

_____
*In the parlance of bond trading, the term "municipal securities" covered indebtedness bonds issued by all local governments—state, county, city, etc.—as well as by local authorities.

bond issues and expressed concern about the financing delay.

Ford Ends Opposition to Federal Aid for City

Ford proposes loan program. President Ford Nov. 26 ended his opposition to federal aid for New York City and asked Congress to approve legislation making up to $2.3 billion in direct federal loans available to the city annually. Ford announced his decision during a nationally televised press conference from the White House.

Ford denied that his support for federal aid to the city marked a reversal of his opposition to a federal "bailout" of the city. Instead, he said, state and city officials had changed their positions.

Ford contended that only after he "made it clear that New York would have to solve its fundamental financial problems without the help of the federal taxpayers has there been a concerted effort to put the finances of the city and the state on a sound basis."

Under such pressure, Ford said, state and city officials now were beginning to make the "tough decisions that the facts of the situation require." Proof of this change in attitude, Ford said, and crucial to his support for federal aid, was the recent adoption of a rigorous "self-help" plan by New York leaders.

As outlined by Ford, the plan consisted of "meaningful spending cuts" in the operation of the city; imposition of $200 million in new taxes; a moratorium on redemption of city notes and a reduction in interest payments to city noteholders; a delay in collection of outstanding loans to the city by banks and their acceptance of reduced interest charges; reform of municipal-union pension plans, including members' contributions to their retirement funds; and additional loans to the city from the city pension system.

New York's self-help program had two aims, Ford said: "to provide financing and to bring the city's budget into balance by the fiscal year beginning July 1, 1977." Prior to adoption of the plan, Ford said, New York City had anticipated a deficit of nearly $4 billion in its operating budget for the current fiscal year.

The President "commended" state and city leaders for their efforts to achieve a balanced budget. Through these actions, Ford said, "New York has bailed itself out."

However, he added, "in the interim," while these steps were being taken to restore the city's fiscal integrity and credibility with investors, New York City would "lack enough funds to cover its day-to-day operating expenses."

Most cities, he explained, paid their daily operating expenses by borrowing funds in anticipation of receiving tax revenues in the spring. Since the credit market currently was closed to New York City, its cash flow problems were intense. Therefore, Ford said, he had decided "it was necessary to give short-term financing on a seasonal basis" to insure the continuation of essential services to city residents.

Ford asked Congress to enact legislation providing New York State with a line of credit through fiscal 1978 so that the city could borrow up to $2.3 billion annually. Under terms of the proposed legislation, the funds would be loaned from July through March, and repaid from April through May.

The aid package included "stringent conditions," Ford said. Repayment of all federal loans outstanding would be required at the end of each year. Ford vowed to terminate the loan program if New York City failed to meet its debt obligations to the federal government.

Ford said the money would be loaned "at a rate no less than" the rate paid by the federal government in borrowing money on the open market. (According to the White House, the government currently paid about 7%.) Ford added that the secretary of the Treasury, who would administer New York's loan program, would have the option to impose an additional 1% interest charge.

For these reasons, Ford contended that the loan program would entail "no cost" to other U.S. taxpayers. He also denied that the loans to New York City were risky, saying the legislation would include a lien providing the federal government with a priority claim against other creditors in the event New York City failed to meet its debt obligations. (Ford also urged

Congress to amend federal bankruptcy laws "so that if the New York plan fails, there will be an orderly procedure available" to reorganize the city's debt.)

Ford said he preferred offering the city a loan rather than loan guarantees, as requested by the state and city officials, because a loan "was a much cleaner transaction," giving the government "better control" than with loan guarantees.

Ford was asked about the potential political liabilities involved in being identified with the "onerous" tax burden voted by the state legislature. Although he said he "approved" of the financial plan enacted in Albany, Ford declined to take responsibility for the program. "Gov. Carey has taken full responsibility for the total package," Ford said, adding that it was a "courageous stand."

Text of Ford's statement:

Since early this year, and particularly in the last few weeks, the leaders of New York State and of New York City have been working to overcome the financial difficulties of the city, which as the result of many years of unsound fiscal practices, unbalanced budgets and increased borrowing threaten to bring about municipal bankruptcy of an unprecedented magnitude.

As you know, I have been steadfastly opposed to any federal help for New York City which would permit them to avoid responsibility for managing their own affairs. I will not allow the taxpayers of other states and cities to pay the price of New York's past political errors. It is important to all of us that the fiscal integrity of New York City be restored and that the personal security of eight million Americans in New York City be fully assured.

It has always been my hope that the leaders of New York, when the chips were down, face up to their responsibilities and take the tough decisions that the facts of the situation require. That is still my hope. And I must say that it is much, much closer to reality today than it was last spring. I have quite frankly been surprised that they have come as far as they have. I doubted that they would act unless ordered to do so by a federal court.

Only in the last month, after I made it clear that New York would have to solve its fundamental financial problems without the help of the federal taxpayer, has there been a concerted effort to put the finances of the city and the state on a sound basis. They have today informed me of the specifics of New York's self-help program.

This includes meaningful spending cuts have been approved to reduce the cost of running the city. Two, more than $200 million in new taxes have been voted. Three, payment to the city's noteholders will be postponed and interest payments will be reduced through the passage of legislation by New York State. Four, banks and other large institutions have agreed to wait to collect on their loans and to accept lower interest rates. Five, for the first time in years members of municipal unions will be required to bear part of the cost of pension contributions and other reforms will be made in union pension plans. Six, the city pension

system is to provide additional loans up to $2.5 billion to the city. All of these steps—adding up to $4 billion—are part of an effort to provide financing and to bring the city's budget into balance by the fiscal year beginning July 1, 1977.

Only a few months ago, we were told that all of these reforms were impossible and could not be accomplished by New York alone. Today they are being done.

This is a realistic program. I want to commend all of those involved in New York City and New York State for their constructive efforts to date. I have been closely watching their progress in meeting their problem. However, in the next few months New York will lack enough funds to cover its day-to-day operating expenses.

This problem is caused by the city having to pay its bills on a daily basis throughout the year; while the bulk of its revenues are received during spring. Most cities are able to borrow short-term funds to cover these needs, traditionally repaying them within their fiscal year.

Because the private credit market may remain closed to them, representatives of New York have informed me and my Administration that they have acted in good faith, but they still need to borrow money on a short-term basis for a period of time each of the next two years in order to provide essential services to the eight million Americans who live in the nation's largest city.

Therefore, I have decided to ask the Congress when it returns from recess for authority to provide a temporary line of credit to the State of New York to enable it to supply seasonal financing of essential services for the people of New York City.

There will be stringent conditions.

Funds would be loaned to the state on a seasonal basis normally from July through March to be repaid with interest in April, May and June when the bulk of the city's revenues comes in.

All federal loans will be repaid in full at the end of each year. There will be no cost to the rest of the taxpayers of the United States.

This is only the beginning of New York's recovery process, and not the end. New York officials must continue to accept primary responsibility. There must be no misunderstanding of my position. If local parties fail to carry out their plan, I am prepared to stop even the seasonal federal assistance. I again ask the Congress promptly to amend the federal bankruptcy laws so that if the New York plan fails, there will be an orderly procedure available.

A fundamental issue is involved here; sound fiscal management is imperative of self-government. I trust we have all learned the hard lesson that no individual, no family, no business, no city, no state and no nation, can go on indefinitely spending more money than it takes in.

As we count our Thanksgiving blessings, we recall that Americans have always believed in helping those who help themselves. New York has finally taken the tough decision it had to take to help itself. In making the required sacrifices, the people of New York have earned the encouragement of the rest of the country.

Reaction to Ford announcement—Gov. Carey hailed the President's statement, saying his proposed legislation offering federal help to the city "represents a vindication of New York's case, of the merit of our position." Mayor Beame said Ford's decision "marks a crucial turning point in our continuing struggle to resolve the city's fiscal crisis."

State Sen. Warren Anderson (R), majority leader of the state assembly and a partner with Carey in winning support for the legislative tax package, sounded a bipartisan note. Ford's action, Anderson said, was the "culmination of a lot of effort on the part of a lot of people, including unions, banks, public-spirited citizens, and public officials of both parties."

Chase Manahattan Bank Chairman David Rockefeller, a spokesman for the major banks which held large amounts of city notes and a strong supporter of federal aid to prevent default, also expressed relief at the President's decision. Ford's action "came in the nick of time. Without it, I think there would inevitably

have been a New York bankruptcy," Rockefeller said.

State legislature's tax package—The $200 million tax package, which state and city officials said was needed to secure Ford's agreement to the federal aid for New York City, had been passed by the New York State Legislature Nov. 25 after days of political brawling.

Among the provisions in the 12 bills approved by the legislature during a late-night session were an average 25% increase in personal income tax for city residents, a 50% surcharge on the estate tax (effective April 1, 1976), and higher levies for cigarettes and various personal services, such as those provided by barbers and beauticians.

White House Statement on City and State Actions To Produce a Balanced Budget and Refinance Debt

Gov. Carey and Mayor Beame have informed Administration officials that the actions listed below are being implemented. New York state and city officials are delivering documentation verifying such actions for the Administration to review.

The following actions are designed to insure a balanced city budget by June 30, 1978:

A. The three-year Emergency Financial Control Board plan will produce a modest surplus in the city's expense budget by fiscal year 1977–78.

B. The state legislature has voted over $200 million of additional city taxes, which will be imposed by the board.

C. A portion of annual city contributions to the pension system has been shifted to the employes by legislation. On an annual basis, the savings to the city would be $85 million and the impact on the employes would be $107 million per annum.

D. The city has laid off about 22,000 employes since Jan. 1 and increased taxes over $300 million this past summer. Additional personnel reductions of over 40,000 employes are contemplated in fiscal years 1977–1978.

E. A partial wage deferral was imposed this fall.

F. The city has reduced its subsidy to the City University by $32 million.

G. The New York City transit fare has been increased from 35¢ to 50¢.

The following actions are designed to enable New York City to meet its financing requirements:

A. Moratorium legislation has been enacted with respect to $2.6 billion of city short-term notes.

B. An exchange offer has been approved by the M.A.C. Board for an exchange of 10-year 8% bonds for the $1.6 billion of city notes held by the public.

C. The New York banks and pension systems have agreed to take 10-year 6% city securities as part of the moratorium in exchange for $1 billion of city notes.

D. The New York banks and pension systems have agreed to take 10-year 6% bonds in exchange for $1.7 billion of M.A.C. bonds bearing higher in-

terest rates and/or shorter maturities.

E. New York City pension systems have agreed to purchase $2.5 billion of new M.A.C. and/or city securities over the next three years. This commitment is subject to appropriate trustee indemnification.

F. M.A.C. has provided about $3.5 billion of financing to the city, of which $1.5 billion is refinancing of short-term debt.

The city and state have implemented the following management changes:

A. Creation of M.A.C. and E.F.C.B. control mechanisms.

B. Extensive management changes are being made in the city, including a new deputy mayor for finance and a new chief of planning.

The following proposals have been made to reform the New York City pension program:

A. The E.F.C.B. has passed a resolution directing the city to terminate the practice of using, for budgetary purposes, all income of the pension systems in excess of 4% per annum. In the year beginning July 1, 1976, this will result in approximately $136 million per annum of additional income to the pension systems and a commensurate increase in the city's expenses.

The E.F.C.B. has also directed the city management to take action and report back within 30 days with respect to termination of the practices resulting in the abuse of overtime in the last year of employment, thereby creating excessive pension burdens on the city.

B. Governor Carey has directed Richard Shinn, president of the Metropolitan Life Insurance Company, to report to the E.F.C.B. by Dec. 31 on the actuarial soundness of the city pension funds.

The E.F.C.B. has directed the city to prepare and submit to the control board such legislative requests and other amendments as may be necessary as a result of the Shinn study to put the funds on a sound actuarial basis and to have those recommendations to the control board no later than Jan. 31, 1976.

Legislators from the suburban commuting areas around New York City blocked imposition of a proposed $10 increase in the city's auto-use tax. To replace the lost revenue, legislators voted an additional 1 percentage point increase for the bank tax, thereby raising the levy from its current level of 11.8% to 13.8%.

Before giving its final approval to the complex tax package, the legislature had been deadlocked for several days by partisan and ethnic feuding over the unpopular measure.

Under initial bipartisan arrangements, it was planned that President Ford would endorse the tax package and urge its passage by the legislature. However, Republican leaders rejected the ploy, fearing that the endorsement would prove a political liability for the President.

Under a compromise worked out between Carey and Senate Majority Leader Warren Anderson (R), the governor took full public responsibility for his tax proposal. The bill's final version also provided that the new taxes would not take effect unless the Emergency Financial Control Board, a state agency created by the legislature to run the city's fiscal affairs, certified the need for the higher levies. By this action, state politicians of both parties were relieved of the stigma of imposing taxes on the city.

A more serious threat to the tax package's passage was posed by the 14-member Black and Puerto Rican Caucus in the legislature. The Democratic group refused to vote for Carey's proposals unless he agreed to name a minority member to the financial control board, supported a residency requirement for new city employes, and limited budget cuts in the areas of social services.

None of their demands was accepted, but the group succeeded in delaying a final vote on the tax package until the last minute. (Swift action was imperative because President Ford had warned he would not support a federal aid plan for the city until the tax package was acted upon. Ford was due to leave for a state visit to China Nov. 29.)

The caucus ended its holdout after winning face-saving concessions from Carey, who agreed to give "strong consideration" to filling the next vacancy on the financial control board with a minority appointee. The governor also agreed to put a res-idency bill on the legislature's agenda for immediate consideration.

The tax package was only one component of an elaborate $6.6 billion financing program devised by Carey to meet the city's immediate cash needs for December and refinance the city's debt over a three-year period in order to restore fiscal integrity and a balanced budget. President Ford's approval of federal aid Nov. 26 completed Carey's arrangements, but final action on the plan was not taken at the state level until Nov. 25 when the tax package was voted and two other key hurdles in the financing plan were cleared.

Carey had asked the city's five municipal unions to make investments totaling $2.5 billion from their pension systems in securities issued by the city and the Municipal Assistance Corp. They also were asked to "stretch out," or extend, maturities on $1.2 billion in city and MAC notes that they currently held. Trustees for the city's teacher retirement system balked at the plan, refusing to purchase their $860 million share of city- and MAC-issued securities.

The trustees relented Nov. 25 when Carey agreed to support their demand for an indemnification bill, protecting them from lawsuits alleging a breach of their fiduciary responsibilities.

An unexpected snag to completion of the plan developed when passage of the indemnification bill by the legislature was delayed until early in the morning of Dec. 5. Without the cash purchases by the pension trustees, the city was unable to meet its expenses. Distribution of payroll checks, payable Dec. 5, was withheld for two days pending resolution of the indemnification issue. The city had been able to pay its bills through Dec. 3 only with a temporary infusion of cash from the prepayment of real estate taxes (discounted to provide an incentive) and bond sales. MAC completed an offer of $150 million in bonds Nov. 25, rounding out the last stage of a $2.3 billion rescue plan passed by the legislature in September.

The second major obstacle to Carey's financing plan also was cleared Nov. 25 when the city's largest banks agreed to extend maturities at a low rate of interest on their holdings of $550 million of city notes and $1.1 billion of MAC bonds.

The banks had refused to join the unions in Carey's refinancing program until the governor took steps to close the state fiscal gap.

The bankers, who became the lone holdouts in the plan to stretch out New York City securities, finally relented and accepted "in principle" Carey's stated "resolve" to balance the state budget.

Debt moratorium; aid for HFA & Yonkers—A major part of Carey's financing plan for New York City had been enacted Nov. 14 when the legislature passed a controversial debt moratorium plan.

At the same time, the legislators also voted temporary aid for the state Housing Finance Agency, and the city of Yonkers, a suburb of New York City. Both faced default Nov. 14 when money was unavailable to redeem notes falling due that day.

Passage of the moratorium measure gave lawmakers time to enact the other parts of Carey's financing plan, which had persuaded the President to offer aid for the city. When the governor had convened the special session of the legislature Nov. 11, New York City was in imminent danger of defaulting on its debt and proving unable to meet operating expenses for essential services.

The Moratorium Act covered three city-note issues totaling $1.6 billion. Holders of the short-term notes, most of whom were unidentified individual investors, were offered a choice: they could exchange their securities for long-term MAC bonds, redeemable in 10 years and paying 8% interest; or, if they refused to make the swap, they could retain their note holdings and accept a suspension of payments on the principal for at least three years (the moratorium could be extended by the legislature). Interest would be paid during the moratorium period, but at a reduced rate. By June 30, 1978, the target date for ending the moratorium, a balanced city budget was projected under Carey's debt restructuring plan.

Spokesmen for Carey insisted that the moratorium was not a "sham default," saying the U.S. Supreme Court had upheld the legality of debt deferral when moratoriums for mortgage payments were enacted during the depression of the 1930s.

The exchange offer was scheduled to begin Nov. 25, but the law was challenged in a suit filed Nov. 17 by the Flushing National Bank of Queens, forcing a delay in the Dec. 10 deadline for completion of the exchange offer. The class action suit, brought by the small New York bank on behalf of all city noteholders, charged that the Moratorium Act violated state and federal constitutions. The suit cited Section 10, Article I of the U.S. Constitution, which stated: "No state shall . . . pass any bill . . . or law impairing the obligations of contracts."

In separate action Nov. 14, legislators appropriated $80 million to the HFA, allowing State Controller Arthur Levitt to use state treasury funds to purchase a portion of the agency's $170.5 million of short-term bond-anticipation notes (plus interest) maturing that day. Four state funds also purchased more than $31 million of HFA notes and several banks accepted $19 million worth. The balance of the notes was redeemed with HFA funds.

Rescue legislation also was voted Nov. 14 for Yonkers, the state's fourth largest city. Under a plan devised by Gov. Carey, the legislature enacted a $25 million aid package needed to pay off $21 million in notes maturing that day and also to provide $4 million in operating funds for the city.

The rescue plan included a $10 million advance from the state in future revenue-sharing funds, and a $15 million investment in city notes with the state insurance funds. The legislature also ordered an immediate wage freeze for Yonkers' municipal employes; established a seven-member emergency financial control board, patterned after the management panel that ran New York City's fiscal affairs, and headed by State Controller Levitt; and mandated a 1 percentage point increase in Yonkers' sale tax, which currently was 3% (a 4% sales tax also was paid to the state), and an increase in the property tax.

Moratorium law upheld—The constitutionality of the Moratorium Act was upheld by a state Supreme Court justice Dec. 23.

The suit challenging the legality of the moratorium measure was filed by the Flushing National Bank of Queens. The plaintiffs argued that the moratorium was "basically a municipal cover-up" and "a political ripoff."

In his ruling, Justice Harold J. Baer said, "We must deal with the subject realistically in light of the financial crisis of the city." A decision against the moratorium law would produce a "Pyrrhic victory," Baer said, resulting in default and bankruptcy, which would be costly not only to city residents but also to note holders who would "lose interest on their investment and a substantial portion of the principal as well."

Baer ruled that the legislature acted "to protect the health, safety and welfare of the citizens." Since "the courts, federal and state, have given priority to the public interest over strict compliance with the contract clause," Baer said, the moratorium law did not violate the U.S. Constitution.

When the deadline for swap offer expired Dec. 29, more than $360 million of city notes had been exchanged for MAC bonds.

Ford signs New York City aid bill. President Ford Dec. 9 signed legislation authorizing the Treasury to loan New York City $2.3 billion annually until June 30, 1978 to help the city meet its seasonal cash flow needs. The House had approved the measure Dec. 2, by a 213–203 vote, and the Senate Dec. 6, after invoking its antifilibuster rule, had passed the bill, 57–30.

Sponsors of the legislation circumvented normal Congressional procedure to speed up passage because New York was expected to default on payment of loans Dec. 11 if the aid were not forthcoming by then. As a result, bond guarantee legislation, reported by the House and Senate banking committees, that was pending but stood little chance of gaining Ford's approval was set aside and the President's plan for short-term federal loans was substituted on the House floor. The Senate leadership, meanwhile, waited for House passage of the loan legislation and then introduced the House-passed measure on the floor. By adopting a bill identical to that of the House, the Senate avoided the need for a House-Senate conference that would have meant further delay.

The bill contained the following provisions:

The Treasury secretary was authorized to make loans to New York City or to an agent authorized by the state to administer the city's financial affairs. No more than a total of $2.3 billion in loans could be outstanding at any one time.

The loans would have to be repaid at the end of each city fiscal year (June 30) at an interest rate one percentage point higher than the prevailing Treasury borrowing rate.

The secretary was authorized to set terms and conditions of repayment and to withhold other federal funds due the city to offset the amount of any unpaid loans.

The secretary was prohibited from making new loans unless all previous loans had been repaid.

The General Accounting Office was authorized to audit the financial records of the city and the state.

Authority to make the loans was to be terminated June 30, 1978.

Senate conservatives who opposed aid to New York delayed passage of the legislation. After the Senate Dec. 5 voted, 70–27, to invoke cloture and forestall a threatened filibuster, the conservatives initiated time-consuming quorum calls and introduced more than a dozen amendments, each of which was either tabled or defeated by an overwhelming margin.

The conservatives, calling the measure a "bottomless pit for the American taxpayer," warned that passage would mean the establishment of yet another federal bureaucracy and result in more federal control over local governments, while serving as a disincentive to sound fiscal management of local government.

The bill's proponents conceded that it might not be enough to keep the city from bankruptcy. Rep. Henry Reuss (D, Wis.), chairman of the Banking and Currency Committee, said Dec. 2 that the "problem will come back to haunt us, possibly as early as next winter."

Appropriation passed—President Ford Dec. 18 signed a bill appropriating money for the federal loan to New York City.

The funds were contained in a $10.3 billion supplemental appropriations bill, which was approved Dec. 15 by the House, by a 275–130 vote, and by the Senate on a voice vote.

Before taking a final vote, the House rejected, 219–187, a motion to recommit the bill to a House-Senate conference committee with instructions to reduce the money available for the loan fund to $1.3 billion. Rep. Robert Michel (R, Ill.), the minority whip, who sponsored the motion, argued that Congress should appropriate only what New York City would need until June' 30, 1976, the end of the city's fiscal year.

Political background to aid issue. The debate over federal aid for New York City, whose fiscal crisis first surfaced in May, quickly developed into a "game of political brinkmanship," the Wall Street Journal reported Nov. 28.

The chief adversaries in the aid debate both were forced to make dramatic public reversals of oft-stated positions: President Ford, the steadfast opponent of a federal "bail out" for New York City, eventually proposed legislation giving the city direct Treasury loans; Gov. Carey, who had insisted repeatedly that he and city officials had done all they could to rescue New York from default, ultimately supported a politically unpopular tax increase as the price for winning modest federal aid.

The opposing strategies were staked out early in May, the Journal recounted. Carey and Beame May 13 met privately with the President to appeal for federal aid to deal with the city's worsening fiscal situation. When Ford asked why they could not raise taxes, cut expenditures, use union pension funds, renegotiate labor contracts, or restructure the city debt to restore fiscal health to New York City, Carey and Beame reportedly replied that nothing could be done without federal help.

Convinced that the New York officials were manufacturing a "crisis" to frighten Washington into mounting a massive rescue effort, Ford May 14 rejected their request for federal aid.

During the summer, Carey and Beame undertook some of the self-correcting measures Ford had suggested. The Municipal Assistance Corp. was created by the state legislature to refinance the city's debt and act as New York City's fiscal agent. Many municipal workers were laid off (but others were rehired). In spite of these limited self-help actions, the fiscal crisis worsened. By August, MAC was unable to sell bond issues on behalf of the city. With the credit market effectively closed to New York City, the threat of default had become dangerously close.

State and city politicians, bankers, and Administration officials tried unsuccessfully during August and September to negotiate a solution to the fiscal crisis. Administration officials favored a voluntary debt-restructuring plan that would make federal involvement in the city's fiscal affairs unnecessary, but New York leaders rejected the proposal, according to the Journal.

The political "hard-ball" season ran from mid-September into early November when positions hardened and each side appealed for public support, the Journal reported. New York politicians and bankers lobbied in Congress and around the nation for federal aid, warning of the "financial doomsday" that would occur if New York defaulted. Others warned of possible "social chaos" and raised fears of international repercussions from default, the Journal added.

The Ford Administration counterattacked with its own lobbying effort "to belittle the danger of default and fuel the widespread antagonisms to federal help for the 'profligate' city," the Journal reported.

However, the Administration's united front of opposition to federal assistance cracked when Vice President Nelson Rockefeller announced his support for short-term federal aid. Arthur Burns, chairman of the Federal Reserve Board, also dissented from the White House position. Burns did not explicitly endorse rescue legislation pending in Congress, but cited the possible adverse consequences to the nation's developing economic recovery if New York City were allowed to default.

According to the Journal, Ford tried to counteract speculation that the White House position was softening by delivering a hard-line speech Oct. 29 vowing to veto federal aid bills before Congress.

The speech was a "pivotal point in the crisis," according to the Journal. Ford's statement rejecting federal assistance for New York "scotched the bail-out bills in Congress; it forced New York to begin mapping a painful alternative solution involving higher taxes; it stunned labor leaders into realizing their labor contracts would be rewritten in a bankruptcy court; and it painted President Ford into a rhetorical corner from which there wasn't any graceful escape."

Although the purpose of the speech was to state Ford's inflexible opposition to pending federal rescue legislation, its actual catalytic effect was quite the opposite, the Journal noted. After the speech polls showed public sentiment swinging toward New York City, now the political underdog, and toward a limited federal aid program.

Two bills passed in Congress shortly after the President's speech reflected this change in public and legislative attitude. According to the Journal, Ford miscalculated by trying to "capitalize upon anti-New York sentiment elsewhere in the nation," and his political plan "backfired."

Meanwhile, the Journal reported, political and economic advisers to the President, such as Treasury Secretary Simon and conservative economist Alan Greenspan, chairman of the President's Council of Economic Advisers, who had supported Ford's hard-line opposition to federal aid for the city, now were urging the President to reconsider his position and take steps to avert default.

Contributing to their worries about the national impact of default was a Federal Reserve study, released Nov. 13, showing that 546 banks across the country held New York State and city securities in "significant" amounts (defined as equalling at least 20% of a bank's total capital). Of this total, holdings by 179 banks exceeded 50% of their capitalization. Banks in New York, Illinois and Florida had the heaviest concentration of holdings. New York City's 11 major banks collectively owned city and state obligations amounting to 28.7% of their capital.

Pressure of another sort was brought to bear on Ford Nov. 8 when Republican party officials in New York state announced they would send an uncommitted delegation to the 1976 Republican nominating convention.

By mid-November, both sides indicated there was movement toward a compromise. Gov. Carey convened a special session of the state legislature to declare a moratorium on the payment of city notes and to enact tax increases.

The White House contended Nov. 13 that the drastic restructuring of debt entailed in the Moratorium Act was in fact, if not legally, a declaration of voluntary bankruptcy, which Ford had set as a precondition for winning federal aid after default. The statement allowed the White House to announce it was reconsidering a plan for short-term seasonal aid to allow the city to maintain essential services.

There were other signs of a shift in the Administration's position. House Minority Leader John J. Rhodes (R, Ariz.) Nov. 11 announced his support for limited federal aid for New York City. With Rep. Henry Reuss (D, Wis.), Rhodes sponsored a scaled-down version of the bill passed earlier by a House committee. The Reuss-Rhodes bill would provide $4 billion in federal loan guarantees over a 5-year period, instead of $7 billion over 19 years, as originally drafted.

Most observers believed Rhodes "received a go-ahead from the Administration" for his sudden shift in position, the Journal reported. Soon thereafter, White House aides began leaking word that Ford was "impressed" by Carey's legislative efforts to solve the city's fiscal crisis.

A few last-minute hitches developed when Carey encountered resistance to his proposals from Republicans and Democrats in Albany, but the seven-month-long struggle to restore New York City's fiscal integrity and save it from default ended with passage of the tax legislation and announcement of White House support for aid legislation.

Urban Problems in Mid-1970s

'Flight From Cities,' Growth of Urban Crime

As the problems of crime, unemployment, racial segregation and municipal insolvency mounted in the cities in the mid-1970s, there was growing evidence of a "flight" from the cities to the small towns and suburban areas.

Migration to cities halts. By 1975 it had become clear that more people were leaving the U.S.' cities than were moving to them.

The population migration to U.S. cities had been halted or reversed, it was reported Feb. 9. U.S. Census Bureau figures showed that in the 15 largest metropolitan centers, more people had moved out than in, but the population increased slightly because births had exceeded deaths. The trend was to towns of less than 10,000 people and to rural living, according to Calvin Beale, head of population studies for the U.S. Agriculture Department. He cited as reasons: an improved economy in smaller towns; fear of the city, particularly among parents; and a desire, particularly among younger people, to return to a more natural environment.

The trend away from big urban areas was revealed in Census Bureau data collected between 1970 and 1973, the New York Times reported June 16. The study showed that the eight biggest metropolitan areas in the country had a net balance of in-migration over out-migration of 2,408,000 (a 5% gain) during 1960–70 but a loss of 664,000 (1.2%) during 1970–73.

Five of the eight areas—New York, Los Angeles, Chicago, Philadelphia and Detroit—experienced a decline in net in-migration from 1970–73. All but Chicago had registered net migration gains during the 1960s. The most striking reversal occurred for Los Angeles, which had a total net in-migration gain of 15%, or 1,164,000, from 1960–70 and a 1.2% loss of 119,000 for 1970–73.

The three other major metropolitan areas—San Francisco, Boston and Washington—had slight gains of in-migration over out-migration during the 1970–73 period.

The nonmetropolitan counties in the country, those with no population center of at least 50,000 persons, gained 4.2% in population between April 1970 and July 1973, according to the study; metropolitan counties, which included suburbs, gained 2.9%.

The combination of decelerating growth rate of the major urban areas and accelerating growth rate of nonurban areas was interpreted by several demographers as unprecedented in the nation.

The experts forecast, on the basis of the new data, a pronounced shift of income away from the Northeast and North

161

Central regions of the country to the Southern and Western portions. The Far West and New England areas were seen as exceptions because their changes were at approximately the national rate.

The net in-migration for the major metropolitan areas, in addition to Los Angeles, for the period 1970–73 (1960–70 figures in parentheses): New York – 305,-000, a 1.8% loss (218,000, 1.4% gain). Chicago – 124,000, 1.6% loss (– 17,000, .2% loss). Philadelphia – 75,000, 1.3% loss (91,000, 1.8% gain). Detroit – 114,000, 2.4% loss (9,000, .2% gain). San Francisco – 23,000, .5% gain (485,000, 13.9% gain). Boston 15,000, .4% gain (32,-000, .9% gain). Washington, D.C. 34,000, 1.2% gain (426,000, 20.3% gain).

Crime seen as worst urban problem. In a Gallup Poll made public July 26, 1975, those adults surveyed in cities with a population of over 500,000 said crime was the worst problem they faced. Of those city dwellers questioned, 21% named crime the top problem while 11% picked unemployment and 5% chose the high cost of living. The poll was taken between June 27 and 30 in over 300 localities both large and small and included 1,500 participants.

When asked whether they were afraid to walk in their neighborhoods at night, 56% of those who lived in large cities said they were, including 77% of the women asked. Nationwide, 45% of those asked said they felt unsafe when outdoors at night.

The survey further revealed that one household in every four had been touched by crime during the previous year in the United States. Nearly one household in three was struck by crime in cities with a population of over 500,000. The poll pointed out how official statistics in this area could be misleading in that almost four in 10 incidents of crime had not been reported to authorities by those polled.

The survey results also indicated that non-whites and lower-income persons were more likely to have been the victims of a crime as opposed to whites and upper-income groups. This was particularly apparent in a survey of crimes against persons.

Low-income U.S. families were most likely to suffer crimes of violence and high-income families personal larceny, according to a nationwide survey conducted in 1973. The study was made by the U.S. Census Bureau for the Law Enforcement Assistance Administration (LEAA) which released the report Aug. 12.

The survey was based on interviews in 60,000 households and 15,000 businesses. It found that males were more often the object of crimes than females while black males were the most likely victims of crime. According to age, males between 16 and 19 had the highest victimization rate while persons over 65 had the lowest.

The data indicated that over 37 million persons had been victims of rape, robbery, assault, burglary, larceny or auto theft in 1973.

Another aspect of the survey, released July 31, revealed that among 13 large cities surveyed, San Francisco and Minneapolis residents suffered the highest levels of violent crime in 1973. The rates of personal crimes of violence per 1,000 residents were 71 in San Francisco and 70 in Minneapolis.

In contrast, citizens of Miami and Washington were least likely to have been victimized by crime that year. Their rates of violent crime per 1,000 residents were 22 and 31 respectively. Other cities in the survey, and their rate of crime per 1,000 population, were: Boston (67), Cincinnati (63), Milwaukee (61), Oakland (59), Houston (53), San Diego (53), Buffalo (49), Pittsburgh (47) and New Orleans (46).

Commercial burglary rates ranged from 253 per 1,000 commercial establishments in San Francisco to 637 in nearby Oakland. In other cities surveyed the rates were: Boston (576), Cincinnati (566), Houston (518), New Orleans (448), Minneapolis (436), San Diego (358), Washington (330), Milwaukee (321), Buffalo (319), Pittsburgh (293) and Miami (292).

The FBI said Dec. 23 that serious crime reported in the United States rose 11% in the first nine months of 1975, a slower rate of increase less than during the same period of 1974.

The report cited an 8% increase in violent crimes and an 11% rise in property offenses: Robbery increased 11%; larceny-theft 13%; burglary 10%; aggravated assault 7%; murder 3%; and forcible rape 2%.

Geographically, the report found a rise of 13% in the South, 10% in the north central states, 11% in the Northeast and 8% in the West.

There was a rise in crime of 9% in cities with populations of 100,000 or more and crime in country locales and the suburbs rose 12%, the report said.

Levi proposes urban handgun curbs—Attorney General Edward H. Levi April 6 urged stricter federal controls on handguns in urban areas with high or rising rates of violent crime. In a speech before the Law Enforcement Executives Narcotics Conference in Washington, Levi proposed heavy taxation of cheap handguns and the outright banning of all handguns in urban areas with violent crime rates significantly higher than the national average, or greater both than the national average and the previous year's local rates.

"In crowded urban areas the handgun has become a medium of terror.... [It] makes an individual in a city too powerful for his environment.... It is a mechanism that translates passion or a passing evil intent into destruction," he said.

Financial Woes

Mayors warn of cities' plight. A delegation representing the U.S. Conference of Mayors told the Senate Government Operations Subcommittee on Intergovernmental Relations Jan. 30, 1975 that many, if not most, of the major cities would soon be forced to reduce services, lay off employes and raise taxes.

"Any federal program to cure the ills of the economy by a reduction in federal taxes without some form of direct assistance to the cities will be offset by increases in local taxes," Moon Landrieu, mayor of New Orleans, testified. "What the hand of the Internal Revenue Service puts into the pocket of the taxpayer, the hand of the local tax collector will take out of his other pocket."

San Francisco Mayor Joseph Alioto, current president of the mayors' conference, said that many current antirecession economic proposals were aimed at aiding the taxpayer in the $8,000–$14,000 income bracket. However, he said, financially strapped local governments would be forced to raise property taxes, which already fell most heavily on middle income groups.

The mayors urged Congressional passage of a one-shot, $5 billion emergency relief act to help balance city and state government budgets and head off tax increases. It should be in addition to the $16 billion tax cut proposed by President Ford, they said. A survey of 67 cities, the delegation said, had indicated that 42 cities would either raise taxes or reduce services if outside financial aid were not forthcoming.

President Ford's budget was criticized insensitive" in a joint analysis issued Feb. 8 by the National League of Cities and the United States Conference of Mayors. The report said the budget projected reduced federal spending in many areas on the unrealistic assumption that the slack would be taken up by hard-pressed local governments.

It said the budget "sets forth economic recovery policies that both help and rely heavily upon the private sector.... Thus the President proposes to shift some billions of dollars in purchasing power to private business and to individuals." Such a policy, the report said, "means that the urgent needs of the cities will go largely unmet." The President's budget itself, it said, "creates emergency fiscal conditions in cities."

The report noted critically that the budget projected high unemployment that struck especially hard at "vulnerable" members of the work force, such as blacks and youth, but it failed to focus any emergency programs on these groups. It also objected to the fact that defense funds had been raised 10% to offset inflation while other expenditures, such as those for housing and transportation, did not get the inflation increment.

New York City Mayor Abraham Beame testified about conflicting state and national priorities before Congress. "Local governments," Beame said, "are being forced to raise taxes, while the federal budget proposes to stimulate the private sector through tax deductions; local governments are laying off city workers, while the federal budget proposes to create new jobs for other unemployed; local officials are forced into unnecessary confrontations with local union leaders, while federal officials are implementing and proposing to expand a national public employment program; local governments are being forced to cut public service in health and welfare, in a pennywise, pound foolish attempt to reduce the federal budget." (Beame's remarks were published in the Times March 28.)

Local and state governments shared many fiscal troubles confronting the federal administration—problems of how to provide adequate services to the increased numbers of persons in need, meet labor demands and pay fuel bills when inflationary pressures had raised the cost of government and recession had caused revenues to shrink.

Neither of the options available to officials—increased taxes or reduced spending on services and personnel—was popular with the electorate. Yet, according to an Associated Press survey published March 16 by the New York Times, 16 states planned net tax increases for fiscal 1976. Only eight states reported they would reduce taxes.

Another survey of 67 various-sized municipalities conducted by the National League of Cities and published in the Times March 28 indicated that 36 cities planned to postpone capital improvements, 21 reported municipal job layoffs or hiring freezes, 43 said they expected revenue short falls during the year, 28 planned to raise taxes and 23 intended to reduce city services.

Austerity budgets combining increased taxes and reduced services were planned by nine cities, the study stated: Anchorage, Alaska; Inglewood, Calif.; East St. Louis, Ill.; Auburn, Me.; Newark, N.J.; Binghamton, N.Y.; Buffalo, Syracuse and Cleveland.

Many local officials blamed their cities' crises on national economic problems beyond their control, such as tight money conditions that made borrowing difficult, and the soaring unemployment rate that caused demands for social services to rise.

National policies for dealing with the recession also were at odds with state and local efforts to deal with the economic slump, these officials said. They noted one of the consequences of a recently

enacted federal income tax cut was a sharp cutback in federal revenues earmarked for states and localities at a time when these government faced budget deficits.

States, localities cut services, raise taxes. Financially-pressed state and local governments, caught in a budgetary squeeze between outlays swollen by inflation and revenues reduced by recession, had been forced to cut about $3.3 billion in services, raise taxes by $3.6 billion, and defer $1 billion in capital spending for 1975—bringing the overall impact of the recession on states and localities to about $8 billion. An estimated 140,000 jobs also would be lost in the budget cutbacks, according to a report released June 6, 1975 by the Joint Economic Committee of Congress.

The Congressional survey analyzed data from 48 states and 140 local jurisdictions. Committee members expressed concern that the recession's cost at the state and local level "may significantly undermine the strength of a [national] economic recovery" because service cutbacks and tax increases were working at cross purposes with the Administration's budgetary plans to stimulate the economy through a tax cut.

Most of the retrenching efforts, the study noted, were occurring in areas with the greatest need for economic stimulus—industrial areas with the highest unemployment rate.

Highlights of the survey:

■ 20 states and 52 local governments had enacted or planned tax increases; four states planed tax reductions totaling $50 million and five localities reported making tax cutbacks.

■ 22 states anticipated cuts in services—about 85% of the reductions were planned for the 18 states whose unemployment rates exceeded the national average; 56 localities reported expenditure cutbacks.

■ 23 states had adopted complete or partial hiring freezes and job cuts; payroll cutbacks totaling 52,000 jobs were planned or had been enacted in 48 local jurisdictions.

City troubles listed. Among reports of financial woes in various cities:

Newark, N.J. shared many of New York City's problems. Its tax base was declining as industry and middle class residents fled the city. Heavy demands were being placed on city services by the large numbers of poor persons filling the population void. Newark Mayor Kenneth Gibson announced Jan. 16, 1975 that 370 city employes would be laid off in an effort to reduce an anticipated deficit of $35.7 million. In a later announcement May 1, Gibson said the public school staff would be cut 20%—1,600 administrators, teachers and workers faced dismissal.

Residents of Willimantic, Conn. ended a taxpayers' revolt Jan. 16 when voters approved a $2.4 million budget that was 9% smaller than the original proposal. Voters had rejected three other budget proposals, saying they feared the spending requirement would necessitate a higher tax rate. Willimantic city government had been paralyzed since Dec. 2, 1974 when the first budget had been voted down at public meeting.

Detroit officials March 30 announced drastic measures designed to bring the 1976 budget into balance. Up to 25% of the city's 23,000 employes were scheduled to be laid off, paring Detroit's payroll by about $96 million. A budget deficit totaling $65-$85 million had been projected. The action was necessary, city officials said, because municipal unions had refused to forego automatic wage raises and accept pay cuts.

Cleveland, also affected by the massive auto industry layoffs, faced a $16 million deficit. To meet the fiscal crisis, Mayor Ralph Perk had laid off about 1,100 city workers, including police and firemen, reduced garbage collection and closed four fire stations. Voters defeated Perk's proposal to raise the city income tax.

One key indicator of municipal financial health was the ratio of debt service (defined as interest charges plus payments of principal on maturing long-term debt) to current budgetary expenditures. Agencies that rated municipal bonds considered "a ratio of 10% to be the separation between better and lesser creditworthiness," analysts said. A ratio of 15% "warrants concern" and it "should never exceed 20%-25%," according to the experts. New York City's ratio of debt to current budgetary expenditures was

17.1%. Cleveland was the only city paying a higher percentage—17.9%

Other cities in precarious financial health:

Buffalo: unemployment rate near 20%; projected $17 million deficit in a $229 million budget for fiscal 1975, ending June 30; 8% delinquency rate for property tax collections; 12.1% ratio of debt service to current budget expenditures; 16% cutback over the past four years in municipal personnel.

Boston: highest combined state and local taxes of the nation's 30 largest cities; near 10% delinquency rate on property tax collections; 10% cut in city payroll over past two years.

St. Louis: a projected $20 million budget deficit for the fiscal year that began May 1 violated a state law against deficit spending; officials proposed to eliminate the deficit with a property tax increase and 4% cutback in city jobs—the city payroll already had been pared 7% over the past four years.

Seattle: near 20% unemployment rate; 9.4% debt service ratio; business and utilities taxes increased Jan. 1.

Detroit: debt service ratio under 8% despite the fact that in only four of the past 25 years, Detroit had recorded no budget deficit; 1,980 city workers, 10% of the total payroll, laid off between February and June; city seeking labor agreements to pare payroll costs by a total 24%.

Mayors push for recession aid. Federal aid was the dominant, almost obsessive, theme of the 43d annual meeting of the U.S. Conference of Mayors in Boston July 7-9, 1975.

The mayors focused on an emergency revenue-sharing measure to provide recession aid of $2 billion to localities with high rates of unemployment. At their final session July 9, they urged Congress to pass this measure, which was sponsored by Sen. Edmund S. Muskie (D, Me.) and opposed by the Administration.

A delegation of mayors at the White House July 10 was told that the Administration "would take another look" at the legislation. Treasury Secretary William E. Simon used that phrase in briefing reporters on the White House meeting, which was attended by 120 mayors, Simon and James T. Lynn, director of the Office of Management and Budget. New Orleans Mayor Moon Landrieu, new head of the mayors' conference, told reporters the issue was so important to the cities that the conference would push for enactment with or without the Administration's help.

The mayors also met with President Ford July 10. He talked of revenue sharing, extension of the regular program, without change. "If we tinker with the formula, it would be my fear, and it should be yours, that the whole program might not be extended," he told them. The Democratic big-city mayors had attempted to have the mayors' conference adopt a revenue sharing resolution urging a revision in the allocation formula to emphasize a city's need, but the conference rejected this July 9 as the Republicans, organized into caucus at the convention and led by Cleveland Mayor Ralph Perk, voted in bloc against it.

Ford also thanked the mayors July 10 for defeat of another resolution at the final session of the conference July 9. The victim of the same political split, this called for taking some funds out of the defense budget and putting them into urban aid.

Host Mayor Kevin H. White of Boston ignored a group of antibusing demonstrators, led by City Councilor Louise Day Hicks, who took over his hotel suite July 8-9 demanding he bring the busing issue before the conference. They left after 13 hours.

The conference chairman for 1975, Mayor Joseph Alioto of San Francisco, referred to the financial plight of the nation's biggest city at a press conference July 5. "The seeds of New York are in every American city," he said. "We want to sound the alarm."

Mayors seek more federal money—A bigger share of the federal tax dollar was a major demand made at the convention of the National League of Cities held in Miami Beach Nov. 30-Dec. 4.

New York Mayor Abraham Beame told the convention Dec. 1 that "perhaps the single most progressive federal effort to help our cities" would be renewal of the general revenue-sharing program by Congress. Beame said he thought New York's desperate fight to avoid financial default had spotlighted urban problems

and "reawakened a sense of urgency in dealing with them."

This was not the message from Carla A. Hills, secretary of housing and urban development, Dec. 3 nor Sen. Edmund S. Muskie (D, Me.) Dec. 4.

Hills cautioned the group that it might be worrying about the wrong thing, the delay in extension of revenue sharing, which was a nuisance to preparation of the city budgets. "Worse than the timing," Hills told then, "is the fact that at present you stand a 50% chance of losing these funds altogether." The combination of "political gamesmanship," which was responsible for the delay, she said, and real opposition to the program was "jeopardizing the most valuable domestic program we have."

She was critical of the mayors for ineffectual lobbying—"the lack of commotion from the cities"—in support of the measure.

She also recommended that the cities mount an effort to attract suburbanites to return to the core city, through provision of services that would attract middle-class residents. She suggested that community development funds from the federal government could be applied to this purpose.

Muskie, in his appearance before the group Dec. 4, also told the mayors a more effective lobbying effort was necessary to avert loss of billions of dollars in federal revenue-sharing aid. Muskie, chairman of the Senate Budget Committee, advised the mayors to make some calls soon to their Congressional representatives to support his proposal for countercyclical aid, which was facing a crucial vote in the House.

Countercyclical aid, or federal aid that was increased in bad times and cut in good times, was endorsed by Democratic mayors meeting in caucus at the convention Nov. 30. The Democrats adopted and issued a major urban policy statement declaring that cities could maintain fiscal health and offer citizens an improved quality of living only through new federal help and a drastic revision of federal spending priorities. It urged increased federal funding of health, transportation, housing, energy and criminal justice programs. Among other things, it called for a full employment policy, federal takeover of welfare costs, a national health insurance program, revision of the local property tax structure and a national ban on handguns. It suggested the creation of regional tax bases as a way to sustain the big cities drained of tax revenue because of the middle-class flight.

Republican mayors, meeting in caucus Nov. 30, also advocated more federal aid. The group's chairman, Cleveland Mayor Ralph J. Perk, proposed formation of a federal municipal bond insurance corporation to bolster city bonds with government backing.

Yonkers averts default. Yonkers, New York State's fourth largest city, averted default at the last minute Dec. 12, 1975 when the state agreed to use $4 million in state funds to buy city notes and nine commercial banks agreed to purchase $3.6 million in other securities issued by Yonkers.

The city needed to borrow $7.5 million by Dec. 12 to pay off notes falling due and to meet its operating expenses. Only a month earlier, Yonkers had been saved from default when the state legislature approved an emergency appropriation.

The fiscal crisis, which had begun with New York City and quickly spread to New York state, had proved contagious for other governmental units and borrowing authorities in the state, as well. In addition to the larger units affected by the credit crunch, such as the Housing Finance Agency and the city of Yonkers, numerous small school districts found themselves shut out of the credit market and facing default.

A state official told the New York Times Dec. 11 that in the previous six weeks, the state had rescued about a dozen school districts from imminent default. When state banking regulators and officials in the controller's office and budget bureau were able to locate lenders, the local school districts often paid a high price for the financing. The yield on some notes was 11.75%.

Study tallies municipal defaults. Mobile, Ala. was the first U.S. municipality on record to default, or fail to make payment, on its debts, according to a study by the Advisory Commission on Intergovernmental Relations reported in the New York Times Sept. 2, 1975.

Since that date in 1838, the report said, 6,195 other municipalities had defaulted on their obligations. About 77% of these defaults occurred during the depression years of 1930–1933.

According to the report, published in 1973 and entitled, "City Financial Emergencies: The Intergovernmental Dimension," most of the municipalities in default eventually repaid the full amount of principal and interest due creditors.

In the years before the great depression, the report stated, municipal defaults resulted from various causes, many of them associated with the national depressions in the 1870s and 1890s: real-estate booms that collapsed; natural disasters that devastated cities and towns; poor financial planning and administration; thieving carpetbagger regimes in the South; and the heavy financing of railroads that failed to meet earnings expectations.

Municipal indebtedness reached a record high in 1933 when more than 1,000 local governments were in default by nearly $2.6 billion. The number of communities in default peaked at 3,251 in 1935, but the total amount of their indebtedness showed a decline from the peak 1933 level.

The report stated that all of the 48 cities (with populations over 25,000) that were unable to pay their debts during the depression had emerged from default by 1938; insolvent smaller communities made almost as many gains in restoring their financial health, the report added.

In reaction to the flood of defaults occurring during the 1930s, many states passed bankruptcy laws, providing for the management of city finances by court-appointed administrators who were empowered to pay creditors out of the remaining city revenues.

The first federal municipal bankruptcy law was enacted in 1934, but was later declared unconstitutional. A second law was enacted in 1937. The present Federal Municipal Bankruptcy Act took effect in 1946. Since then, the report noted, more than 500 communities had filed for bankruptcy.

Eight case histories of municipal default cited in the panel's study:

Grand Rapids, Mich.—The city defaulted in 1933 because of mounting tax delinquencies, increasing debt service costs, and bank closings. Earlier, the city had slashed expenditures by one-third to close a fiscal gap caused by heavy relief payments and declining revenues associated with the depression. In 1934, the state assumed relief costs. With tax revenues increasing in 1935, a refunding plan was established to ease the city's debt pressures.

Fall River, Mass.—The city was prosperous in 1920 when more than half of its assessed valuation was in 121 textile mills. By 1932, however, only 20 mills were left. Despite this sharp loss of revenues, city officials made no cut in expenditures, failed to increase taxes, and financed the deficit through borrowing against uncollectible property taxes. Default came in November 1930 when the banks refused to extend further credit. Faced with a taxpayers' revolt, the state legislature set up a 10-year receivership with absolute control over city finances.

Asheville, N.C.—The town, a booming resort area that discouraged manufacturing to preserve its tourist appeal, was overcome by the depression. Capital was raised by issuing large amounts of short-term notes, but bank failures ended that source of funding and the city defaulted in 1931. Eventually, creditors allowed the city to scale down its debt and some fiscal balance was restored.

Fort Lee, N.J.—The borough on the Hudson River lost 40% of its assessed land valuation through condemnation for two major highway projects from 1928–1932—the building of the George Washington Bridge and the Palisades Interstate Park and road system. Fort Lee defaulted in 1933. A state commission assumed fiscal control and filed a debt-refunding plan in 1939.

Akron, Ohio—Heavily dependent on the rubber industry, Akron was hard hit by the depression. Higher operating deficits were not matched by adequate cuts in expenditures. The city defaulted in 1932 when financing became unavailable. Solvency was restored in 1936 after the city cut municipal workers' salaries by 25%, laid off other employes, and reorganized its debts.

Jackson, Mich.—Jackson, dependent on the auto industry, saw its revenues shrink by 50% early in the depression. Officials responded by cutting expenses

48% from 1930–1933, but bank failures restricted the city's borrowing ability. Jackson defaulted in 1933 when cash reserves ran out and credit was impossible to obtain. The city ran a small surplus in 1934 after employment and production improved and some relief costs were assumed by the state and federal governments.

Detroit, Mich.—In 1930, Detroit was the fourth largest city in the nation but its fiscal practices were inadequate for dealing with a booming growth rate as the auto industry expanded. Detroit defaulted in 1933 after a number of cost-cutting measures failed to close the widening gap between receipts and expenses: in 1931 and 1932, the city had dismissed municipal workers, left vacancies unfilled, cut salaries, curtailed services, and sought prepayment on property taxes.

(Detroit had the highest tax delinquency rate in the nation during that period, according to the Times Sept. 7. With the city unable to meet its payroll in 1931, Henry Ford made a $5 million interest-free loan as an advance on his taxes.)

The final crisis occurred in February 1933 when the national bank holiday coincided with a huge issuance of city tax-anticipation notes. After defaulting, Detroit mounted the largest refinancing effort in the country so that its debt would not fall due at the same time. Ultimately, creditors were paid without state intervention.

Frank Murphy, Detroit's mayor during this troubled period, organized the Michigan Conference on Mayors to bring pressure on the federal government during the urban crisis, according to the Times Sept. 7. The Michigan conference later became the U.S. Conference of Mayors.

Cities report aggregate surplus. U.S. cities received $52.8 billion from all revenue sources in fiscal 1974 and made expenditures totaling $52.2 billion for the year ended June 30, 1974, according to the Census Bureau Oct. 21, 1975. Total revenue increased $4.4 billion, or 9%, from fiscal 1973; spending rose $4.2 billion, or 8.8%, over the fiscal year.

City governments' general revenue climbed $3.8 billion to $44.2 billion in fiscal 1974—44% of that total ($19.4 billion) was derived from city-imposed taxes. Other sources of municipal tax revenues were property taxes ($12.2 billion); general sales and gross receipts taxes ($2.4 billion); selective sales taxes ($1.6 billion); and licenses and miscellaneous taxes ($3.3 billion).

Municipalities received one-third of their general revenues ($16.6 billion) from federal and state grants-in-aid and shared taxes. In the past 10 years, an increasing proportion of city general revenue had come from intergovernmental sources, according to Commerce Clearing House Oct. 28. Federal support to cities increased from 3.5% of general revenue to 12.4% over the decade, and state aid rose from 17.4% of revenue to 23.7% during the 10-year period.

(CCH also reported that there was a related 10-year decline in the percentage of city revenue derived from property taxes from 41.2% to 27.7%. The portion from nonproperty taxes was steady at about 16%-17%, and contributions to general revenue from miscellaneous sources declined slightly from 19.3% to 18.3%.)

Almost 69% of all municipal expenditure in fiscal 1974 ($35.9 billion) was for current operations; capital outlays, chiefly for construction, totaled $9.9 billion.

General expenditures (for purposes other than utilities, liquor stores, and pension funds) totaled $42.5 billion in fiscal 1974. As in past years, the largest share went to education (15% or $6.5 billion). The proportion of general expenditures allocated for public welfare had been rising over a 10-year period, from 5.8% to 8.2%, but government officials noted that the trend was reversed at the end of fiscal 1974 because the federal government assumed direct basic grant payments to aged, blind, and disabled recipients on Jan. 1, 1974. As a consequence, cash assistance payments by municipalities declined for the first time since 1963.

Public works bill vetoed. President Ford vetoed a $6.1 million public works employment bill Feb. 13, 1976 as largely "an election year pork barrel."

He said that the bill "would do little to create jobs for the unemployed" and that the most effective way to create new jobs was "to pursue balanced economic policies that encourage the growth of the private sector without risking a new round of inflation."

In his argument against the bill, Ford said it would create only 250,000 jobs at most, instead of the 600,000 to 800,000 jobs advertised for it, and almost none of them immediately when they were needed but in late 1977 and early 1978. He said the cost of producing the jobs would be "intolerably high, perhaps in excess of $25,000 per job."

He found some merit in the bill's "counter-cyclical" provisions, or revenue-sharing grants to states and cities to areas of high unemployment, but he criticized the section for tying the aid to the spending levels of the state and local governments, which he thought would encourage waste.

The veto was sustained Feb. 19 when a 63–35 Senate vote to override came three votes short of the two-thirds majority needed to cancel a veto. The 319–98 House vote to override earlier Feb. 19 had produced 41 votes more than needed.

Revenue-sharing attacked. A study conducted over 2½ years by four public-interest groups attacked the federal revenue-sharing program for not insuring that funds were directed where most needed. The study, made public March 2, 1976, was made by the League of Women Voters Education Fund, the National Urban Coalition, the Center for Community Change and the Center for National Policy Review.

The revenue-sharing program, with funding of $30.2 billion, was initiated in 1972 and was due to expire at the end of 1976. President Ford had proposed a 5¾-year, $39.85 billion extension of the program.

The study charged that the "averaging of per-capita income within a jurisdiction [on which basis federal funds were allocated] may conceal substantial pockets of poverty and need." The distribution of funding, the study said, "allowed cities to get blacker and poorer and the suburbs whiter and richer by perpetuating [the] status quo with no requirements to share the wealth."

The study also charged that the Office of Revenue Sharing had allowed some governments to use the funds in a racially discriminatory manner, and that there was little accountability or public knowledge concerning how the funds were eventually spent by the state and local governments.

Priscilla Crane, a spokesman for the Office of Revenue Sharing, acknowledged March 2 that some governments receiving revenue-sharing funds had engaged in racial discrimination, but said that enforcement "initiatives" of the office had recently won court orders against discrimination. She cited court orders against employment discrimination issued in Miami, Fla. and East Providence, R.I.

John Gunther, executive director of the U.S. Conference of Mayors, criticized the study for attacking a program essential to the well-being of cities. He said March 2: "With these kinds of 'friends' of the cities, who needs enemies?"

Municipal bankruptcy bill. A compromise bill reforming municipal bankruptcy law was passed by voice votes of both houses of Congress March 25, 1976 and was signed by President Ford April 8.

In its final form, the bill:

■ Allowed municipalities to file for bankruptcy provided state law did not prohibit such action (the consent of the creditors was not required).

■ Provided for an automatic delay on proceedings to collect debts from the city once a bankruptcy petition had been filed.

■ Allowed a city to continue borrowing while in bankruptcy.

■ Barred the bankruptcy court from interfering with a municipality's governmental powers.

■ Required a city in bankruptcy to file with the court at a time set by the court a plan for meeting outstanding claims; instructed courts to approve such plans provided they were equitable and feasible; and required that such a plan, to go into effect, had to be approved by creditors holding two-thirds of all claims held by those who voted on the plan. Also, a numerical majority of creditors within each class had to approve the claim (the bankruptcy court was required to designate classes of creditors, determined on the basis of similarity of claims). The municipality was required to give the court a list of all known creditors, and inform those creditors of the bankruptcy proceedings.

Housing & Urban Development

1976 budget. The fiscal 1976 budget, submitted Feb. 3, 1975, augmented the program for the Housing & Urban Development Department by 29%. Funds were increased to $7.1 billion, from $5 billion in 1975. The community development program authorized by Congress in 1974 accounted for much of the increase. It was projected to expand from $225 million in fiscal 1975 to $1.3 billion for the first full year of spending.

Housing subsidies for the poor were to rise from $2.1 billion to $2.6 billion in fiscal 1976, with the government paying the difference between the fair market rental for apartments and the 15%–25% of income required from eligible families.

Subsidies for new and existing apartments were expected to be in the 200,000-unit range for fiscal 1975 and 400,000-unit range for fiscal 1976.

HUD would continue to carry the heavy burden of a discontinued program of insured home loans to low-income buyers in the inner cities. Net outlays for mortgage defaults under the program were budgeted at $792 million in fiscal 1975, $730 million in fiscal 1976.

"Tandem plan" programs begun in 1974 to spur the housing market were responsible for a deficit in HUD's special assistance programs, which required $390.4 million for fiscal 1975 and $513.2 million for fiscal 1976. Under the "tandem plan," HUD subsidized below-market mortgage rates by offering to buy low-interest loans from lenders. The loans subsequently were sold by HUD to private investors.

Rent ceilings end on U.S. housing. HUD April 4, 1975 issued interim rules exempting any housing projects owned or insured by the federal government from local rent control laws. Local rent control was "a significant factor in causing owners of FHA [Federal Housing Administration] projects, especially subsidized projects, to default on their mortgage payments," the department said. While some tenants would face higher rents, the department said, the poor and near-poor would be protected by federal regulations setting maximum rents.

Housing bill vetoed. President Ford vetoed a $1.2 billion emergency housing bill June 24, 1975. He said that "its cost, ineffectiveness and delayed stimulus" would damage the housing industry and the nation. The bill would have subsidized mortgage interest rates as low as 6% and provided federal loans to unemployed home owners facing foreclosure.

The President announced at the same time his own plan to help speed the housing recovery—release of $2 billion remaining from $7.75 billion authorized in the 1974 housing bill under which the Housing and Urban Development Department (HUD) bought home loans made at below-market interest rates and then sold them at existing market rates. The government's loan rate was pegged to its own cost of borrowing money. HUD Secretary Carla Hills said June 24 the $2 billion program was expected to cost the government $60 million and would finance about 65,000 mortgages at a 7.75% interest rate, compared with the current market rate of slightly less than 9%.

The President also asked Congress to extend the 1974 housing bill another year and to authorize another $7.75 billion for it. As for the jobless home owners, Ford said he would support "a workable plan" to prevent foreclosures and he endorsed a House measure for mortgage-relief loans or a coinsuring of lenders refraining from foreclosing.

Ford contended that his plan to stimulate housing and create jobs would be cheaper and faster than the one he vetoed, which he said would take months to get going, hamper a recovery already under way in housing and cause $2 billion in federal outlays, adding $1 billion to the federal deficit in fiscal 1976.

The veto was deplored June 24 by officials of the housing industry and the AFL-CIO.

Veto sustained in House—The veto was upheld in the House June 25 when a motion to override failed 268–157 (249 D & 19 R vs. 122 R & 35 D). It was 16 short of

the two-thirds majority necessary to override.

Philadelphia wins housing grant. The Department of Housing & Urban Development June 3, 1975 approved a $60.8 million federal revenue sharing grant to Philadelphia for the demolition and rehabilitation of housing and neighborhood improvements.

The city received $5 million of the grant in advance and expected to receive about $800 million overall over eight years.

City aid program reviewed. Carla A. Hills, secretary of housing and urban development, reported Jan. 8, 1976 that a new HUD program of federal aid to cities had been generally successful. The program, carried out under the Housing and Community Development Act of 1974, was intended to consolidate older, piecemeal programs, making it simpler for local authorities to obtain federal funds and giving them more independence. A total of $2.5 billion had been allocated for the program, but only $600 million had been spent by the time Hills made her statement.

In a HUD report released by Hills, it was shown that 2,950 localities participated in the program, a larger number, Hills said, than had benefited by all of the programs which were replaced. According to the HUD report, the primary aims of the participating localities were to provide an adequate housing supply, and to prevent urban blight and slums. They sought to do this by providing funds for the rehabilitation and restoration of neighborhoods, instead of (as was done earlier) tearing down slum neighborhoods and constructing new housing.

The new HUD program had, however, been subjected to criticism, chiefly on the grounds that it resulted in too little being done for minorities and the poor. Roger Starr, head of New York's Housing and Development Administration, said Jan. 8 that the program's emphasis on local citizen participation did not leave the city a free hand to concentrate on those neighborhoods most in need of aid. The National Urban League, in a report issued in 1975, said that the federal funds had not gone to "the intended lower income beneficiaries."

Fiscal 1977 budget. The fiscal 1977 budget, submitted Jan. 21, 1976, alloted $7.2 billion for HUD. HUD planned more emphasis on community development grants to local governments and on housing subsidies and less emphasis on older programs, such as urban renewal.

On programs to aid housing by purchase of home mortgages made at below-market interest rates, the budget assumed "that there will no longer be a need for these temporary programs . . . as conditions in the mortgage market return to normal." Despite the same assumption in the previous budget, HUD had injected $8 billion into the housing market in 1975 to buy mortgages in an attempt to spur the market.

In HUD's apartment-subsidy program, under which rent aid was provided for low-income families, the Administration projected subsidies for 400,000 units. The department planned to use part of the funding to ease the problem of defaults on government-insured mortgages by apartment projects. The apartment subsidies were to be applied in both fiscal 1976 and 1977 to up to 110,000 units in apartment projects near default or owned by HUD as a result of default.

School Desegregation

Judge orders HEW to enforce integration. U.S. District Court Judge John H. Pratt ordered the Department of Health, Education & Welfare March 14, 1975 to act swiftly to enforce desegregation guidelines in 125 school districts in 16 Southern and Border states. Ruling on a suit by the NAACP Legal Defense and Educational Fund, Inc., Pratt also ordered HEW to move firmly in another 39 school districts whose voluntary desegregation efforts had been unsuccessful.

"There appears to be an overreliance by HEW on the use of voluntary negotiations over protracted time periods and a reluctance in recent years to use the administrative sanction process where school districts are known to be in noncompliance," Pratt said in his ruling.

Pratt's ruling gave HEW 60 days in which to notify each of the 125 districts that it would have to answer the charge that a "substantial" racial disproportion existed in one or more of its schools. The point at which racial imbalance occurred, Pratt's ruling said, was when there was a 20% disproportion between local minority pupils and their percentage for the entire district.

The court also set up a procedure for handling future complaints of noncompliance: HEW would have 90 days to determine if a district was in compliance with the law. When a district was found to be in noncompliance, it would be given an additional 90 days to take voluntary corrective action. If, after 180 days, the district was still in noncompliance, HEW would commence within 30 days enforcement proceedings "through administrative notice of hearing or any other means authorized by law." (Knowledgeable observers noted, however, that a school district could lengthen the enforcement process with court appeals.)

The 125 districts were in Arkansas, Delaware, Florida, Georgia, Kentucky, Louisiana, Maryland, Mississippi, Missouri, North Carolina, Oklahoma, South Carolina, Tennessee, Texas, Virginia and West Virginia.

Expert pessimistic about integration. James S. Coleman, sociologist and the principal author of a 1966 study often cited to justify school desegregation, said that the flight of whites from desegregating city school systems threatened to defeat the purpose of integration, it was reported April 6, 1975.

Addressing the American Educational Research Association in Washington, Coleman offered a somber assessment of the impact of desegregation during the past few years. More attention should have been paid to how middle-class whites would react to rapid racial mixing of their schools, he suggested. Given the premise that culturally disadvantaged children tended to learn better when their classmates came from culturally advantaged homes, Coleman said, the flight of the middle class from the cities dimmed the prospect of black children being more successful in school through desegregation.

Careful analysis of whites' reactions and

the other indirect effects of desegregation might yield results advocates and opponents of desegregation would find preferable to what was currently happening, Coleman contended. Federal, state and local officials were fearful of political consequences, Coleman said, and left desegregation almost entirely to the courts. As the courts were necessarily "blind" to such factors as white flight, they turned out to be "probably the worst instrument of social policy," he said. "Desegregation through the courts probably will have served in the long run to separate whites and blacks more severely than before," Coleman stated.

Boston violence & court action. Sporadic violence troubled Boston during much of 1975 and on into 1976 as the issue of busing for school integration was fought in the streets as well as in the courts.

The Supreme Court May 12, 1975 let stand lower court decisions that Boston school officials had deliberately maintained an unconstitutionally segregated public school system.

U.S. District Judge W. Arthur Garrity Jr. May 10 had issued his final plan for desegregating the Boston public school system. Superseding a proposal by four court-appointed experts March 21, the new plan called for the busing of 21,-000 pupils, 4,000 more than required by the interim court-ordered desegregation plan in effect for the 1974-75 school year. In contrast to the interim plan, which affected students mostly in the upper grades, the new plan required the busing of 12,000 children in grades one through five.

In his 104-page order, Garrity rejected the traditional system of assigning children to neighborhood schools because it would not "achieve substantial desegregation in Boston due to the geography of the city and racial and ethnic distribution in the city."

Among the provisions of the new plan: Boston would be divided into eight districts, seven of them containing a portion of the city's predominantly black center. Twenty-two schools with special programs—so-called "magnet schools"—would draw students from throughout the city and reflect Boston's racial and ethnic make-up. Twenty schools would be closed

to promote integration by consolidating their student bodies.

Under the new plan, predominantly white South Boston, a focal point of anti-busing sentiment, would continue to share its schools with neighboring black areas. South Boston High School, the scene of considerable violence during the first three months the interim desegregation plan was in effect, was to have a student body of 1,500 whites and 900 blacks.

Garrity put South Boston High School in federal court receivership Dec. 9, removing the school from Boston School Committee jurisdiction. Charging the committee, an elected policy-making body, with obstructionism, Garrity stripped it of control over security in the schools and implementation of a court-ordered desegregation plan.

Garrity's ruling was upheld Jan. 14, 1976 by the U.S. Court of Appeals in Boston. The three appeals judges unanimously approved the lower court integration plan in all its features. The opinion, written by Chief Judge Frank M. Coffin, said: "The overriding fact of the matter is that the District Court in this case had to deal with an intransigent and obstructionist school committee majority . . . [who] engaged in a pattern of resistance, defiance and delay."

The School Committee had opposed the integration plan on grounds that it represented an illegal attempt by the district court to frame educational policy, instead of a measure merely designed to eliminate segregation. The committee had also argued that the "white flight" which followed implementation of the plan had left the schools just as segregated as they had been before the plan went into effect.

Judge Garrity Feb. 24, 1976 imposed a 20% quota for employment of black administrators in Boston's public schools, and ruled that blacks had to be hired in equal numbers with whites until the quota was reached. The upgrading of acting principals or headmasters to permanent rank would be exempted from the judge's order. Also, the quota could be suspended if there were no qualified black candidate for a position.

Garrity's plan barred use of the national Educational Testing Service examination; only tests approved by the U.S. Equal Opportunity Commission could be employed.

On Feb. 15, a violent confrontation had taken place between police and anti-busing demonstrators in front of South Boston High School.

The clash came when police halted an anti-busing "fathers' march" (in which organizers had urged only men participate), estimated by police at over a thousand, before it reached South Boston High School. Demonstrators claimed they had a permit allowing them to give speeches on the school steps; police cited a standing order of Judge Garrity barring assemblies within 100 yards of the school.

Police the next day showed reporters a videotape of the riot in which demonstrators could be seen throwing rocks and other objects. From the videotape it appeared that the protesters had been the first to use tear gas.

Police Commissioner Robert J. Digrazia Feb. 16 said that the police department "will no longer tolerate . . . illegal violent behavior" on the part of demonstrators. He said the department, recognizing the widespread opposition to busing and the rights of citizens to demonstrate against it, had "for almost two years . . . had a tolerance policy."

Digrazia said, however, that "some people, in the name of liberty, have been trampling on the liberties of others." He said that "300 to 400 hoodlums" were engaged in a "conspiracy against public order."

Pasadena voters back busing foes. A drive to oust antibusing members of Pasadena, California's school board failed March 4, 1975, when voters rejected a move to recall three members and elected a fourth busing opponent to the five-member board. While the issue of busing underlay the election, both sides avoided mention of it. The antibusing forces concentrated their attack against "militant" teacher unions and the coalition seeking recall emphasized the board members' "antics" and a trend toward fundamentalism in education. Two teachers unions were part of the recall coalition.

Busing plan in Los Angeles suburb ended. Superior Court Judge Max F. Deutz May 10, 1975 authorized school officials of the Los Angeles suburb of

Inglewood to abandon a five-year old plan to desegregate the city's schools. "As a practical matter, we are now busing black children from predominantly black schools to other predominantly black schools," said Deutz, who noted in his decision that the district's 17 schools had gone from 62% white in 1970 to 19.5% in 1975. School authorities said that families with school-aged children had moved out of the district or sent their children to private schools.

Louisville order. U.S. District Judge James F. Gordon July 30, 1975 ordered the desegregation of Louisville, Ky. public schools under a plan that called for the busing of 22,600 pupils.

The plan went into effect with the start of the new school year Sept. 4. Violence broke out two days later and 1,020 National Guardsmen were called in. But calm was soon restored, and the Guardsmen were sent home Sept. 16.

Schools reopen integrated in 1975. Students in the Omaha public school system began classes Sept. 2 under the first phase of a court-ordered desegregation plan. The first phase included integration of faculties, classes for 4,000 fifth graders at three "learning resource centers" and use of the formerly predominantly black Tech High School as a magnet school offering specialized courses.

Schools in Stockton, Calif. opened Sept. 2 with 1,500 of 5,425 high-school-age students being bused as part of a desegregation plan adopted under court pressure. Unlike other U.S. cities, Stockton did not appeal a court finding of illegal segregation and instead immediately set about integrating its schools.

Schools in Racine, Wis. were voluntarily desegregated Sept. 2 under a plan calling for the busing of 2,186 elementary pupils. Desegregation of high schools already had been accomplished through the building of new schools and the shifting of school boundary lines.

A voluntary plan that used magnet schools and the busing of 3,600 children went into effect in Dayton, Ohio Sept. 3.

Texas order. The U.S. 5th Circuit Court of Appeals Sept. 16, 1975 ordered the Midland, Tex. school system to redraw its school boundary lines to mix black and Mexican-American students with the city's other students. The appellate court's decision overturned an earlier ruling by U.S. District Court Judge Ernest Guinn Jr., who had rejected a desegregation suit on the ground that the Midland schools were already operating in a unitary fashion. The appellate court said that as late as the 1974–75 school year, 99% of all black elementary children and 86% of all Mexican-American elementary children attended seven schools in minority neighborhoods.

Atlanta plan upheld. The U.S. 5th Circuit Court of Appeals Oct. 24, 1975 upheld a plan for desegregating the Atlanta public school system that left more than 60% of the city's schools black. "Based on live, present reality," the court said, Atlanta's school system "is free of racial discrimination and . . . wears no proscribed badge of the past."

The 1973 plan had called for the desegregation of the school system's administration and staff and the redistribution of teaching assignments in exchange for limited voluntary busing. As a result of the plan, the system's superintendent was black, two-thirds of all administrators were black and 60% of the teachers were black. (The system's student population of 80,000 was 90% black.)

"The aim of the 14th Amendment guarantee of equal protection . . . is to assure that state-supported educational opportunity is afforded without regard to race; it is not to achieve racial integration in the public schools," the court said.

"Conditions in most school districts have frequently caused courts to treat these aims as identical. In Atlanta, where white students now comprise a small minority and black citizens can control school policy, administration and staffing, they no longer are," the court said.

The decision was praised by Warren Fortson, legal counsel to the Atlanta school board, who said the appellate court had recognized that "the mere fact people are segregated doesn't necessarily mean that they are discriminated against."

However, a spokeswoman for the Atlanta branch of the American Civil Liberties Union said the decision showed that "desegregation could not be accomplished within a city system" and that the only solution was the merger of all public school systems in the Atlanta metropolitan region.

NYC principal quota voided. A U.S. Appeals Court in New York City ruled Jan. 19, 1976 that a lower court decision setting up race quotas for principals in the New York City school system was "constitutionally forbidden reverse discrimination."

The overturned decision—a federal district court ruling of Feb. 1975—was designed to protect members of minorities who lacked seniority in their jobs as school principals. Prior to the February ruling, if a school district had to eliminate a position, it would do so by transferring, demoting or dismissing "the least senior person in the job classification." This procedure was called "excessing." The February ruling, however, ordered that the percentage of minority members on an "excessing list" for a school district could not exceed the percentage of the group in the district.

As a result, non-minority members with greater seniority were sometimes excessed instead of minority members with less seniority.

The appellate court, on a 2–1 vote, voided the quota system and restored seniority as the basis for "excessing."

Judge Ellsworth Van Graafeiland, in the decision, said that racial quotas in hiring, to provide "remedial relief" of past discrimination, might receive "limited approval," but there was no justification for extending the quotas to "excessing practices" which were not in themselves discriminatory.

In a dissent, Judge James L. Oakes argued that the quotas were a legitimate means of remedying past discrimination.

Integration ordered for Milwaukee schools. Judge John Reynolds of the U.S. District Court in Milwaukee ruled Jan. 19, 1976 that the city's public schools were segregated, and that steps should be taken immediately to desegregate them.

As of Oct. 1, 1975, black students made up 34% of the Milwaukee public school enrollment of 114,180, with other minorities contributing 6%. Most black students went to predominantly black schools.

Segregation up in Chicago schools. The New York Times reported Jan. 25, 1976 that an annual survey conducted by the Chicago Board of Education had provided evidence that schools in Chicago had grown more segregated than in the previous year. The survey showed that only 37 of the system's 674 schools were integrated, as judged by the standards of the Illinois Office of Education. The previous year, 44 schools had been in compliance with those standards. (Those standards required the racial and ethnic composition of a school student body to be within 15% of the composition of the student population of the system as a whole.)

The survey found that 415 schools—as opposed to 412 the year before—were at least 90% black or 90% white.

The continuing decline in Chicago's white population was seen as a major difficulty for integration efforts. In 1975, white students accounted for only 26.8% of the school population, a drop of 1.4% from the year before.

The survey also found that school faculties had made no progress towards integration. By the guidelines of the city board of education, only 43.4% of the schools had integrated faculties.

Detroit busing starts peacefully. Schools experienced virtually no disturbances as a court-ordered desegregation plan went into effect in Detroit Jan. 26, 1976.

The Detroit school system, with about 247,000 students, was the largest thus far to bus students under court orders. The desegregation plan required 21,653 children to be bused, and 4,179 more to change schools for integration purposes.

About three fourths of the pupils in the Detroit school system were black. The court plan did not seek to make every school in the system reflect the overall racial composition. Rather it attempted to increase to just over 50% the percentage of black children in those schools which were still predominantly white.

The limited nature of the desegration plan—busing less than 10% of the stu-

dents, and affecting only 107 of the system's 240 schools—was cited by some to explain the peacefulness which attended its implementation. However, the plan also drew criticism on the ground of its limitedness; the National Association for the Advancement of Colored People (NAACP) had appealed it as inadequate to the U.S. Sixth Circuit Court of Appeals. The NAACP preferred a busing plan which included the suburbs with the city of Detroit. The Supreme Court in 1974 ruled against such cross-district busing, a ruling which observers said had pacified the most vigorous opposition to busing in the Detroit area.

Some observers also attributed the lack of incidents partly to the harsh winter weather of January in Detroit. It was also thought that the frequent statements in support of desegregation by the public officials of the city and the school board may have helped smooth the way for the plan.

The plan had been ordered Nov. 4, 1975 by U.S. District Court Judge Robert E. DeMascio, who had devised it with the aid of Prof. John E. Finger of Rhode Island College. DeMascio said the plan's purpose was to keep white students from moving to avoid an integration order.

Judge sets Dallas desegregation plan Judge William M. Taylor, ruling in U.S. Court in Dallas March 10, 1976 ordered the city school district to adopt a desegregation plan that called for the busing of about 20,000 students, and would divide the city into five subdistricts. The plan included the use of "magnet concept" schools for grades 9 through 12.

City Employes

Teacher strikes & pay deals. Milwaukee's public schools reopened Feb. 6, 1975 after the settlement of a 17-day strike by the system's 5,800 teachers. The teachers struck when contract negotiations with the city's board of education stalemated over the question of salary increases. Under the terms of the settlement finally reached, the teachers were to receive an 8% pay increase the first year,

9% the second and improved fringe benefits. Initially the teachers had sought a 16% raise the first year, and the board had offered 6.5%. The strike affected 180 schools and 110,000 students.

The Camden (N.J.) school board June 10 ratified a two-year pact with the city's 1,200 teachers that called for average raises of $2,000 for each teacher over the life of the contract. Under the new contract, salaries for teachers with bachelors degrees would range from $9,600 to $15,500 in the second year.

The opening of schools in September was marked by a rash of teachers' strikes. Teachers in 12 states were on strike by the first week of September. The action affected at least 961,000 elementary and high school pupils, according to United Press International count. Of the total, 530,000 were in Chicago, where 27,700 teachers walked out Sept. 3.

The issues largely were wages, class size and contract retractions. In Chicago, teachers were seeking a cost-of-living pay increase, a reduction in class size and improved fringe benefits. The board's budget did not contain funds for a pay raise and called for elimination of 1,525 teaching positions. (The Chicago strike was settled Sept. 17 under terms that included a 7% raise and retention of the 1,525 teaching jobs.)

Strikes also were affecting 40,000 other Illinois schoolchildren; 140,000 pupils in Pennsylvania; 80,000 in Rhode Island; 47,000 in Michigan; 41,000 in New York; 24,000 in California; 16,800 in Montana; 15,000 in Massachusetts; 14,200 in Delaware; 8,000 in New Jersey; and 5,500 in Ohio. A strike in Indiana at Marion ended after a day when the teachers agreed to a 7% pay rise Sept. 4. It involved 400 teachers and 11,000 pupils.

The statistics jumped considerably when New York City joined the ranks of strikers Sept. 9, the second day of the new term. The strike, by members of the AFL-CIO United Federation of Teachers, effectively halted the education of 1.1 million public schoolchildren. Only 1,300 of the 60,000 teachers in the system reported for work, and many of the 37,129 pupils who went to school were sent home that day. The union had called the strike on charges that contract provisions on class size had been violated and conditions

in general were chaotic on opening day. But the union's contract expired at midnight Sept. 8 and negotiations on a new one were stalemated. The major issues were the school board's demands for increased teacher productivity and the union's stand against yielding benefits and working conditions negotiated in previous contracts.

By Sept. 10, with some strikes resolved and others newly begun, the strike statistics involved nearly 2 million pupils.

One of the hardest-hit states was Florida, where 140,000 pupils were affected by the strikes, all of them in the Fort Lauderdale district. Pennsylvania had strikes in 20 districts, affecting 113,000 pupils.

Some 14,200 pupils were affected in Delaware by a strike in Wilmington, which began Sept. 3. It was marked by mass arrests of teachers, 209 on Sept. 22. Half of the teacher union's 800 members there had either been arrested or cited for contempt of court.

The teachers in Fort Lauderdale agreed Sept. 23 to return to work while contract negotiations continued, and the three last strikes in Rhode Island—in Pawtucket, Woonsocket and Tiverton—ended Sept. 24. The settlement in Pawtucket and Woonsocket included release of 14 union leaders from jail.

Boston teachers struck Sept. 22, halting the start of the city's desegregation plan. They ended the walkout Sept. 30 under a new one-year contract providing a 6% raise, job security and money for teaching materials. Superior Court Judge Samuel Adams fined the union $60,000 for the strike (Adams had enjoined a walkout) and fined the union's president and executive vice president $1,000 each for leading the strike.

The six-week strike by Wilmington, Del. teachers was settled Oct. 10 with agreement on a three-year pact providing an 18% pay rise in three equal steps. The settlement covered reinstatement of more than 500 teachers and 44 school secretaries who had been fired because they struck.

A teachers' strike in Salt Lake City affecting 60,000 students was resolved Oct. 17 after a week's walkout.

A settlement of a teacher's strike in New Haven, Conn. was reached Nov. 23. It began Nov. 10. The city's 46 public schools, having 20,000 students, were closed Nov. 19 after having been kept open by some nonstriking teachers, substitutes and administrators. Some 90 teachers were jailed during the strike action, which was illegal for teachers under state law. The settlement was attained under threat of a citywide strike by all organized labor in New Haven.

In New York state, a 28-day strike by teachers in Nyack ended Nov. 24 with ratification of a two-year pact increasing the base salary, which was $10,550, to $11,000 the first year and to $11,800 the second year. The walkout, which affected 3,700 students and began Oct. 14, involved penalties for defiance of the state's Taylor Law forbidding strikes by public employes.

An eight-week strike by teachers in Pittsburgh ended Jan. 26, 1976 with ratification of a new 30-month contract providing salary increases of 24.7%. The current salary range of from $8,700 to $16,700 annually would rise in September to $9,900–$18,300 and in March 1978 to $10,500–$20,300. The strike, which began Dec. 1, 1975, involved 3,800 teachers and 800 para-professionals and affected 62,000 pupils.

Ratification came about 10 hours after a tentative agreement had been reached by negotiators. A general agreement on terms had been reached the week before on proposals presented by a special commission appointed by Common Pleas Judge Donald E. Ziegler. The teachers union was under fines of $105,000 from Ziegler for defiance of an injunction to return to work.

Ending a strike that began Feb. 3, teachers in Newark, N.J. ratified a new contract Feb. 8 with an average salary increase of 8.5% over a two-and-a-half-year period. The pay range would go to $9,741–$15,929 beginning in September and to $10,131–$16,901 the following year.

The strike involved 4,000 teachers and 78,000 students in 102 schools.

Detroit averts police layoffs. The planned layoff of 10% of Detroit's policemen was averted May 21, 1975 when city officials and representatives of the police force reached agreement on a plan calling for all officers to take 14 consecutive working days off without pay between June and the end of 1976. The police also agreed to accept straight-time pay for holiday work.

In return, the police received additional compensatory time and an extra seven days of paid vacation by June 1976.

The labor dispute had its origins in Detroit's worsening budget situation, but charges of discrimination and reverse discrimination related to the planned layoffs caused racial tensions to rise. Mayor Coleman Young initially announced that 1,500 city employes, including about 550 police officers, would be laid off in an effort to reduce a projected $50 million budget deficit. However, representatives of black and female police officers obtained injunctions barring the city from implementing its layoff plan on May 1, contending that their dismissal would violate the city's commitment to affirmative action for the hiring of minority and female workers.

The court orders would have forced the city to layoff about 825 white officers with more seniority than the junior-ranking black and female officers. The police union, most of whose members were white, charged that the court action would violate contracts requiring that layoffs and demotions start with junior officers.

Mediation by a federal court judge was required to settle the labor dispute.

San Francisco police-fire strike. Mayor Joseph J. Alioto invoked emergency powers Aug. 21, 1975 to impose a pay settlement and end a strike by the city's police and firemen. The strikers accepted the settlement, which included the 13% pay raise they sought, but it was rejected by the city's legislature, an 11-member board of supervisors, which had offered a 6.5% increase.

The strike by the 1,935-member police force began Aug. 18 despite Alioto's threat to dismiss officers failing to report for work. It continued despite a state court's temporary restraining order against it and a later order that the pickets be disarmed. Although in civilian dress, some of the picketing policemen wore their weapons.

There were some picket-line incidents, such as broken windshields and slashed tires, and Alioto denounced "vicious attacks" on the pickets while deploring the strike itself.

Elsewhere, with only 45 officers on duty throughout San Francisco to protect its 671,000 residents, there were reports Aug. 20 of looting and of robberies—some of patrons in restaurants—and of violence— a pipe bomb exploded outside Alioto's home.

As public concern mounted, the board declared a state of emergency Aug. 20 and requested the mayor to get state highway patrolmen to secure the city.

The pressure for settlement increased when the city's 1,781 firemen joined the strike Aug. 20, a move that threatened to close the city's airport, which received firefighting coverage from the city.

Another complication, the threat of a strike by 1,900 transit workers, set for Aug. 22, dissolved Aug. 20 when a 6.9% pay hike was accepted for settlement.

Alioto, who was attempting to mediate between the board and the unionized police and fire unions, announced a settlement Aug. 21 for the 13% pay hike, effective Oct. 15. It would raise starting pay for policemen and firemen from $16,-044 to $18,816. Part of the settlement was that no reprisals would be permitted against the strikers.

The board unanimously rejected the settlement, but Alioto immediately invoked emergency powers under the city's charter and imposed the settlement as law in the interest of public safety. "The strike is over," he declared. "San Francisco will be fully normal tomorrow."

The policemen and firemen accepted the settlement and began to return to work immediately.

Racial quotas set for Chicago police. Judge Prentice Marshall, ruling in federal district court in Chicago, ordered the Chicago Police Department to establish racial quotas for the future hiring of police officers. The ruling, made Jan. 5, 1976, also enjoined the Treasury Department from sending revenue-sharing funds (now amounting to $76 million) to the city until his orders had been obeyed.

The quotas specified by the judge were: 42% black and hispanic males, 16% women, and 42% white males. At the time of the ruling, blacks and hispanics made up 17% of the police force (in contrast to a 40% share of the general city population).

Judge Marshall also reaffirmed a previous ruling of his, made in December 1974. In that ruling, the city was required to admit groups of 200 for police training, the groups to be composed of 100 black or hispanic males, 33 women, and 67 white males.

The occasion of Judge Marshall's ruling was a suit, charging racial and sexual discrimination in hiring and promotion practices by the Chicago Police Department, filed by the Afro-American Patrolmen's League, the Justice Department, and a group of Spanish Americans. It had been in litigation since 1970.

N.Y. transit strike averted. A New York transit strike halting the city's subway and bus service was averted by a last-minute settlement April 1, 1976 on a two-year contract without a direct wage increase.

The contract, covering 34,000 workers, did contain a cost-of-living clause to provide a one-cent per hour wage boost for each .3% increase in the local consumer price index. The one-cent boost had been pegged to a .4% price jump. Under the new formula, the boosts were to be applied every six months.

The average wage of the transit worker was $6.96 an hour for a 40-hour week.

The pact covered 32,400 members of the AFL-CIO Transport Workers Union and 2,300 bus drivers and shop employes represented by the AFL-CIO Amalgamated Transit Union.

Other Developments

Doctors strike N.Y. hospitals. Interns and resident doctors at 21 New York hospitals went on strike March 17, 1975 to shorten work schedules. It was the first major doctors' strike in U.S. history. It ended March 20 with an agreement to limit work hours and to set up scheduling committees at individual hospitals.

More than 2,000 doctors went on strike at the hospitals, which had 14,000 beds, a third of the city's total, and normally handled 10,000 outpatients daily. Medical service was maintained by private attending doctors and staff and faculty members. The striking union, the Committee of Interns and Residents, pledged to cover emergencies where doctor shortages existed. The state health department also sent doctor-nurse teams to monitor patient care during the action.

Formed in 1958, the committee had labor contracts with municipal, voluntary and independent hospitals. It struck 15 voluntary ones and six affiliated municipal hospitals to get relief from schedules it said ran up to 110 duty hours a week with uninterrupted stretches of up to 56 hours. Federal mediators assisted the negotiations.

The union received an unexpected assist March 18 from the American Medical Association, whose two top officers said "in important respects, it is a strike for better patient care." Dr. Richard E. Palmer, board chairman, and Dr. Malcolm C. Todd, president, said 50 hours straight or 100 hours a week were "tough" on the doctor and a threat to quality patient care. They noted that patients were covered during the strike, which was not a right the AMA believed a doctor had, the right to strike against a patient.

The work hours would be limited, under the agreement, to not more than one night's duty in a three-day period unless approved by a committee, to be established, of union and hospital representatives. The committee would devise guidelines for schedules focusing on "optimum patient care" and "the health and well-being of house staff officers, including their reasonable social needs and providing for adequate rest." The guidelines were to be implemented by the hospitals "subject to budgetary limitations."

Disturbances follow Detroit shooting. The shooting in Detroit of a black youth by a white tavern owner July 28, 1975 touched off two days of racial disturbances that city officials feared for a time would escalate into full-scale riots.

The trouble erupted when Andrew Chinarian, 39, the owner of a bar in the city's northwest section, fatally shot Obie Wynn, 18, whom Chinarian claimed to have found tampering with his car. Chinarian told police he fired in self-defense

when Wynn turned on him with a shiny object he thought was a knife.

When Chinarian was questioned by police and subsequently released on $500 bail, residents from the predominantly black northwest section gathered at Chinarian's bar, demanding that they be allowed to destroy it. Riot police were dispatched to the area, but they failed to stop roving crowds from setting fire to two police cars, looting nearby stores and severely beating a passing white motorist, Marian Pyszko, 54, who later died.

Detroit's mayor, Coleman Young, a black who had once owned a tavern across the street from Chinarian's, immediately went to the scene, to try to cool the tempers of the protesters. From 11 p.m. until after sunrise, the mayor was out on the streets, the New York Times reported Aug. 1, "pleading, cajoling, agreeing, identifying with the anger of many of the black residents of the neighborhood."

During the first night, Detroit police made 63 arrests, but never fired a shot. One of the mayor's first acts after the fatal shooting had been to order as many black policemen as possible into the area in an effort to reduce tensions.

Young also appeared at the bar the second night and urged a crowd attempting to ram a car into the bar to disperse. Young left when a thrown object narrowly missed him.

The disturbances were further quieted July 30 when Chinarian's bail was raised to $25,000. Chinarian posted bail and was released.

Cairo racial ills unchanged. A report issued by the U.S. Civil Rights Commission Aug. 13, 1975 said that federal, state and local officials had done little in the past 10 years to ameliorate racial hostility in Cairo, Ill. The report, entitled "A Decade of Waiting in Cairo," documented racial troubles in the southern Illinois town of 6,000 persons. (The agency had conducted an investigation in 1972 and had found discrimination against blacks in all facets of their lives.)

The latest commission report said whites in Cairo had made little effort to change the racial climate there. It blamed whites for their continuing resistance to dialogues with blacks but also cited failure of state and federal agencies to take corrective action.

Among the report's findings:

The Internal Revenue Service continued to accord tax-exempt status to private, all-white schools set up to avoid desegregation. No action had been taken to prevent a recurrence of the breakdown of law and order that occurred in the late 1960s and early 1970s. Health care had not improved during the past decade. Government agencies had been inefficient in attacking housing problems and had "accomplished little [in] their programs to arrest deteriorating housing ... and provide decent housing for large numbers of low and moderate income families."

Index